My Partner, My Enemy

Published by Rowman & Littlefield
A wholly owned subsidiary of The Rowman & Littlefield Publishing Group, Inc.
4501 Forbes Boulevard, Suite 200, Lanham, Maryland 20706
www.rowman.com

Unit A, Whitacre Mews, 26-34 Stannary Street, London SE11 4AB

British Library Cataloguing in Publication Information Available

Library of Congress Cataloging-in-Publication Data
Names: Leventhal, John Michael, author.
Title: My partner, my enemy : an unflinching view of domestic violence and
    new ways to protect victims / John Michael Leventhal.
Description: Lanham : Rowman & Littlefield, 2016. | Includes bibliographical
    references and index.
Identifiers: LCCN 2016006184 (print) | LCCN 2016013470 (ebook) | ISBN
    9781442265165 (cloth : alk. paper) | ISBN 9781442265172 (Electronic)
Subjects: LCSH: Family violence—United States. | Victims of family
    violence—United States. | Abusive men—United States.
Classification: LCC HV6626.2 .L49 2016 (print) | LCC HV6626.2 (ebook) | DDC
    362.82/92—dc23
LC record available at http://lccn.loc.gov/2016006184

Printed in the United States of America

This book is for my late father, Harry, my very best friend;

for my late blind mother, Elizabeth, who saw with her heart;

and for the joys of my life, my sons, Adam and Danny.

It is also for the late Honorable Judith S. Kaye,

the mother of problem solving courts and

a mentor and inspiration to us all.

Acknowledgments

I would like to thank all those who encouraged me in my work as a judge handling domestic violence cases and in the writing of this book. First, I mention my sisters, Vivien Landau and Barbara Friedman, who are always there with a supporting ear or a loving suggestion, and of course, Sheryl.

Next, I want to thank all those who toil in the quarries of domestic violence, but in particular those persons who have made my work doable and labored right beside me—Hon. Charles Troia, Hon. Guy Mangano Jr., Jezebel Walter, the late Gail Kohn, Gloria Moloney, John Gallo, Karen Boyd Gillen, Monte Ruschwerger, James Imperatrice, and all of the court officers who served in my part. I wish to mention and express my admiration to the Domestic Violence Bureau of the Kings County District Attorney's Office, formerly headed by Wanda Lucibello; the defense bar; Brooklyn Defender Services, headed by Lisa Schreibersdorf; the Legal Aid Society headed by Dawn Ryan in Brooklyn; the Center for Court Innovation, especially Emily Sack and Liberty Aldrich; victim advocates, especially Safe Horizons, Sanctuary for Families, and My Sister's Place; and all the partners of the Brooklyn Domestic Violence Court for their dedicated service day in and day out in handling these very difficult and challenging cases.

I would also like to give credit to Hon. Guy J. Mangano Jr. for suggesting that I write this book; the Hon. Mark Dillon, the late Hon. Nicholas Clemente, the Hon. Anne Feldman, Ben Darvil, Ted Taub, and the late Betty Taub for reading through the first draft and giving me constructive criticism; Mel Harris, Matt Weiner, and Samantha Perlstein for making suggestions and for editing my final draft; and my friends Howard Blum, the Hon. Barry Kamins, Mark Schulman, and Bruce Taub for their constant encouragement. I want to thank my editor, Kathryn Knigge, who kept my eye on the ball and believed

What comes to my mind when dealing with domestic violence is the lyrics of the 1983 song by the Police, "Every move you make . . . every step you take . . . I'll be watching you!"[2] This may have been the perpetrator threatening the victim. Now, we are changing it to the judge warning the perpetrator.

These deadly vignettes or stories are based upon true cases and events that, except in four instances, came before me in my capacity as a judge in the Domestic Violence Court. "Lucky Laurie" was a woman whom I represented as a defense attorney when I was engaged in the private practice of law years prior to my ascension to the bench. "The Ax Murderer" was a case that came before me months prior to my assignment to the Domestic Violence Court. It resulted in a plea bargain that I first declined to agree to impose. "Deadly Dave" was a counselor at a batterers' intervention program that I used to monitor defendants in the first two years after the opening of the Brooklyn Domestic Violence Court. He never came before me as a defendant. Dave delivered reports to the court every Tuesday pertaining to the monitoring of the participation of those defendants who were placed in a batterers' intervention program as a condition of bail or release. Dave's tragic story confounded me as it did everyone else whom he knew and who was interviewed in the newspapers.

"Yuri the Hunter" was tried before me prior to my being assigned to the Domestic Violence Court. Yuri killed his in-laws with a hunting knife, duct taped his son to a chair, and attempted to rape his estranged wife, culminating in a hostage situation where Yuri unsuccessfully tried to orchestrate his "suicide by police." This introduction was an eye-opener and scared me to become hypervigilant so that this situation would not easily arise with any of the cases that I would come to preside over as a judge in a dedicated domestic violence part.

My first trial in the specialized court involved a man, Desmond, who was convicted of attempted murder of his girlfriend, Enid. He had shot her two times in the back of the head while she was asleep. His motive was to prevent her from testifying against him when she refused to drop the pending felony assault charges where he cut her across her upper lip with a jagged Tabasco sauce bottle. I wanted to take steps to avoid any violence on my pending cases so incidents like this would not happen.

All of these accounts of the proceedings and trials are based upon cases resulting in death or near death or having deadly overtones. All of the cases have been completed. They have been appealed or the time to appeal has expired or the defendant has waived the right to appeal as part of a plea agreement. Nonetheless, the names of victims, family members, and witnesses as well as the perpetrators have been changed in most instances. I did, however, cite press reports when the victim openly talked to the media or when the victim was murdered or when the New York newspapers covered the criminal incident or trial. I have also taken artistic license in describing certain background information and events to protect the privacy of the victims and their families. The essence of the facts gleaned at the trials or hearings remains true to what was in fact revealed at the proceedings of those cases.

1990s to show that domestic violence has been—and continues to be—an issue of national proportion even before the highly publicized domestic violence cases, such as the Nicole Brown Simpson/O. J. Simpson drama, caught the nation's attention. The horror of these statistics is only magnified by the realization that incidents of abuse are gravely underreported, and even more so in minority, religious, wealthy, and gay, lesbian, and transgender communities. Domestic violence perpetrators and victims are not peculiar to any class, race, religious, or ethnic group.[2] It is a crime committed across all strata of the population, like driving while intoxicated.

Domestic violence is the leading cause of injury to women between the ages of fifteen and forty-four in the United States—more than rapes, muggings, and automobile accidents combined.[3] A woman is beaten every fifteen seconds in the United States.[4] There are at least four million reported incidents of domestic violence against women every year.[5] A woman is nine times more likely to suffer a violent attack in her home than on the streets.[6] Over 50 percent of the women killed in the United States are killed by male intimate partners or ex-partners.[7] The 11.6 percent of married women or those in relationships of cohabitation experience some physical violence within a given year.[8] Battered women are often severely injured—22 to 35 percent of women who visit hospital emergency rooms are there for injuries related to ongoing abuse.[9] Domestic violence is a significant cause of miscarriage and birth defects.[10] Approximately 50 percent of homeless women and children in this country are on the streets because of violence in the home.[11] In over 50 percent of all domestic violence situations, children are also abused.[12] Nearly fifty thousand restraining orders pertaining to violence against intimates have been issued in Massachusetts alone each year.[13] There are an estimated six hundred women in California prisons convicted of killing an abusive partner.[14] Where the relationship between the murderer and the victim are known, 49 percent of women murdered in New York City are killed by their husbands or boyfriends.[15]

Domestic violence has a profound, and often everlasting, effect on children. Between 3.3 and 10 million children are exposed to domestic violence each year.[16] Fifty to 75 percent of batterers abuse the children as well as the domestic partner.[17] Forty to 60 percent of child victims of physical abuse have witnessed the abuse of their mother by her male partner on at least one occasion.[18] Witnessing domestic violence can be as traumatizing for children as being the victim of the abuse.[19] Child witnesses experience stress-related problems, including headaches, peptic ulcers, stuttering, and depression.[20] Exposure to domestic violence impairs children's academic performance.[21] Children are aware of domestic violence even when they do not observe it.[22] A child need not directly witness domestic violence to experience emotional trauma;[23] close proximity to domestic violence, without actually seeing it, will cause a child to suffer serious emotional consequences.[24] The biological processes that occur when children are exposed to stressful events such as witnessing domestic violence can disrupt the early development of the central nervous system, potentially impeding their ability to cope with negative or disruptive emotions and leading to problems with emotional and behavioral self-regulation later in life.[25]

Domestic violence is about power and control—physical, sexual, verbal, economic, legal, emotional, and psychological.[26] When the intimidation and coercion becomes physical or has physically coercive overtones, then this domestic violence becomes criminal. The power and control persist throughout the prosecution of the case, where it is estimated that approximately 40 percent of the complainants become uncooperative. In the felony domestic violence part, over which I presided for nearly twelve years, complainants would often (and continue to) refuse to testify, recant, claim that they had committed perjury, and sometimes, actually testify on behalf of the defendant/purported batterer. By way of example, in one matter long ago concluded, the wife was the complainant in an allegation regarding a burglary and misdemeanor assault. The defendant's girlfriend bailed him out of jail. Subsequently, the defendant had a disagreement with his girlfriend, who in turn asked the court to exonerate the defendant's bail. The defendant was then placed back in prison pending trial. At a later point in time, he made up with his wife. She posted his bail and retained an attorney for his criminal defense where she was the complainant. This is a microcosm of what we sometimes see. I again emphasize that this is not victim blaming as will be explained below.

Why do women stay with their abusers? These women should not be criticized as weaker persons than those who do cooperate in the prosecution and punishment of their batterers. In some cases, there is direct manipulation by the abuser—threats of harm to the victim or her family if she should proceed with the case or threats of legal action to remove a child from the parent through accusations of child abuse or neglect. In other instances, there is indirect manipulation—fear and low self-esteem that may be the result of years of ongoing abuse. Sometimes the women may still truly love their batterer—they simply want the abuse to stop. There are other legitimate and concrete concerns that these survivors of violence have about their families' economic well-being. Many are financially dependent upon the batterer—the rent needs to be paid or the children have to be watched when a woman goes to work or school. There is no day care for many battered women. A criminal conviction or incarceration, moreover, would deprive the family of essential income, health insurance for a sick child, housing, overall economic security, and many times survival. Some domestic violence victims remain because

Chapter Two

Build It and They Will Come

The Genesis of the
Brooklyn Domestic Violence Court

In February 1996, a New York City Criminal Court judge lowered the bail for Galina Komar's boyfriend who was being held on an assault charge against her. Three weeks after being released, he obtained a gun and killed Ms. Komar. As sometimes happens, the boyfriend then committed suicide. Governor George Pataki and Mayor Rudolph Giuliani called for the impeachment of the judge who had reduced the bail set on the case for the boyfriend's previous assault of Ms. Komar. Although a judge cannot be impeached for a discretionary bail determination, he was nonetheless universally vilified in the media. He became a magnet for disapproval, and the judicial conduct commission called for his removal, not for the bail decision in this case, but for a finding, after hearings, of an anti-prosecutor and anti-woman bias. In all fairness to the judge, there had been many different judges and several prosecutors handling the case and information may have not been communicated down the line.[1] This event highlighted the need for a dedicated domestic violence court.

Galina Komar's murder came shortly after O. J. Simpson's acquittal for the murders of Nicole Brown Simpson and Ron Goldman. The nation had been transfixed on O. J. Simpson riding in the white Ford Bronco leading the police in a low-speed chase on a Los Angeles freeway. The drama of the subsequent trial brought domestic violence to the nation's collective attention. Although it was not an easy task to start a "domestic violence court," the time was right for its creation.

In June 1996, just four months after Ms. Komar's murder, I was asked to preside over the Brooklyn Domestic Violence Court (BDVC), the first court of this kind in New York, and the first felony domestic violence court in the nation. My first trial in the specialized court involved a man who was

may expand the choices available to them? If domestic violence defendants present a particular risk of future violence, then why not enhance monitoring efforts to deter such actions? If cases slip between the cracks of a fragmented criminal justice system, then why not work to improve coordination and consistency? If domestic violence cases do not fit the traditional paradigm of court cases, then why not change the mold?[3]

From June of 1996 until January of 2008, I had the privilege, as well as the awesome responsibility, of being the presiding judge of the nation's first felony domestic violence court.[4] In April of 1998, I was joined by a terrific judge, the Hon. Matthew D'Emic, who is now the administrative judge of the Supreme Court, Criminal Term in Kings County and still presides over the Domestic Violence Court as well as the first Mental Health Court in New York.

Have we been successful? We had far fewer dismissals than there have been historically when domestic violence crimes are processed in conventional courts. Our court fulfilled the traditional role of courts in protecting the constitutional and procedural rights of the defendants. We also, however, worked as a problem-solving court to ensure the safety of the complainants. This is where we deviated from a traditional court. We engaged in intensive judicial supervision and monitoring throughout the case, returning defendants to court in front of the judge every few weeks even though there may not have been any motions, hearings, or trial proceedings.[5] At various times, as many as five defendants were placed on curfews as part of the conditions of bail. The judge would spot-check that the defendants were home by calling the defendants. The court placed muscle behind the protective order by reinforcing that the order of protection was the court's order and the name of the case was the state (not the wife or girlfriend) versus the defendant. It was emphasized that the case is an evidence-based prosecution, not a matter of the defendant's wife or girlfriend controlling the outcome. This also fostered defendant accountability to the court and lessened any overt or subtle pressure by a defendant upon the complainant to drop the charges.[6] The judge not only supervised the defendants while the cases were pending, but also after the cases were adjudicated through the monitoring of probationers and parolees who had to return to court by appointment. Over a decade, our probationers in the Brooklyn felony domestic violence court had one-half of the violation rate when compared to the general probation population. This was a significant reduction, especially when considering that the complainant and the defendant not only knew each other, but they were once intimately involved. Anecdotally, the Division of Parole reported that the violation rate for the Domestic Violence Court parolees was far less than the rest of the parolee population. This was the predecessor of what then U.S. Attorney

General Janet Reno had championed and is now termed a "reentry court." Throughout the process, emphasis was placed on the defendant's awareness that the judge was watching.

After a year, the court created a newly developed position, the resource coordinator, whose job is to help the judge in monitoring defendant compliance and victim assistance. Before each court appearance, the resource coordinator obtains compliance information from the batterers' program and Probation Department, information from the district attorney's office about rearrests and any violations of court orders, and information from victim advocates about violations of orders of protection and victim safety. The resource coordinator presents the judge with this information on each case before the court appearance so that the judge can have full information available and will be able to take any action that may be necessary, including advancing a case that is not scheduled to be heard until a later day. This further promotes victim safety and defendant accountability and further emphasizes that the judge is watching.

We developed a partnership, or what some call a coordinated community response. The judge served and continues to serve as a catalyst to bring all of these agencies and groups working on domestic violence together. We held scheduled meetings with our partnership—police, prosecutors, the defense bar, victim advocates, probation and parole officers, corrections personnel, the family court, drug and alcohol abuse programs, and elder abuse organizations. We communicated directly and through the resource coordinator and through the resource coordinator with the Family Court to see whether there were cases pending with the defendant and the complainant.[7] This coordinated community response facilitated a concentration of resources in combatting domestic violence crime. The partnership was constantly expanding, recognizing that other agencies and organizations play important roles in addressing the problems of domestic violence in the community. The partnership worked, and still works, in concert at these meetings—and between formal meetings—to solve problems and to address concerns relating to domestic violence issues and crime. For example, it was discovered during discussions with both the State Division of Parole and State Department of Corrections that they were unaware that an order of protection was in place when a defendant had been convicted of a felony and/or had been sentenced to state prison time, say felony assault, attempted murder, or kidnapping. Steps were taken to develop a simple protocol to alert these institutions of the existence of the protective order. No longer would the felon be able to call, write, or have a visit with the victim in prison, nor would he be able to live with her upon his release from incarceration. The judge or court clerk needed only to attach a copy of the order of protection to the state commitment order

Chapter Three

Lucky Laurie

The pens in the courthouse were quite the experience. Laurie was placed with other females who were also waiting to be arraigned before a judge. She imagined that almost all of the other women in there with her were in jail for prostitution, drug addiction or pushing, shoplifting, or maybe for a petty assault. Laurie viewed them as the real criminals, not herself. Upon brief reflection, she recognized the irony of the situation. If they knew why she was incarcerated, they would regard her as the true criminal and themselves as only amateurs. The wait was an ordeal and the smells were horrific. The pen in which she was placed was crowded. Many of the women stank of urine and sweat that dried a long time ago. There was one toilet in the pen without a scintilla of privacy. No one could blame the women for not wishing to relieve themselves in such an open place. Despite the public nature of such a setting, Laurie actually contemplated urinating in the cell potty until she had noticed that the one roll of toilet paper had been exhausted. She would simply have to hold it in. She mused over how she could be found in such a position. She knew, but it was still unbelievable to her. Laurie thought that she was dreaming that she was in a play where she was wrongly accused of committing a crime. Only this was no play. It was surreal, yet unfortunately quite real . . .

I will never forget her. I was just caught by surprise when she called me in the spring of 1995. How long had it been? It must have been more than ten years since I had represented Laurie on charges of assault in the first degree and criminal possession of a weapon in the second, third, and fourth degrees. That case had been an eye-opener for me, and since then my eyes have never been closed.

When Laurie walked into our law offices in 1984, I was not an expert on domestic violence. In fact battered women's syndrome was not formally recognized in New York by an appellate court as an accepted syndrome until

They spent more and more time together. Steve would have a few drinks when they ate out at a restaurant. Then Laurie would notice that he started to have a few cocktails before dinner and drinks after dinner even when they dined at home. As time went on, she started to smell the odor of alcohol when she saw him on a weekend afternoon. She also detected anger and almost a rage about him when he had more than a few drinks in him.

Laurie thought that she could still deal with Steve. He never acted violently toward her, and his wrath was not directed at her. She would speak to him about his drinking, and everything would be as before. Oh, were it so easy!

She continued to talk to him about his drinking. He became less responsive as time went on. Laurie attempted to discuss the issues surrounding his alcoholism and tried to persuade him to seek professional help or to join Alcoholics Anonymous. Steve listened less and less and became more and more defiant. Their relationship gradually grew dysfunctional—ugly, nasty, and then violent.

On one occasion, he threw a beer bottle at her when she chided him for his drinking. Laurie forgave him—for a while. He apologized profusely and sent her flowers. Steve told her that it would not happen again. Yet the drinking, anger, and arguments soon continued. This type of behavior escalated one terrible day when he hit her with a blow that luckily only glanced off of her cheek during a spat over the same old stuff.

"Get out of my house and stay out. I don't ever want to see you again." Laurie trembled.

Steve stood his ground without any indication that he was intending to leave.

"If you don't leave right now, I will call the police!" Laurie screamed.

Steve hesitated, then walked out, slamming the front door behind him. That was it—over, finished, caput, or so she thought.

Just like Steve was unable to stop the drinking, the anger, or the arguments, he was unable to put Laurie out of his mind or out of his life. He would call her repeatedly at work and at home. When he had a snootful to drink, he sometimes threatened to kill her. Laurie was fearful, but she thought that Steve would not make good on any of his threats.

One late Thursday afternoon during the school Christmas vacation, Steve called and called and called. Laurie repeatedly hung up on him. Yet she knew that these calls were somehow different from the others. Steve sounded more agitated, and yes, there was something else—he was chillingly determined.

In the past, after Laurie had hung up on him several times, he would seem to get the picture and stop calling. This night Steve was relentless. Call after call after call after hang-up after hang-up after hang-up, he would call again and again. She decided that she would talk to him to tell him to stop calling. She thought that maybe the holidays were getting to him. Perhaps that was it; he was alone for the holidays. Then she caught herself. She was making excuses for him, again. Sure enough he called one more time.

Laurie started to speak, but when Steve actually heard her voice, he seemed to become infuriated. She thought it was almost as though he felt cheated when she did not hang up on him because he was deprived of another opportunity to call and to drive her crazy. Her very voice seemed to make him more enraged. He was breathing oh so heavily.

"I will break your arms, legs, and neck if you ever hang up on me again," Steve bellowed.

Laurie told him, "Calm down!"

Steve threatened, "I'll break every fucking bone in your body if you don't see me right now!"

"I will never ever see you again," Laurie stated simply.

Steve roared back, "You'll be real sorry that you were ever born. Bitch, you will pay real soon for all that you did to me!"

She thought, "What did I do to him?" She recalled how she shared with him her innermost thoughts and how she gave him her most precious gift, her love. These sentiments quickly passed as she conjured up the indelible memory of his alcohol-laden breath blowing upon her. Then the present once again became real.

Steve screamed, "I am going to come over tonight to kill you!"

When he had hung up, Laurie realized that this time was truly different than the other times when Steve had called in a drunken stupor. He had never hung up on her before. She had always hung up on him while he was in the midst of his blind ravings. He had also never made threats of such an immediate nature.

Laurie could not simply attribute these calls to Steve's loneliness during the holidays. Although she did not call the police, Laurie did think that Steve was serious, perhaps deadly serious. She did call her son at work. She described what had transpired over the phone and how scared she was. Although she thought of leaving, Laurie asked her son to sleep at her house that night as she did not want to be alone. Her son said he would leave in fifteen minutes and be there just as fast as possible.

Her son said in an attempt to reassure her, "Steve probably was just drunk and saying anything that came to his mind." Yet her son had his doubts and left his office within five minutes.

Laurie calmed down slightly as she hung up the phone. She instantly calculated that her son was twenty to twenty-five minutes away by car even without traffic. She added the fifteen minutes to his trip and realized that he would not arrive for another forty minutes. She thought that maybe it was a mistake to stay and wait for her son.

Here was a woman who was the envy of all her friends and acquaintances for her ability to live and to survive on her own. As a single parent, Laurie supported herself while she returned to school. She raised her children in the same house where she now lived. She had resided there alone for the past six years when her nest became empty. The prospect of being alone in her house never bothered her. She admittedly did not prefer it this way and sometimes felt lonely and on many occasions longed to have a man friend for romance and companionship. Still she loved her privacy and valued her time spent puttering about the house. Yet right then, Laurie was very uneasy at the prospect of being isolated for forty minutes, a time period that all of a sudden seemed as though it were eternity. She second-guessed herself, thinking that maybe she should have left her house.

Laurie's thoughts were immediately interrupted by a loud crashing sound on the front entrance to her house. She looked out of the bedroom window and spied Steve lowering his shoulder into her front door. She was unable to see the actual point of contact, but she now felt justified in spending the extra money on replacing her old door with a newer, heavier model and in purchasing sturdier locks. It was clear that the new door and locks could withstand whatever Steve had to offer. She trembled at the realization that he would eventually secure entry either by breaking a window or by going through the side door, which she had not yet replaced.

Laurie contemplated calling her son or the police. She quickly realized that her son was en route and even the police would not arrive fast enough should Steve succeed in entering her home. This was a time when there were no cell phones. She knew what she had to do.

After Laurie and her ex-husband had separated many years ago, she had purchased a handgun legally when she was on a vacation with her then-small children down south. In the back of her mind, she always planned on applying for a license in New York City. It was never a priority, and the issue of the license was invariably shuffled to the back burner. Days turned into weeks, weeks into months, and months into years. Laurie's procrastination in this matter led to complete inertia. She had originally purchased the weapon as safety insurance for the protection of her children. She never had used the gun, nor had she ever taken it out of its hiding place.

When she had purchased the handgun, she had contemplated that she could possibly need it to deter would-be burglars or robbers that might come into her house and threaten her babies. Laurie thought that in the unlikely event that she would need to resort to the use of the weapon, it would be because of an intruder, a stranger. She never conceived that she would need to use a weapon against someone she knew, especially someone with whom she had shared an intimate relationship.

Yet it was clear to Laurie that the time had come when she would need the gun not only to protect herself, but perhaps to save her life. Laurie ran to the back of her bedroom closet, to clear away some shoe boxes covering the removable wooden tile that concealed a drop box below. She reached down to lift open the tile and then to grasp the almost forgotten, and until now, the never before removed, fully loaded, .38 caliber handgun.

She ran down the stairs clasping the gun in her right hand, her shooting hand. As she approached the large window in the kitchen, Laurie observed Steve running in the middle of the street across from her house carrying what appeared to be some small kind of bat. She quickly reasoned that her better course of safety would be to be outside her house in the open. There, others might see her plight and help her. She feared that if Steve secured entry into her home, the mayhem that he would inflict upon her would go unnoticed.

This calculus was done in an instant as Laurie sprang toward the front door, opened it, jumped down two steps, and spotted Steve entering the curtilage of her property by the metal chain link gate. It was then that she observed that the object in Steve's hand was not a small bat but a metal pipe. The gravity of the situation was not lost on her. Even while failing to slow her rapidly beating heart, reflexively she instantly raised her arm, breathed out, aimed the weapon, and fired.

Steve went down like a felled rhino. He stopped in his tracks and slumped to the ground motionless. Laurie thought that she had killed him for sure. She was almost in shock. Laurie had not practiced her shooting since she was a teenager. Until her late teens she used to enjoy going with her father to the firing range. Her dad was so patient with her. He would inculcate the basic lessons of shooting: breathe out, relax, aim, and steadily squeeze the trigger. These early lessons served Laurie well during the only time, she hoped, they would ever be needed.

When the reality of the moment hit her, she realized that she must call the police. She entered the house, placed the gun on the kitchen counter, and removed the phone from its receiver and called 911. A few minutes after she replaced the phone into its cradle, she heard the blare of sirens growing louder, signaling the imminent arrival of the police. Laurie felt a sense of relief that help had at last arrived. To Laurie the last few minutes seemed endless.

When Laurie exited her house once again, she realized the police were not there to rescue or to comfort her, but they had come for her. A muscular rather young-looking officer with fire-red hair read her Miranda warnings. Although she indicated that she would answer the officer's questions without the presence of a lawyer, he only wanted to know where she put the gun.

Laurie directed the police officer to the kitchen counter, but before she could accompany him into the house, he handcuffed her. His partner led her toward the patrol car.

On the way, she passed Steve, still supine and motionless, being administered to by ambulance and EMS personnel. Her fear had vanished earlier when she had pulled the trigger and had shot Steve. Although she reckoned that she had killed him, she prayed that she had not.

Now passing Steve, who was lying on the ground motionless, she palpably felt her fear returning. Laurie was certain that she would be charged with Steve's murder. At the same instant that she felt this overwhelming fear, she also experienced a flood of confusion.

She asked herself a multitude of rhetorical questions seemingly at the same time. Didn't they see the lead pipe lying only a few feet from Steve? Didn't the police know that Steve was trying to kill her? Why didn't they ask her what had happened so that she could remain at home? Didn't they know that she called 911? Why was she handcuffed behind her back so tightly that her wrists hurt and why was she being stuffed into the backseat of a police car like a common criminal? "Why? Why? Why? Why?????" She wondered aloud as her thoughts were unconsciously transformed into speech. They didn't see; they didn't know; they didn't ask. She started to sob uncontrollably.

Laurie was transported to the station house. She was placed into what she believed to be some kind of interview room. After what seemed like a couple of hours, a hard-faced detective with closely cropped hair reread her Miranda warnings.

Once again Laurie consented to speak with the detective without the benefit of having an attorney present. Even though he had stubbled and craggy skin and a smile never seemed to cross his face, she was certain that once he heard the truth, he would understand and let her go home. He had given her a Big Mac and a Coke when she had told him she had been hungry. He had allowed her to use the bathroom when she said she had to go. Laurie was quite surprised, after she had finished her rendition of the pertinent events of the evening, when the detective asked her whether she would agree to sign the written statement that he had prepared based on what she had told him. She became even more perplexed when after she had signed the statement, the detective told her that an assistant district attorney would be arriving soon to talk to her. Again? What could she possibly add to what she had already recounted? The detective told her that if she were willing, the assistant district attorney wanted to memorialize her statement by videotaping it.

Laurie all at once realized that no matter what she told them or how many times she said it, they were not going to release her. She told the detective that she would not answer any more questions without a lawyer being present. The detective never asked her another question, nor did she get to see an assistant district attorney.

Within five or six hours, she was sent to Central Booking. She spent more than ten hours there waiting to be interviewed for the processing of her arrest. There she was asked for pedigree information such as her name, address, date of birth, height, weight, job, next of kin, and so forth. After being transported to the local criminal court, she spent the next five and one-half hours waiting for the return of her fingerprints from Albany.

The pens in the courthouse were quite the experience. Laurie was placed with other females who were also waiting to be arraigned before a judge. She imagined that almost all of the other women in there with her were in jail for prostitution, drug addiction or pushing, shoplifting, or maybe for a petty assault. Laurie viewed them as the real criminals, not herself. Upon brief reflection, she recognized the irony of the situation. If they knew why she was incarcerated, they would regard her as the true criminal and themselves as only amateurs.

The wait was an ordeal and the smells were horrific. The pen in which she was placed was crowded. Many of the women stank of urine and sweat that dried a long time ago. There was one toilet in the pen without a scintilla of privacy. No one could blame the women for not wishing to relieve themselves in such an open place. Despite the public nature of urinating in such a setting, Laurie actually contemplated using the cell potty until she had noticed that the one roll of toilet paper had been exhausted. She would simply have to hold it in. She mused over how she could be found in such a position. She knew, but it was still unbelievable to her. Laurie thought that she was dreaming that she was in a play where she was wrongly accused of committing a crime. Only this was no play. It was surreal, yet unfortunately quite real.

None too soon her name was called, and she was brought up with five other women to the holding cell just outside of the courtroom. Although the holding cell seemed spacious compared to the pens where she had just been, Laurie still experienced the cramped, almost claustrophobic feeling that pervaded her being since she had been placed in the station house cell. At last she thought, she would soon see a judge, an objective party, to whom she could tell her side of the story to clear up this mess.

After about twenty minutes, a man in his late sixties called out her name. "I am J. J. Thomas. I will be your attorney for the Criminal Court arraignment."

He motioned her to a part of the cell that had an entry and a chair and a board that served as a desktop. The lawyer sat down in his part of the "interview room." They were still separated by mesh steel and a Plexiglas panel similar to a divider in a bank between the customer and the teller.

The bespectacled Legal Aid attorney wore a bow tie to go with his double-breasted suit that always remains in fashion. He was impeccably groomed and dressed. He had a full head of hair that was brushed to the left side and held in place by some gel or mousse. Laurie's mind wandered to the old Brylcream commercial, "A little dab will do ya."

He did not fit the stereotype of a public defender. J. J. Thomas was obviously a career man. Laurie had always imagined that public defenders were all young men and women who stayed a few years to gain some trial experience before moving onto their own private practices. The physical juxtaposition of Joshua J. Thomas with the young public defender working alongside him was striking. The younger man wore a brown rumpled Sears's type suit. He had a straggly beard. They both exhibited an enthusiasm and exhibited a caring respect for their clients that made it appear to Laurie that they loved their work.

J. J. Thomas, Esq., was quick, yet seemingly patient and fatherly in explaining to Laurie that since she was working, made a decent living, and owned her home, she would have to hire a private attorney. He seemed very bright and attuned to her situation. She wished that she would have qualified for this particular public defender.

He asked her information about her job, family, and how long she had resided in her home. He asked Laurie whether any family members would be in court when the case would be called and whether any of her relatives would be able to post the bail that would almost certainly be set in a case where the top count was attempted murder. J. J. Thomas stated that the fact that Laurie had not previously been arrested, had been steadily employed, and had long-standing roots in the community would mitigate in her favor when the judge determined what an appropriate amount of bail would be.

Laurie had a delayed reaction to the import of her attorney's statement. She was incredulous, and her feeling of helplessness and depression momentarily disappeared and was replaced by a sense of relief.

"What?" she cried. "Steve's not dead?"

The lawyer informed her that he had conferenced her case with the assistant district attorney in the arraignment part during a court break. She told him that although Steve lost a lot of blood and his condition was serious, he was not dead nor was he likely to die.

Laurie finally answered her lawyer's questions, telling him that she thought that either or both of her children may be in court. She thought that she could put up to forty thousand dollars toward a bail bond. The lawyer from the Legal Aid Society reminded her that she would need to hold some of her money in reserve to retain an attorney.

J. J. Thomas then asked Laurie to tell him about the events of the previous evening and any pertinent background information. After she concluded her description of the incident, she asked whether she would be able to address the judge directly. She was shocked when the attorney told her that he would do all the talking to the judge on her behalf. She understood why she should be silent after the reasons were explained to her by Joshua J. Thomas, mainly that she might incriminate herself unknowingly.

Laurie was impressed by the speed in which the lawyer collected, recorded, and processed the information that she had provided. His answers were clear and concise and given with great alacrity. The entire duration of her discussion with the attorney from the first moment when he introduced himself to his last words—"I will see you soon when you go before the judge"—lasted no longer than twelve minutes. Laurie realized that he afforded her more time than any of the other four women that he had interviewed. He gave no more than eight minutes to each.

Laurie had a bad feeling. Nothing seemed to be breaking her way. It was 4:45 p.m. when the interview with her attorney was concluded. At about 5:10 p.m., J. J. Thomas had completed the consultations with his assigned clients in the holding cell. He informed the group that the court was breaking from five to six o'clock, when the night court shift would begin. Much to her relief, J. J. Thomas explained that he would handle the arraignments of all those whom he had interviewed.

After another jailhouse dinner, this time consisting of an American cheese sandwich, the third case to be called after the resumption of court was Laurie's. In five, maybe eight minutes, the entire arraignment proceeding was over. Laurie's attorney was nearly perfect in forecasting what would occur. Joshua J. Thomas waived the reading of the charges against her and entered a plea of not guilty on her behalf.

The assistant district attorney, a pretty woman with dark brown curly permed hair and dressed in an expensive Evan Picone navy blue suit, recited what she believed to be the events of the incident. Her depiction of the facts clearly laid the entire blame on Laurie. The prosecutor requested that the judge set bail in the amount of two hundred thousand dollars.

Laurie's attorney reminded the judge that the assistant district attorney's rendition was only an allegation. Then her attorney provided the magistrate with Laurie's view of the facts. J. J. Thomas was quick to point out to the judge that Laurie's children were both in the courtroom. She was gainfully employed and had worked in the same job for more than fifteen years. She owned the home in which she lived, and she had never before been arrested. Her lawyer informed the judge that Laurie would be hiring private counsel as she was financially ineligible to have an attorney appointed by the court. He asked the judge to set bail in an amount more reasonable than that requested by the prosecutor.

The judge, a most serious-looking man in his late fifties, was bald with a black crown of hair with more than speckled gray throughout and seemed interested in what J. J. Thomas was saying.

Peering over his glasses, which were casually perched on the tip of his nose, the judge asked J. J. Thomas, "What do you consider a reasonable bail to be?"

Thomas replied, "Under these circumstances, Judge, a fifty-thousand-dollar bond or in the alternative, twenty-five thousand cash bail." That was the precise amount of bail set.

Laurie was given a short court room visit with each of her children. She blew kisses to them and whispered, "I love you."

Then they all talked about putting up the bail. All at once a light bulb went off in Laurie's head. She realized that the banks would be closed for the weekend and on Monday, New Year's Day. She then quickly resigned herself to spending the next three days in jail.

Laurie was transported to Riker's Island and placed in the women's prison, the Anna Cross Center. All the prisoners were either awaiting trial or had been sentenced to jail terms of one year or less. The conditions at the prison were not great but were far superior to those at Central Booking or at the pens at the courthouse.

Laurie's roommate was a young black woman who had been sentenced to a six-month period of incarceration for shoplifting. This had not been her first arrest for this offense. In fact, she had been through the criminal justice system five times before her punishment for her most recent crime. In this context, she was a good cell mate who kept mostly to herself. When she did speak to Laurie, she was not intrusive or nosy.

Thankfully the days that Laurie spent at Riker's Island passed relatively quickly and uneventfully. After her children secured the fifty-thousand-dollar bond from a bail bondsman on Tuesday, she was released and her son drove her to freedom across the Riker's Island Bridge. Now Laurie faced the unenviable task of hiring a criminal attorney to defend her.

Laurie searched the yellow pages under criminal attorneys. There were ads and more ads. Instead of being enlightened, she became more confused. How was she to know who was good for her case? Then she called the local bar association for a suggestion. It was explained to her that she would be referred to the next criminal defense attorney on a rotating list. The attorney would then provide her with a free consultation. At that point Laurie could determine whether to retain the suggested lawyer to represent her. She thanked the local bar association representative but said no thanks. Laurie did not like the idea of hiring an attorney next on a list, the luck of the draw so to speak. Thankfully one of Laurie's friends recommended a noted criminal defense firm whose office was near the courthouse.

Laurie met with one of the named partners of the firm. He was a short, sturdy man in his late forties. He was all business and very thorough in obtaining the facts of the incident and the relevant background information. His earnestness was further emphasized by his Wall Street–style suspenders and his perfectly knotted bow tie. Laurie liked him and his manner. She hired him, or so she thought. She signed the retainer agreement and paid some money.

Her attorney called the district attorney's office and ascertained which assistant was assigned to the case. He then phoned the assigned assistant and spoke with her for about five minutes. Then he turned his attention to Laurie. Over and over she related the events of the incident and the facts leading up to that fateful evening. The named partner informed her that she would be testifying before the grand jury on the day after tomorrow. Laurie made another appointment to meet with the named partner after five o'clock the next evening.

When she arrived, she again went over her story, the true story. At the end of the session, the named partner told Laurie, "You are well prepared. You will be fine. I will be unable to accompany you tomorrow when you testify before the grand jury."

The named partner explained that an old client had been arrested and charged with others with being involved in a large drug conspiracy. He had to be in federal court the next morning for his old client's arraignment.

Laurie was unnerved. Those words stung as though salt were being poured on an open wound. All her confidence had dissolved when she heard those words that the named partner would not be there with her. The named partner unsuccessfully attempted to relieve Laurie's anxiety by informing her that another attorney from the law firm would appear with her the next morning at the grand jury proceeding. The named partner gave her the attorney's name.

"Unfortunately, I cannot introduce you to him now as he had to leave early today," the named partner stated in a rather lame attempt to reassure her.

Laurie frantically exclaimed, "I engaged you, someone who is familiar with my case. I didn't hire another attorney whom I have not yet met."

The named partner explained that in fact she had retained not only him but also the entire law firm. Any of the attorneys qualified to handle Laurie's case could be assigned to represent her. Further, he told her that this was fully laid out in the retainer agreement that she had signed.

The named partner attempted to reassure Laurie. He told her that the attorney who would go with her to the grand jury had been fully briefed as to the circumstances of her case. The named partner then spent the next ten minutes explaining to Laurie the important but limited function that a defense attorney serves in accompanying a targeted suspect who testifies before a grand jury under a waiver of immunity.[4] Although counsel is present and available to confer with the client, the attorney may not otherwise participate in the grand jury proceeding. He concluded by informing her that she was lucky that this was not a federal case. There, he explained, the target must testify without the attorney's presence in the grand jury.

Laurie left the law office feeling alone, abandoned, and somewhat betrayed. She had a fitful sleep that night. The next morning, Laurie arrived at the courthouse devoid of any of the self-assurance that she had earlier possessed.

She met the young lawyer associated with the law firm she had retained. He seemed nice enough. He was with the firm for one year since completing his four-year commitment with the district attorney's office. He did not exude the authority that she felt in the named partner. Consequently her confidence was deeply shaken in being able to convey her feelings and the related factual background to the grand jury for the incident for which she was charged.

Although the assistant district attorney gave Laurie wide latitude in rendering her version of the evening's events, Laurie's portrayal of the incident and her recitation of the scope and nature of her relationship were abysmal. She almost forgot to mention that Steve had a lead pipe when he came barreling down the street. The only positive outcome achieved by this exercise was that the grand jury did not indict Laurie for attempted murder.

Laurie was relieved and in fact grateful that she was no longer facing a charge of attempted murder. The indicted charges of assault in the first degree and criminal possession of a weapon in the second degree, however, were both C violent felonies for which Laurie would receive mandatory state prison time that could be as much as fifteen years should she be convicted after trial.

She could not imagine going to prison for years. Yet Laurie sensed that there was nothing else she could do to prevent this. "It was inevitable," she thought to herself. No one was hearing what she had to say. If they were hearing, they certainly were not listening.

Laurie was unhappy with the prospect of having the firm that she had originally engaged continue to represent her. She did not approve of the way she was shuffled off at the last instant from the named partner with whom she had developed a rapport to the young well-meaning associate whom she did not know at all. She objected to the last-minute switch as well as to the "take it or leave it" manner in which it was done.

Laurie was determined to retain another law firm to defend her. She was recommended to a named partner in the firm where I had worked and where I would later become a partner. Laurie once again gave all the appropriate information germane to her case. She did not object when I was given her case as I was present throughout the initial interview. Thereafter, I always dealt with her.

Laurie was aware that Steve was fired from his employment at the phone company, but she was fuzzy as to the reasons for his discharge. Since her release from jail, Laurie had done some word-of-mouth investigation and had come to believe that Steve had been terminated for aggressive behavior. The circumstances attendant to the shooting incident warranted the making of a motion to dismiss the indictment in the furtherance of justice. Steve's employment and character were certainly relevant factors in the court's exercise of its discretion in deciding whether to grant or to deny a motion to dismiss in the interest of justice. Thus, it was proper and relevant to subpoena Steve's employment records to the courthouse, especially since a good-faith basis existed to believe that he was terminated for cause.

Sure enough, Steve's personnel records provided a treasure trove of helpful information. Over a period of at least the last three years prior to his being discharged, Steve had been verbally abusive to his superiors. On a few occasions, he had threatened supervisors with bodily harm. The last incident leading to Steve's dismissal involved him shoving a coworker. These incidents were memorialized by a company looking to make a record to be utilized ultimately for the disciplining and perhaps the termination of one of its employees. These documents were now going to be used for quite another purpose. If Steve would threaten his superiors at work, the same people who were responsible for recommending whether he should be given a raise or a promotion or whether his employment should be discontinued, then why would anyone doubt that he was capable of threatening Laurie with mayhem and acting out on such a threat?

Although it was improbable that Steve's personnel files would ever be seen by a jury, the judge properly considered these records during the hearing on Laurie's motion to dismiss the indictment in the interest of justice. After listening to Laurie's son testify and after reviewing Steve's employment record, the judge had a good picture of the type of complainant that had been shot—a colossal and aggressive bully who listened to no one, but who was governed by his feelings of anger, rage, and sense of entitlement as well as his thirst for alcohol.

The judge was given a preview of the issues that would be explored at trial. The issues were fully crystallized for the court when the prosecutor called Steve to testify at the hearing. His true personality came out and across to the judge loud and clear. Although he had not yet regained all the weight that he had lost due to the injuries suffered from the shooting, he was still a huge, physically formidable figure.

His answers to the questions posed to him by the prosecutor were cantankerous. His responses to the queries put to him by me bordered on downright nasty and were often sarcastic.

When he was asked where he had lived prior to his then current residence, Steve replied in an almost defiant tone, "Wherever I wanted." When asked why he had been fired by the utility company where he worked, he responded, "No one knew what they were doing. I was the only one there who knew anything."

There was one poignant moment where I did something that I had never done before and have never repeated since as a lawyer. I did the unthinkable and unpardonable. I asked a question whose answer I did not know. As the words were forming on my lips, my mind remembered that fabled example given by law professors everywhere to demonstrate to their students that one should never ask one question too many especially when the answer is unknown to the inquirer:

Question: "Did you ever see Mr. Jones bite your ear off?"

Answer: "No."

Question: "Then how do you know Mr. Jones bit your ear off?"

Answer: "I saw him spit it out."

The answer to that question should have been known to that lawyer. I did not know the answer to my last question and with a sense of dread the words were uttered:

"Do you wish to see Laurie go to jail for shooting you?"

The question was allowed without objection as it was pertinent to two of the relevant hearing criteria, namely, the attitude of the complainant with respect to the motion and the purpose and effect of imposing a sentence authorized for the offense.

The answer came slowly and uncharacteristically seriously and sincerely. "No, I do not. I love her."

Steve probably did in his own twisted way.

The judge called the attorneys up to the bench where he strongly recommended to the assistant district attorney that Laurie be offered a plea to the reduced charge of criminal possession of a weapon in the third degree with a promised sentence of five years' probation. The assistant agreed with the judge's suggestion.

Laurie was also to receive a certificate of relief from civil disabilities, which would in most instances prevent a private employer from using her criminal conviction as a reason for firing or not hiring her. In addition, her civil rights to vote, to hold public office, and to serve as a juror were restored. The State Department of Education declined to convene a hearing to suspend or to revoke her license as an occupational therapist.

While my consciousness returned to the present conversation on the telephone with Laurie and away from those memorable events from a decade ago, I suddenly realized why she was asking me whether she had been convicted of a felony. After the conclusion of her criminal case, I had represented Laurie at an administrative hearing. The local board of education once again authorized her to serve the handicapped students that she loved so much.

Laurie's life and psyche would forever be marked by this indelibly painful experience. Yet all in all, Laurie was lucky. She was a victim who was alive, a survivor. Although she was subjected to the criminal justice system, she stumbled through it relatively unscathed.

A few observations come to mind. Even if battered women syndrome would have been available to Laurie in 1985 as part of a justification or self-defense to the felony assault charge, the possession of the gun charge was still problematic. Usually justification is not a defense to the illegal possession of a firearm. In addition, in New York the illegal possession of a firearm is a felony unless it is in the accused's home. Laurie was faced with the prospect of remaining in her home where she could be trapped by Steve or going outside to prevent him from entering. I certainly do not advocate that anyone should possess an illegal weapon. I do note that it would be very difficult for someone like Laurie to obtain a gun license in New York City. However, if Laurie had not had a weapon and Steve had been able to assault her with the metal pipe he was holding either inside or outside her home, the outcome could have been quite tragic for her.

Although Laurie did commit a crime by having an illegal handgun, Steve committed crimes of domestic violence, arguably attempted burglary and definitely attempted assault with a dangerous instrument, criminal possession of a dangerous instrument with the intent to use unlawfully, trespass, and aggravated harassment by his phone calls. Had there been, as there is now and since 1994, a mandatory arrest policy for crimes involving domestic violence, Steve would have been arrested and charged. The police armed with probable cause now arrest those who are alleged to have committed misdemeanors against intimate partners. Through proper training, the police now can evaluate who is the primary aggressor in a situation where the man, in an effort to avoid arrest or to have the woman arrested, alleges that the woman hit him. Factors include size differential, type and severity of injuries, prior calls to the house or prior incidents, and other firsthand observations.

I came through this episode of my professional life with a new awareness that I would not soon forget. With a smile on my face and joy in my heart, I informed Laurie that although she had been convicted of a felony almost ten years ago, this would not disqualify her from serving jury duty for which she had been summoned.

Chapter Four

Yuri the Hunter

"Sir, your attorney has informed me that you wish to waive your right to be tried by a jury. Is that correct?" I asked.

Through an interpreter, the defendant replied, "Yes."

As the Court TV crew left the courtroom, I knew at that moment that I alone, and not a jury, would have to decide the fate of Yuri, the Russian defendant who was accused of a double homicide and who now stood before me . . .

The Ural Mountains run north to south to the Ural River, which flows into the Caspian Sea. The Urals separate the European or western portion of Russia from the Asian or eastern side. Siberia lies in Asia, east of the Urals. Siberia is harsh and unforgiving. The people also are hard in order to endure the long, cold winters where the temperatures routinely go down to more than one hundred degrees below zero. The living conditions are most difficult. Virtually none of the houses have running water.

Yuri grew up in Siberia. His family had to pump water from an artesian well into buckets, which had to be carried into the house for cooking, washing, and cleaning. Outhouses were then the norm rather than the exception.

Hunting and trapping were necessities rather than sport for many in the Siberia of Yuri's youth. One had to hunt and trap to feed oneself and one's family in order to survive. Yuri hunted animals, including moose and wild ox for their meat. His weapon of choice was a rifle. He trapped mink and sable for their valuable fur.

Yuri was also very good with a knife. He gutted and cleaned his kills with hunting knives. Yuri hunted for food, but he also enjoyed and in fact loved the hunt and did not mind the killing at all. In fact, he delighted in it.

Although Yuri loved the isolation and the primitive aspects of Siberia, it was difficult for him to make a good living. It was nearly impossible to support his family as a hunter and trapper. He had recently been divorced and was still financially responsible for supporting his three-year-old son, Alex.

Yuri decided to relocate to Leningrad, which he did in the early 1980s. He worked as a taxi driver when he met Irina.

They were truly an odd couple. He was a strapping hunter and fur trapper from the wilderness of Siberia. He was hard in every way, including his drinking. His face was craggy, reminding one of the unevenness of the Ural Mountains, the western border of Siberia not far from where Yuri was raised. The coarseness of his appearance was further accentuated by the days' growth of hair that seemed perpetually frozen on his face. He was nearly ten years older than Irina.

Irina was so different than anyone he had ever known. She was petite in stature, soft-spoken, and almost doll-like in appearance with nearly perfect features, light brown hair, and vibrant blue eyes. Her cheeks dimpled whenever she would smile.

Irina was Jewish and only knew the city way of life. She worked in a scientific institute, which was most uncommon for Jews even in Communist Russia. This was the residue of the pre-Communist anti-Semitism. She was quite surprised to have landed her position as the administrator of the bioengineering patent department. When she was a child, she had been a chess prodigy. As a sixteen-year-old, she was skilled enough to represent the Soviet Union in international matches, but the regional tournament director would not give Irina the opportunity to enter a playoff to determine the regional champion that would challenge for the national championship. The director was determined that no Jew would represent Mother Russia if he had anything to do with it.

After Yuri and Irina married, she taught kindergarten. The vestiges of czarist pogroms and sentiments of pre-revolutionary Russia left a deep-seated feeling of anti-Semitism among the populace. Yuri, through no fault of his own, also harbored anti-Semitic feelings. It was handed down from generation to generation.

Yuri did not find the city way of life suitable to his nature and disposition. He felt confined in the city with so many buildings and so many people all close together. When he was driving a cab and before he had met Irina, Yuri would spend his free time in the country whenever he had a rare day off. He missed the hunting, trapping, and free-spirited manner of life.

It was later rumored that Yuri could not return to Siberia as he had been convicted of manslaughter several years prior. Even though Yuri had completed his prison sentence, the family of the man that he had killed wanted to exact their own style of Russian frontier justice.

Yuri had been involved in a heated argument with another hard-drinking man at a local establishment in Siberia when words were replaced by fists and perhaps weapons. No one was sure what exactly occurred, but after it was all over, the other man was dead. He had sustained a crushed skull by the orbital of his left eye. Some say Yuri hit him only with a crashing right fist; others say that some sort of stone or heavy metal object concealed in Yuri's hand caused the man's death. No one knew or asked exactly how much time Yuri had actually spent in prison. Irina only heard about this episode years after they were married.

When Yuri started to date Irina seriously, he would spend his days off with her. Invariably they stayed within the boundaries of Leningrad. This only exacerbated Yuri's feeling of confinement.

Yuri longed for Siberia. Although he could not return, he did the next best thing. He sought and gained employment as a forest ranger in the rural area outside Leningrad. This work was more to Yuri's liking. He reveled in the days with the wind in his face and the sun on his back. He cherished his freedom. More accurately, he loved his sense of feeling free.

He did not miss the restraints of the taxi cab at all. He often wondered how Earth would seem to aliens observing humans entering and driving automobiles. The uninitiated might think that humans were parasites living off of these host-vehicles.

Yuri enjoyed the solitude of his nights in his own special way. Unimpeded, he would be able to pour down his beloved vodka without hesitation or reservation. Every once in a while, a friend from home would visit his quarters and spend the night. On those occasions, the two would drink together and talk until well after midnight.

Yuri and Irina's relationship evolved into a serious one. They were married in 1985. Although he moderated his drinking at the beginning of their marriage, within six months Yuri returned to drinking to the near point of intoxication on a nightly basis. His drinking once again tapered off to moderation when Irina became pregnant.

In 1987, they had a beautiful baby boy named Mikhail. For many months after the birth of their baby, Yuri was able to curtail his intake of vodka. Yuri had started to physically abuse Irina on several occasions even when he was not intoxicated. When their child became two years old, Yuri continued to drink heavily.

They had separated a few times while they lived in Leningrad, each time after Yuri had beaten Irina. They would inevitably reunite after a short period. Yuri and Irina decided that they would immigrate to the United States in late 1992 or early 1993. Two weeks prior to their departure from Russia to the United States, Yuri once again struck her forcefully. Irina, this time with blackened eyes, once again left Yuri to move in with her parents. As she was exiting through the door, Yuri threw a package of rubles at her, sneering and saying through angry, contorted lips, "Take it. This is for your funeral."

Yuri did not like Irina's parents. In fact, he despised them. He tried to separate and isolate Irina from her family. He did not ever want Irina to visit her mother and father. Perhaps he resented the safe harbor they provided her whenever she left him. Maybe it was deeper than that.

Yuri was able to overlook the "Jewishness" of his wife. He thought he loved her, and he did, as much as he was capable of loving anyone in his very limited and misguided way. Irina's parents were a different story. Yuri thought Vladimir and Tatiana were the Jews that deserved to be the objects of the derisive jokes and subjects of the demeaning caricatures that were abundantly common in the Siberia of his youth. His disdain for Irina's parents spilled over and was transformed into an intense hatred of her sister, Petrova. Yuri could not countenance that Petrova was Irina's confidante. He detested the fact that his wife told Petrova her most secret and intimate thoughts. This was something that Irina had not shared with him for several years. He also realized, and could not bear, that Petrova knew about all their fights and the beatings and his drunken episodes. Yuri's intense hatred for and jealousy of Irina's family would portend badly for her parents.

Irina and Mikhail immigrated to the United States in 1994 along with Irina's parents, Vladimir and Tatiana, and her sister, Petrova. Irina lived with her parents and sister. Later the same year, Yuri also came to America. They reconciled and rented an apartment in the Brighton Beach section of Brooklyn.

Irina worked at various jobs to make ends meet. It was not easy. She also went back to school to study to be a medical secretary. Financially and emotionally, Yuri and Irina's relationship became further strained when Yuri's son from his first marriage, Alex, immigrated to the United States and lived with them. It did not ease the tension or help their marriage when Yuri was unable to find work after months of searching. There simply was no great demand in New York for a Russian forest ranger-hunter-trapper who did not yet speak English.

Although Yuri had promised to change, he was unable to do so. He still was unhappy when Irina went to visit her parents and sister. Not only would he not go with her, he again tried to deter her from having any connection with them. On the few occasions that her parents came to visit at the apartment that he shared with Irina, Yuri would leave prior to his in-laws' arrival and come home late in the night cockeyed drunk. As the days of unemployment turned into weeks and the daily strains of life began to wear and tear at the fragile, thin fabric of their marriage, Yuri's drinking became noticeably worse.

After one evening of too many shots of vodka followed by beer chasers, Yuri poured a bottle of beer over Irina's head. One humiliating gesture achieved what several beatings could not and pushed Irina out of Yuri's life for good. Irina called her parents who brought Mikhail and Irina to their apartment. Irina would never return to live with Yuri again.

Over the next few months, Irina and Mikhail, then ten years old, continued to reside with her parents. Petrova had married her fiancé, Sasha, and moved out of her parents' apartment.

Several times, Yuri would telephone Irina at her parents' apartment or stop her on the street to ask her, to beg her, to come back to their apartment. Each time, he promised he would change his personality and stop drinking. Each time he assured her that he would be okay, that they would be okay. Each time for the sake of their child she wanted to believe him. Each time, because of their son, she knew that she could not afford to trust him. Irina noticed no perceptible change in his personality, behavior, or drinking habits since they were together in Russia. The only real difference in their situation, in his situation, is that he no longer worked.

In early January of 1995, Irina arose at 5:40 in the morning to ready herself for work. She moved in silence in order not to awaken her sleeping parents and son. After showering, dressing, and putting on makeup, she had breakfast with Mikhail as was their custom on most every school day. She left the apartment at about 7:00 a.m. to catch the D train to school.

The early morning sun was ineffective in combating the cold that seemed to penetrate every pore and joint of her body despite the fact that she was dressed in layers and was wearing a long down coat specifically purchased to provide shelter from the severe Russian winters. The morning nor'easter swept the dampness in from the Brighton Beach shore more chillingly than usual. Irina had an uneasy feeling that the morning's eerie chill was a warning of something cruel or even evil to come. She did not have to wait very long.

As she neared the corner where Ocean Parkway meets Kings Highway, she was startled to see Yuri's car parked with the motor running. Yuri opened the window on the driver's side and called Irina over to the car. She walked slowly on the sidewalk toward the front door.

"Can I drive you to school?" Yuri asked Irina in Russian.

Irina was taking her classes in lower Manhattan to become a medical secretary. Although she was reluctant to enter Yuri's car, she was cold and was content to avoid the windswept five-block-trek to the train station as well as the cold and often long wait for the D train.

The car ride, from Brighton Beach to the Belt Parkway to the Brooklyn Queens Expressway, then over the Brooklyn Bridge to the southernmost part of Broadway by the tip of Manhattan, where the technical institute that Irina attended was located, had taken an hour and twenty-five minutes because of the usual Monday morning rush-hour traffic. The actual travel time on the subway normally lasted no more than forty minutes. Irina lamented her choice to take Yuri up on his offer to give her a lift to school, not merely because she arrived five minutes late for her class, but also since she was a captive and a most grudging participant in a conversation that had been held many times before and that had been conclusively resolved, at least in her own mind.

Yuri had once again professed his undying love for her and asked Irina to come home and to give him another "final" chance. He had assured her that he had changed. He promised that he would never hit her nor would he ever drink again.

Irina, with a resolve that she had felt in her heart but that she had never previously articulated to Yuri, told him with tears welling up in her eyes, "I do not believe you and I cannot forgive you. I am planning to start my life over without you."

Uncharacteristically Yuri did not indulge in a violent or even a surly reaction. Irina was truly surprised and even relieved. Yet she was truly mystified that Yuri revealed absolutely no response at all. He simply looked straight ahead, finished the last few minutes of their journey, pulled the car over to the curb when they arrived at Irina's technical school, and said good-bye, uneventfully, as she exited the automobile. Irina was puzzled at this poker-styled attitude by a man who was never able before to subdue his passion.

Irina did not have the luxury to reflect on Yuri's lack of emotion or reaction. She was late to class and had to hurry. After class ended at 12:15 p.m., she walked seven blocks uptown, then gobbled down her brown-bag lunch when she arrived at her workplace. She worked a five-hour shift as a paralegal in the patent section of a small intellectual property law firm.

At six o'clock, she walked the three blocks from City Hall to Grand Street to catch the D train back to Brighton Beach. She had intended during the train ride home to mull over the events of the early morning and Yuri's unfamiliar behavior in the car. Yet after about five minutes of musing, Irina succumbed to the droning sounds of the train's wheels on the tracks and fell into an uneasy sleep. She awoke at Neck Road Station, two stops from her destination. Irina exited the train at the Brighton Beach stop and walked the five blocks from the station to her parents' apartment in the silent darkness of the early winter night.

She opened the front door to the apartment and immediately sensed that something was terribly wrong. As she entered the hallway, she spied a reddish-brownish paint smudged haphazardly on the walls. She then peered into the living room. The television was on, and the volume was very loud. The linens and towels were strewn all over the floor seemingly covering every square inch of surface.

Irina was hit with a heavy right fist that crashed into her left cheekbone. She crumbled to the floor where Yuri continued to hit her, to beat her. He tried to push her eyes and teeth out with his thumbs and fingers, which were covered with thick work gloves.

While Yuri was beating her, Irina was crying for help. As Yuri was about to deliver one more telling blow, she heard Mikhail cry out to his father from what she believed to be another room.

"Papa, you promised that you would not hurt Mama!"

Yuri's quickly descending fist instantly opened. He picked Irina up by her coat like she was some light bag of laundry. He carried her into the living room.

Unfortunately the blows dealt by Yuri did not sufficiently blur her vision. Irina screamed, "Oh, no!" over and over again. Her parents were lying side by side motionless on the floor covered with towels and sheets. Yet their bodies were partially exposed.

She shrieked, "How could you? How could you?"

Irina's father was lying on his back. The dark red blood by his stomach where he was apparently wounded was drying and turning to a brownish hue on the blood-soaked sheet that covered him.

Irina looked at Yuri and saw a cruel smile resting on his face. He had been drinking, but he was not nearly intoxicated. Irina knew all the different stages of Yuri's drinking. She noticed the blood spread over his body, face, and clothing.

Fearing for her own life and surging with adrenaline, she summoned all of her remaining strength in an effort to run out of the living room to escape. As a great polar bear would swipe through the ice to snare a seal pup for a meal, Yuri snatched Irina up with one arm and brought her into the kitchen where Mikhail was seated. A closer inspection by Irina revealed that Mikhail's arms and legs were taped to the chair.

Mikhail had come home from school at about 3:30 p.m., his usual time. He rang the downstairs intercom to gain admission into the building. Mikhail took the elevator up to the fifth floor. As he rang the bell to his grandparents' apartment, he saw that the door was slightly ajar. When he had passed through the front door, Mikhail saw his father standing calmly in the entry hallway. Yuri was wearing a green shirt and jeans. The shirt had what Mikhail thought to be tomato juice or sauce on it. His father's face and arms were also covered with the stuff. Later he would learn that it was in fact the blood of his grandfather. Yuri then took Mikhail into his grandparents' bedroom.

Once inside the bedroom, Yuri told Mikhail in Russian that he loved him very much. Yuri then proceeded to fasten the upper arms of Mikhail to his chest with duct tape to immobilize his son and to prevent him from using his arms. Yuri once again told his son how much he loved him and then continued to tape Mikhail's mouth shut. Yuri lifted Mikhail up with great care and placed him on the bed in a supine position.

Yuri then left the bedroom of Vladimir and Tatiana. When he returned ten minutes later, Mikhail through a taped mouth managed to ask in Russian, "Where are Grandma and Grandpa?"

Yuri replied, "You don't have them any longer."

"Did you kill them?" Mikhail inquired, frightened at the prospect that his father may have murdered his grandparents.

All his fears were realized as his father responded with a simple, matter-of-fact "Yes."

Mikhail's little heart was beating rapidly as he strained to be understood through the tape. "Are you going to kill Mother too?"

Yuri answered with complete silence and a hellish stare.

After pregnant moments had passed, the son pleaded with his father, "Please don't kill Mama!"

Yuri, sensing the deep turmoil in his son's heart and soul, promised, "I won't kill your mother."

Yuri again left the bedroom. Mikhail remained lying on the bed with all sorts of thoughts going on in his head. Would his father keep his promise? Would his father harm him? He did not think so, but he did not ever imagine that his father would kill his mother's parents, nor would he have guessed that his father would tie him up. Upon reflection, he knew that his father would never hurt him, but he was not so sure whether his mother would remain safe.

After a few minutes, Yuri came back into the room, picked Mikhail up, and tenderly carried him into the kitchen. Yuri then seated Mikhail into a chair and secured Mikhail's legs and torso to the chair with duct tape. Gingerly Yuri removed the tape from Mikhail's mouth. Yuri exited the kitchen and appeared to head toward the living room. Worried and emotionally exhausted, Mikhail fell asleep within minutes.

The child woke up with a start. Immediately he wondered how long he had been sleeping. He realized that the sound that had awakened him was a loud hammering noise coming from what he thought was the hallway. It was the television. He then heard his mother scream. With great effort and without the use of his hands, Mikhail was able to rise up off the floor on his tiptoes and take a few steps with the chair fastened to his body. As he reached the kitchen doorway, he peered into the hallway where he saw his father repeatedly hitting his mother.

He cried out, "Papa, you promised me that you would not hurt Mama!"

Mikhail saw his father abandon the attack and gather up his mother. With a momentary sense of relief, he relaxed his leg and calf muscles, which had been flexed in an unnatural position in order to maintain him in a quasi-standing posture while being affixed to the chair. The young boy's muscles were exhausted to the point of cramping. He fell backward, and miraculously the chair landed firmly on all four legs after sliding back a few feet toward the center of the kitchen.

It was evident to Irina that her father had put up a valiant struggle to save himself and his beloved Tatiana. Broken crystal and glass was scattered all over the living room floor despite Yuri's best efforts to place the contents of the linen closet over the entire surface in order to obfuscate the two corpses from his son's view. Much of the living room furniture and some chairs in the kitchen were also busted up. This later led the detective investigators to believe that the fighting started in the kitchen and ended in death in the living room.

Vladimir, Irina's father, was going on seventy-two years and was no match for the savage hunter, Yuri. Vladimir had the heart of a lion and had seen war firsthand and close up as a teenaged soldier in Stalin's army during the courageous defense of Leningrad in World War II against the onslaught of the German army. He apparently defended his wife and best friend and lover with the same ferocity that he had displayed many years ago. This time his struggle was valiant, but of no avail.

Only later did Irina learn how her parents were murdered. Even when she identified their bodies at the city morgue, she had no idea of the extent of their injuries. The assistant medical examiner unzipped the two plastic body bags just below the neck to reveal only the faces of her parents. "Those sweet faces would smile and move no more," she thought at the time.

Yuri did make statements to the police and later testified at his trial. After driving Irina to work, Yuri had returned home to the apartment that he had shared with Irina prior to their separation. He gathered a few rolls of duct tape, a bottle of vodka, and his two favorite hunting knives, the ones he used to skin the large animals that he had hunted in Siberia. He then went to his in-laws' home.

Yuri claimed that he only intended to talk to Vladimir and Tatiana when he rang their bell and when they so graciously allowed him to enter. They gave him coffee. Yuri talked about finding work and about the possibility that he and Irina may reconcile. Yuri stated that he brought the knives along because he had no desire to live, and depending on the outcome of his conversation with his in-laws, he was prepared to die there that very day.

The autopsies performed on the bodies of Irina's parents revealed the hatred and rage that Yuri possessed. There were multiple injuries to both Vladimir and Tatiana, six wounds to each. Almost all of the wounds were at least two inches deep and were inflicted with substantial pressure. There were several wounds to Vladimir's back that ranged from four to six inches in depth. The deputy chief medical examiner had testified at trial that there was one wound in Vladimir's chest that was delivered with such force that his sternum was cracked by the impact of the knife upon it.

Irina was standing in the kitchen on wobbly legs, her brain jumbled by the sudden events thrust upon her. Her mind tried to assimilate all that had occurred and what was happening. She was certain that her parents had been murdered, her son had been tied down to a chair, and she had been beaten by her estranged husband. She wondered if he would kill her.

As soon as that thought entered into her consciousness, she felt an immediate and immense sense of guilt. Her first concern was for Mikhail's safety. She thought it unlikely that Yuri would kill his own son. She reconsidered this premise almost as soon as she thought it. Mikhail was also her son. Did not Yuri murder Vladimir and Tatiana simply because they were her parents? In light of what she had just observed, all of her considered judgments and her foundation of beliefs were suddenly and irrevocably shaken. Her immediate concern was to protect Mikhail, who was sitting within five feet of her and affixed to a chair.

This cognitive process lasted only seconds. It was abruptly and explosively interrupted when Yuri picked up a long hunting knife from the kitchen table, held it in his fist, and pointed it at her.

In a calm voice delivered in a steady monotone, which made the words even more menacing, Yuri stated in Russian, "I won't kill you if you spend the night with me."

Mikhail was crying and shaking as he exclaimed to his mother in English, "Mama, do whatever he tells you! What will happen to me if something happens to you?"

These words took hold of what was left of Irina's tattered heart and rendered her will subservient to one end—the survival of her son and, if possible, herself.

Irina nodded in assent to Mikhail as much as to Yuri. Yuri placed the knife in his left hand, and with his right hand, he grasped Irina's left hand and walked her into the master bedroom. Irina was further upset at the specter of being forcefully taken in her parents' bedroom, a place of love, honor, and respect. The sacrilege was further exacerbated by the realization that her attacker had only a short time ago killed her parents and snatched away her security and safe harbor.

Yuri took Irina into the adjoining bathroom. He told her to wash the blood from her face and nose where she had been beaten. After she finished cleaning herself, Yuri ordered her to undress. When Irina removed her last item of clothing, Yuri ordered her to get on her knees. Yuri unzipped his pants and ordered Irina to perform fellatio upon him. Yuri placed his penis in her mouth. She consciously forced herself to move her mouth upon him.

Irina soon realized that Yuri could not get an erection. After a few minutes, he told her to lie down on her parents' bed. Yuri unsuccessfully attempted to have intercourse. Irina was unsure whether Yuri's limp penis had in fact entered her. Nonetheless, the horror and humiliation of this episode were not lost on her. A man whom she had once loved had forced himself upon her in the bedroom of her parents, her loved ones, whom her assailant had murdered only a short while ago.

When Yuri had seemingly abandoned his attack by putting his pants back on, Irina reached into her closet in the hall of the bedroom and placed on her mother's robe.

Yuri started to weep convulsively while exclaiming to Irina in Russian, "It is your fault that your parents are dead. If you only had come back to live with me, none of this would have happened. I have to die now too. I don't know if I should die in the electric chair or if I should kill myself. For forty years I always did whatever I wanted. Now a bunch of Jews try to tell me what to do."

Then Yuri's mood changed inexplicably. He started to giggle and declared that he would now telephone his mother in Russia. He called his mother and talked with her for about five minutes as though nothing had happened. He never suggested to her that anything was awry.

As soon as he had hung up, the phone rang. Yuri would not allow Irina to pick up the receiver. Irina quickly convinced Yuri to allow her to answer the phone. She explained that she was expecting a call from relatives and they may be suspicious if no one were to be home. Yuri warned Irina to speak only in Russian.

Sure enough, it was Irina's sister, Petrova. Yuri directed Irina to tell her that everything was all right.

Irina said in Russian, "Everything is fine here. Call me back in the morning."

Petrova asked, "Irina, may I talk to Momma and Papa?"

Irina replied, "They cannot come to the phone right now. They are out. You can call them in the morning as well."

Petrova, surmising that something was amiss as her parents specifically told her they would be home, asked, "Is everything all right?"

Irina responded simply but with a pounding and excited heart, "Nyet."

Petrova then inquired, "Should I call the police?"

Irina did all she could to deliver her answer in a short and unrevealing manner, which might yet, she thought, save the life of her son. Unemotionally she said, "Da," and then hung up the phone.

Yuri grabbed Irina's hand and informed her while walking toward the bed, "I will be alive only until the morning."

Yuri once again removed his pants. A few minutes after they both went to lie down in bed, they heard someone knocking hard on the front door. Yuri directed Irina to place the robe once more over her body. He held her tightly by the hand and walked her to the front door of the apartment. Irina looked through the peephole and with a sense of great relief saw the police.

Irina, thinking that Yuri may surrender, told him, "The police are here."

Yuri told her to tell the officers, "Everyone is okay, no one called, and nothing happened."

Irina instead informed the officers in English of what had transpired in as calm a voice as she could muster. "My husband killed my parents. He said that he would be dead in the morning. Please don't leave."

Yuri then took Irina back into the kitchen. He then released her hand and ordered her, "Go to the door; tell the police to leave as everything is fine here."

Irina placed her hand on the door handle, then looked back at Yuri who was standing near the entranceway to the kitchen. He looked angry. Irina was ever mindful that Mikhail was in the kitchen very near to Yuri. Yet she realized that the only hope of survival for both her and her son lay with the police. She turned the doorknob, yanked the door open, and ran to safety.

As she ran into the outer hallway, she yelled to the police officers, "My son is in the kitchen and my husband has a big knife!"

Three burly police officers, one bigger than the next, rushed into the apartment with guns drawn. The officers could not help noticing the blood smears on the inner hallway walls. They observed Mikhail, sitting behind a table, facing them. The dried blood on Yuri's clothes, arms, and face immediately reminded the officers of the deadly situation into which they were thrust.

This bear of a man before them, who they were told had just murdered two people, picked up a huge knife and placed it on the small boy's chest. The officers' weapons were all aimed at Yuri's heart.

One of the officers in a loud, firm voice both ordered and implored Yuri, "Put the knife down!"

Almost as though he understood, Yuri placed the knife on the kitchen table. For an instant, he had mesmerized the police. Before they could reach him, drag him to the floor, and handcuff him, Yuri was able to turn around and away from the officers and point, by reaching behind and up, to the middle of his back. It was as though he were directing the police to shoot him at the very spot where he was pointing. Even now he was attempting to orchestrate the final act of his twisted play. The police exercised great restraint in not firing their weapons at Yuri. After a short struggle, they subdued him with much effort.

Yuri was arraigned and remanded. After almost a year of motions and an exploration of a psychiatric defense, the case was set down for trial. Court television staffers were in the courtroom and ready to cover the trial. Just as the court clerk was about to summon a panel of jurors, the court room was stunned by the statement made by Yuri's counsel.

"Your honor, my client wishes to waive his right to be tried by a jury. He requests a bench trial."

"Sir, your attorney has informed me that you wish to waive your right to be tried by a jury. Is that correct?" I asked.

Through an interpreter, the defendant replied, "Yes."

I further explained to Yuri on the record what his waiver of a jury trial would mean to him. Among other things, he was informed that if he were tried by a jury, he could only be convicted if he were found guilty by a unanimous vote by the jury. If one juror held out for a verdict of not guilty, he could not be convicted but would instead receive a new trial. Uninfluenced by an explanation of the nature of his waiver and statistics that I had cited from a federal judge's report that convictions were at a higher rate for bench trials as opposed to jury trials, Yuri persisted in demanding a bench trial and executed a written waiver of his right to be tried by a jury.

As the Court TV crew left the courtroom, I knew that I alone, and not a jury, would have to decide the fate of Yuri, the Russian defendant who was accused of a double homicide and who now stood before me. Court television was not interested in broadcasting a non-jury trial. A bench trial would be too quick for television with little time for the hired attorneys and ex-judges to comment on the trial evidence and the lawyers' respective tactics and overall strategy. I was somewhat relieved as this was my first trial presiding over a domestic violence case. This double homicide was tried by me before I had gained any expertise with domestic violence. My only legal experience dealing with cases involving domestic violence until then was as an attorney defending Laurie. Our specialized Domestic Violence Court had not yet come into being. Yet it was a homicide case and I had experience in trying those cases, and I had previously presided over several bench trials.

At Yuri's trial, the medical examiner testified that Vladimir and Tatiana each suffered six wounds that were delivered to the area of the chest, back, and heart. They were all aimed to incapacitate and then kill. It was not deemed to be the work of a madman opined the prosecution's psychiatrist.

Yuri interposed a psychiatric defense based in large part on a dissociative-type disorder resembling most closely dissociative amnesia (i.e., once a person concludes a traumatic act, that person loses or has no memory of what had occurred). Yuri claimed he did not remember what had transpired after a certain point of that tragic day, a time prior to the deaths of his in-laws. Thus Yuri purportedly did not remember the events of the incident when his in-laws were killed.

This defense was rejected. It was established that Yuri knew what he was doing when he was doing it. The act of bringing two hunting knives and duct tape was strong evidence that not only were his acts intentionally performed, but that they were in fact premeditated. Yuri was convicted of a number of crimes, including two counts each of intentional murder and kidnapping in the second degree. Yuri was sentenced to two terms of twenty-five years to life for each murder. Each sentence was to run consecutively, in effect, fifty years to life in prison.

Yuri's case is concluded. Vladimir and Tatiana feel no more pain. Can there ever be any real resolution for Irina and for little Mikhail? While the physical pain has healed and perhaps the very unpleasant memory of testifying at Yuri's trial has faded, the psychological, mental, and emotional anguish will surely endure for their lifetimes.

Yet this case was truly an eye-opener for me. I realized how deadly the consequences of domestic violence could be. Little did I know that soon my judicial life would be all about these type of cases. Yuri's case made me eternally vigilant in my approach to my new role. I instantly became aware of the effect that domestic violence has on the children involved.

Chapter Five

Desmond and Enid

Enid's injuries were very bad. Some were permanent. Upon her arrival at the resuscitation area of the emergency room at the Kings County Hospital Trauma Center, Enid's throat was immediately intubated to clear her air paths from blood that was impairing her ability to breathe and that could cause her to choke to death. She was somewhat responsive to the doctor's questions, but she was not clearly awake or alert. Enid sustained multiple fractures to her face and to the orbital bones surrounding her eyes. She had to undergo surgery to repair her colon, which was perforated by the bullet that had entered her lower chest. The doctors, despite their best efforts, could not heal the blindness in her left eye or the deafness in her right ear as a result of the three gunshot wounds to her head. She spent more than three weeks in the hospital.

My first trial as the presiding judge of the nation's archetypical court part exclusively dedicated to handling domestic violence felonies began in early July 1996. I remember that during the early days of jury selection, a colleague from Cleveland, Judge Ron Adrine, had called to discuss various issues about setting up a DV court in Cleveland as he was soon to be assigned to head a misdemeanor DV court in his jurisdiction. After answering all his questions as best as I could, I recall telling him that I was still learning and we should talk again in a few months. The next day, I was asked to speak at some community event about domestic violence.

When I informed one of my sisters of this speaking request, she underscored reality: "What makes you an expert after three weeks on the job?"

Every day, I reflected on those words, even after nearly twelve years of presiding over DV cases. Vigilance and hard work are essential, but we must never think that we are experts with all of the answers. Despite everyone's best efforts, the nature of our work places us within a heartbeat of a potential tragedy each and every day. Those words, "What makes you an expert?" continually ring in my ears. I will never fail to remember them, nor will I ever forget my very first trial in the DV part.

Enid had immigrated to the United States from French Guyana in May of 1992. She was an illegal alien. Perhaps that is why she put up with so much from her boyfriend, Desmond. Enid started dating Desmond shortly after Thanksgiving of the same year.

She thought she was lucky.

She was glad to have a boyfriend in a strange and new land. Desmond owned a small construction company and earned a very good living. Enid was the envy of the very few friends she had in Brooklyn and her lone relative in the United States, her sister. They all thought that Desmond was rich. He did take her to nice restaurants and clubs as well as many terrific parties. They had some great times early on in their relationship. She was grateful that she had met someone who was interested in her and who was willing to spend some money to make her happy.

Desmond had also emigrated from French Guyana. His brother was married to one of Enid's sisters (Enid's three children were living with that sister in French Guyana). After a few weeks of dating, they had become intimately involved. Within several months, Enid had given Desmond a set of keys to the apartment where she resided in Brooklyn. She shared the kitchen and the bathroom with a roommate, but she had her own bedroom, where Desmond would often spend the night.

After about six months of dating and living together part time, Enid started to notice certain changes in Desmond. He showed an argumentative side that she had not previously noticed. During one verbal dispute on an evening in July 1993, Desmond had told Enid that he was going to spend the night with another of his women.

She screamed, "Go right ahead and don't ever come back!"

Desmond went his own way and Enid hers.

Later that night, Enid was at a party not far from her apartment. She felt Desmond's firm, and what she thought to be friendly, hand on her shoulder.

He asked her, "Please go outside with me. I have something to say to you." Enid was hoping for an apology. Instead, Desmond head-butted Enid and punched her in the face, causing her to sustain a broken nose and bruises to her cheeks. He beat her and kicked her.

He repeatedly reminded her, "You are mine! You are mine and no one else's!"

They had argued several times earlier, but never had he turned their quarrels into physical altercations. Enid would soon learn that this would be the first but not the last time.

Desmond refused to allow Enid to seek medical attention as he feared, for obvious reasons, that the police would become involved. Desmond had an out-of-state felony drug conviction, which would translate to mandatory state prison time should he again be convicted of any felony. Instead, he insisted that they engage in sexual intercourse. Desmond perversely thought that this was the only "medical attention" that Enid required. This episode was never reported to the police. Enid did, however, receive medical treatment at Kings County Hospital a few days later for her injuries.

The cycle began. Days later, he asked Enid to forgive him. He promised that he would change and that there would be no recurrence of his assaultive behavior.

She wavered and gave in. She had her three children in Guyana to support. Also, she was concerned that her children lived with Desmond's brother, who was married to Enid's sister. Desmond was generous to her in that she never had to spend any money for entertainment, eating out, or socializing when she was with him.

Money was always a consideration. She had to work hard for what she earned. Enid was a home care attendant. When she worked, Enid often had to do twelve-hour shifts, sometimes working a double-duty period without getting paid overtime. She would attend mostly to the elderly who were home-bound and needed twenty-four-hour care seven days a week. Many were bedridden and had to be fed, led to the bathroom, and even have their clothes and bedding changed if they were incontinent. It was a physically demanding job that was often a depressing one. She never complained because there were times when there was no work to be had. Enid was grateful for the work, for this was one of the few positions readily available to an immigrant woman who was without a green card.

Things were better between Enid and Desmond for almost two months. Then in September of 1993, they had a very heated dispute. Enid had requested that Desmond return her apartment keys. She was upset with Desmond and was troubled that he tried to extend his will over what she could and could not do. Without any indication that their verbal disagreement was about to turn violent, Desmond punched her, catching her flush on the head with full force, the point of impact being delivered by a large ring that he was wearing.

Enid reported this incident to the police after seeking medical attention at Kings County Hospital for the lump on her head. The police were prepared to make an arrest.

The officers asked her, "Where does Desmond live?"

Although Enid knew that Desmond lived in the Bronx when he was not with her, she had no idea of his street address. At first she was annoyed, even furious, that she was standing there with blood coming out of her head and all the police wanted to know was "How can you go out with a guy and not know his address?"

But then as the words "I don't know" were rolling off her tongue and leaving her mouth, she realized how silly she sounded and how stupid she had been. How could she not have known where the man with whom she resided for part of each week lived the rest of the time? She thought how absurd the entire situation was and how it must appear to the two policemen standing before her now. She was determined that Desmond would never harm her again.

Her resolution went untested as Desmond seemed to disappear for more than one month. During that time, Enid realized that she had no real support group in the United States. Her one sister living in Brooklyn repeatedly resorted to a talisman expression that "things will get better." While her few friends, more like acquaintances, told her, "You will be okay." No one offered her real help or suggested concrete solutions or even approaches to resolving her problems.

Such was Enid's sense of isolation when Desmond came knocking at her door more than five weeks after she had been assaulted by him. Once again she let him in rather than having the police arrest him. Once again they became intimately involved.

"With little money and nowhere to turn, Enid felt she had no choice but to open her door to Desmond whenever he returned. Her consent to have sex with him was as much a surrender of the spirit as of the body."[1]

Again the fantasy continued. Desmond showed Enid his good side and kept hidden the dark side that was ever ready to erupt. They dined out, shared the same bed, went to movies and clubs, and pretended that nothing had ever occurred.

Then nine months later in July of 1994, Desmond, during an argument over something quite unremarkable that started during dinner at a restaurant, chased Enid down the street while holding a knife.

He yelled after her, "I am going to bust your face in with an ax!"

Although Desmond did not have an ax on his person, he did have one in his van parked nearby. This incident climaxed when he insisted on having sex with her. Enid complied without being physically taken but with the threat of force being ever present.

A few days later, the two argued when Desmond became jealous of another man. This was a central motif in many of their disagreements.

Desmond said, "I am leaving."

"I will leave," Enid replied.

This statement caused Desmond to explode. He threw a hot bowl of food onto Enid's head, causing her to sustain a lump. Enid did not seek medical attention, nor did she report this incident to the police.

Again they made up and things went along without incident for some months. On May 8, 1995, violence once more reared its ugly head. Enid was cooking dinner when Desmond fixated on a man he had seen talking to Enid in the street.

Desmond grabbed a bottle of hot pepper sauce, cracked it open, and cut Enid clear through her upper lip. She was unable to find a way out of her apartment as all of her energy was spent on parrying Desmond's attacks. Although in great pain and bleeding profusely from her upper lip, she at last managed to escape Desmond's onslaught and to run upstairs to a neighbor's apartment.

Feverishly, she alternately rang the doorbell and smashed her fist against the door screaming, "My man stabbed me!"

Enid, with the help of her neighbor, called 911. The police responded, and Enid filed a complaint. When the officers went to Enid's apartment to arrest Desmond, they discovered that he had fled. Enid, her face covered with blood, was taken by ambulance to Brookdale Hospital, where she received seventeen stitches to close her gaping wound.

Amazingly, that night Desmond returned. From the street, Enid saw the lights on in her apartment and saw Desmond moving about. She did not enter the apartment but instead called the police from her neighbor's apartment. She met the officers in front of the building. Enid devised a plan to lure Desmond out of the apartment. She was to be the bait. The police officers were most hesitant and uncomfortable to permit Enid to be placed in jeopardy even for an instant, but she was adamant.

Enid knocked on the front door and taunted Desmond before he could open it. Once opened, Desmond dashed through the doorway following Enid down the stairs. He vaulted over the banister to head her off as she was running away from him. He was able to catch her and forcefully grabbed her by the shoulders. At this time, the officers jumped out of the shadows of the staircase landing and apprehended Desmond. The next day the officers returned to retrieve evidence, the broken hot sauce bottle from the garbage.

Desmond posted the six-thousand-dollar bail set by the judge at his arraignment in the criminal court. There was no record of the previous attacks and assaults that he had perpetrated upon Enid. The judge issued a full stay-away order of protection directing Desmond, among other things, to stay away from Enid and to refrain from contacting her. Yet shortly after his release from jail upon posting bail, he called her in violation of the court's protective order.

Enid did not accede at first to his entreaties. She told him that she did not want to see him. Oftentimes she even hung up the phone. Yet his persistence was gradually wearing down her resistance.

Nine days after his latest assault upon her, Desmond showed up at Enid's girlfriend's apartment where she was now staying. Enid was so emotionally downtrodden that she let Desmond literally in the door and figuratively back into her life. This was a grave mistake.

The two resumed their relationship. They went to a party one Friday night and then left to go to a hotel, where they had sex. Over the next few days, Desmond would call and tell Enid that if she would drop the charges, he would pay for the plastic surgery necessary to clear up the ugly scar that he had caused above her upper lip. This vile, jagged mark was left as an indelible reminder of how cruel and violent Desmond could become in one of his jealous rages. Other times, he would ask her how much money she needed in order for her to drop the case. On another occasion, he took Enid to a jewelry store to replace earrings that she had lost. They had again gone to a hotel in one of the first few days in June for a tryst.

During the few weeks since the latest incident, they dated, partied, dined together, spoke on the phone, and had sex together. Despite Enid's willingness to resume their relationship, there was a marked change or transformation in her will, which had become steely strong. Enid would not provide Desmond with a key to her new apartment. Significantly, she remained steadfast in her refusal to drop the felony assault charges despite their resumption of sexual relations and all the subtle pressure concomitant with bedroom talk. Desmond would constantly and repeatedly request that she withdraw the charges against him.

Whether at dinner, at a party, or in the bedroom, Enid was unhesitating and firm with her answer: "No, I will not drop the charges."

Enid had been through a lot with Desmond. She had experienced much physical pain. She thought that she knew the universe of his anger and bully-boy tactics. Enid underestimated his resolve to have the criminal case against him disappear.

On June 7, 1995, Desmond was arraigned on the indictment in the Supreme Court for the felony assault charges arising from his cutting Enid with the broken bottle on May 8, 1995. The judge issued a new order of protection directing Desmond to stay away from Enid and to refrain from having any contact at all with her (e.g., phone calls, letters, etc.).

This event appears to have been too much for Desmond. At last he realized that Enid was never going to drop the charges against him. It was clear to him that he no longer had control over her or his precarious situation. He may have thought that dire measures were needed. He certainly acted in a desperate fashion.

On June 9, 1995, Desmond knocked on Enid's apartment door a few minutes after eight in the morning. Enid's female roommate opened the door and allowed Desmond to enter. This act by her roommate would prove costly to Enid. Enid's roommate explained to Desmond that she was about to leave for work and Enid was still asleep.

The night before Desmond had called Enid a number of times asking her to have sex with him for his birthday. Each time Enid told him no. She was unable to get to sleep until half past four in the morning.

When Enid awoke at half past eight, she thought that she had a massive headache due to lack of sleep. She was somewhat bewildered when she saw Desmond standing near her with a gun in his hand. She now felt as though someone had hit her on the head several times with a sledgehammer. Still she had not yet realized that her pain was not caused by want of sleep.

Desmond had taken his .25 caliber handgun and shot Enid two times in the back of the head and once above the temple while she was lying helplessly on her stomach fast asleep on the couch. Miraculously she did not die. She still had not realized the extent of her peril until she went into the bathroom and saw the blood streaming down profusely from the back and side of her head, meandering around her neck, and cascading down her shoulders.

Immediately when she exited from the bathroom, Desmond said to her: "I am here to kill you, and you will die a slow, painful death."

He then placed the gun under her breast and screamed, "Fuck you, bitch!" as he pulled the trigger.

Blood started to flow freely from a hole that Desmond had just made in Enid's body. Remarkably Enid was still alive.

Desmond telephoned his "common law" wife with whom he had four children. He told her what he had done to Enid. Desmond informed his "wife" that he was going to kill Enid and then himself. He asked to speak to his children one last time.

While Desmond was on the phone, Enid's mind was racing in an attempt to save her life and to be able to see her kids again. With three bullets in her head and one in her belly, Enid not only remained alive, but incredibly was also able to retain her wits and her strong desire to survive.

When Desmond hung up the phone, she begged Desmond, "Don't kill me! Don't kill me!"

He answered, "I am going to kill you, bitch, because you want to send me to jail so you can be with someone else."

Enid was fast running out of energy. With adrenaline pumping her up, her mouth was working as fast as her mind. She was able to convince Desmond not to kill her in exchange for a promise.

"Call an ambulance for me. I will tell the police that burglars broke in and did this to me. Please help me! Don't kill me," she pleaded.

Desmond thought a minute and agreed but not before reminding Enid: "If you fuck with me, I'll kill your kids! Remember I know where they are."

Enid again assured him that she would do and say what he demanded as long as he would call an ambulance. Desmond then proceeded to carry out what they had planned.

After cleaning his gun, he threw it out the kitchen window. He dressed Enid, who had been sleeping in a bra and panties. Desmond did not want the police or the paramedics to see Enid's body.

He called 911, reported that someone had broken into his girlfriend's apartment, and shot her several times. When the 911 operator asked him who shot his girlfriend, he replied, "I don't know." He then helped Enid move to the staircase outside of the apartment.

When the police arrived a few minutes later, Enid was sitting on the stairway steps. She was staring straight ahead and appeared to be in shock. Desmond was standing directly behind her, tightly holding a white towel to her head with both of his hands. The towel was quickly turning crimson from the blood flowing from the three bullet holes in her head.

One of the first two officers to arrive at the scene asked her, "What happened?"

Enid, with Desmond still hovering behind her, replied, "I am not sure."

When the Emergency Medical Service (EMS) unit came about eight minutes later, the paramedic observed Enid looking toward her but unfocused. Enid had blood coming from her three head wounds and dark circles under her eyes indicating a head injury.

When asked, "How are you doing?" Enid replied, "I can't see."

The paramedic further inquired, "What happened?"

Enid answered, "I was shot."

Her pulse was rapid, and it was clear that she was in shock. Bandages were quickly applied to her head wounds. Enid was rushed to Kings County Hospital Trauma Center in critical condition.

After Enid was taken to the hospital, Desmond was questioned by the investigating detectives about what had occurred. He stated that he had come to the apartment at about 8:00 a.m. He then left and returned about one and one-half hours later. Enid had answered the doorbell crawling. She was shot, and Desmond had observed blood on the floor. He related to the detectives that Enid did not know what had happened when he had asked. Desmond told them that he was the one who called 911.

After about twenty minutes, Desmond left the crime scene. He was not yet a suspect. He was free to go.

It was only on the ambulance trip to the hospital, when Enid felt somewhat safe from Desmond, that she told the EMS paramedics that it was her boy-friend who had shot her. Later that afternoon the police arrested Desmond in the Bronx at the home that he shared with his "common-law wife."

Enid's injuries were very bad. Some were permanent. Upon her arrival at the resuscitation area of the emergency room at the Kings County Hospital Trauma Center, Enid's throat was immediately intubated to clear her air paths from blood that was impairing her ability to breathe and that could cause her to choke to death. She was somewhat responsive to the doctor's questions, but she was not clearly awake or alert.

Enid sustained multiple fractures to her face and to the orbital bones sur-rounding her eyes. She had to undergo surgery to repair her colon, which was perforated by the bullet she had received to her lower chest. The doctors, de-spite their efforts, could not heal the blindness in her left eye or the deafness in her right ear as a result of the three gunshot wounds to her head. She spent more than three weeks in the hospital.

At Desmond's trial, Enid testified as to the events that had occurred on May 8 and June 9, 1995. She talked of her injuries, including the blindness in her left eye, the deafness in her right ear, her perforated colon, as well as the numerous operations to her face and to the orbitals surrounding her eyes. Her roommate testified that she had let Desmond into her apartment with Enid sleeping and uninjured at around 8:00 a.m. on June 9, 1995. Various police officers, EMS technicians, and doctors from Kings County Hospital also took the stand regarding both of the incidents that were the subject of the trial. Enid's statement in the ambulance to the EMS technician that Desmond had shot her was admitted as an excited utterance exception to the rule against hearsay.

Desmond testified on his own behalf. He claimed that Enid attacked him with the broken bottle on May 8, 1995. He stated that she was accidentally injured when he pushed her arm away and the bottle struck her in the mouth.

Desmond then contended that he was not the person who shot Enid three times in the head and one time in the stomach on June 9, 1995. He admitted that he went over to Enid's apartment that morning and was let in by her roommate. He was advised that Enid was sleeping on the couch. He went into the apartment as the roommate left. Desmond then woke up Enid and had a brief conversation with her regarding their plans for the day. Enid then fell asleep again. After five to ten minutes, Desmond left the apartment to do some errands. He was, however, unable to specify what those errands were or where he went. He later returned to the apartment after about one and one-half hours to find Enid, who had already been shot. He called 911. The police and EMS responded to the scene and attended to Enid.

Desmond described Enid's motive to label him the perpetrator of these crimes as one of greed. He maintained that he helped to support her kids and yet she invariably would demand more money. He recounted how Enid would call him after he was locked up in jail.

Desmond claimed that she said, "If I had ten thousand dollars, I would go back to French Guyana."

Desmond also alleged that Enid tried to shake him down for thousands of dollars in order to obtain her green card. After all, hadn't he paid for her nurse's aide course already?

He denied calling his wife on June 8, 1995, the day Enid had been shot. The phone records produced at trial revealed that on that day, phone calls had been made from Enid's apartment to Desmond's "common-law" wife's house. Desmond's "wife" testified that Enid called her on June 9, 1995, looking for Desmond. This patently made no sense since it had been undisputed that Desmond was in Enid's apartment on that day.

Desmond was convicted of all twelve counts in the indictment. At his sentencing proceeding, his family members submitted letters appealing for leniency. Several made statements.

One of the questions posed to Desmond by the prosecutor at trial came to mind: "What did you tell your wife when you were out on a date or when you slept away from home for a night or nights?"

Desmond replied, "I don't have to tell her anything." Such was his sense of entitlement.

Enid also made a statement at Desmond's sentencing. She vividly described the events of that day. She referred to the constant reminders that she bears and will continue to live with forever—the permanent loss of hearing in one ear and the loss of sight in one eye as well as the emotional and psychological scars. Desmond was sentenced to two and one-half years' to five years' imprisonment for assaulting Enid with a bottle and twelve and one-half to twenty-five years' for attempting to murder her, each sentence to run consecutively, in all a total of fifteen to thirty years' incarceration.

What about Enid? Weeks after the shooting, Enid was forced to endure the first of many operations and procedures for her injuries. Repairs were made to the numerous fractures in her face. Although her scars have become faint and have all but healed after a few years, she continues to carry a metal plate under her blinded eye because one of the bullets exploded the orbital bone surrounding it. She hardly needed this as a reminder of that fateful morning. About one year after the incident, a bullet fragment was removed from her jaw as she was experiencing great pain. Enid required speech rehabilitation in order to learn to talk correctly.

Enid has now returned to her native country. Although blind in one eye and deaf in one ear, she portrayed a very upbeat spirit when being interviewed by a reporter eight months after the trial: "'Every week, I play the lottery,' she says with a faint smile. 'If I won, I would open up a home for battered women. I'd open two or three or four homes. And I'd say to these women, 'You can make it. You can go forward.' She spreads her arms wide and continues, 'After all, look at me.'"[2]

She has gone forward. Although she may not know it yet, she has already won the biggest lottery jackpot. She is alive and has survived with a terrific attitude about life intact.

Had I been there along with the Brooklyn Domestic Violence Court in May of 1995, the day of the assault that Enid reported, she might still have her full hearing and sight. I would have monitored Desmond closely by placing him in a domestic violence accountability program and by returning him to court every three weeks as a condition of bail. Had the laws been changed earlier to prevent the deportation of battered women who are illegal immigrants, then Enid may have sooner sought the courts' protection from the indignities and assaults that Desmond had perpetrated upon her. Just maybe, we could have kept her out of harm's way. Desmond's failed attempt to control Enid by having her drop the assault charges frustrated him, so he tried to murder her when he couldn't have his way. This was a classic case of power and control that was nearly deadly.

Chapter Six

Deadly Dave

The headline read, "Enraged Ex Guns Down 2 Lovers on Street."[1] It did not tell the entire tale. Dave's story still bewilders me and always will. I will never, ever be sure that one is incapable of being a perpetrator of domestic violence no matter who he is or what he may do . . .

Perhaps Dave Castor was experiencing the loneliness of the approaching Christmas and New Year's holidays. These holidays are often a time of introspection and reflection, not only upon the events of the past year but also on one's relationships throughout life. It must have been exceedingly painful for Dave to confront the fact that Denise Stevens no longer lived with him or loved him.

She had moved out of the apartment that they had shared when she broke up with him several months ago. Although they had parted, he had persisted in trying to revive the relationship by calling her and visiting her at work unannounced.[2] Dave held a strong conviction that Denise had made a big mistake, which he would do all in his power to rectify. His overtures fell on deaf ears, and there was nothing that he could do to reach Denise.

Things went from bad to worse during their telephone conversation right before the Thanksgiving holiday. Denise informed Dave that not only did she not wish to reconcile, but she now had a new boyfriend whom she believed she loved. This disclosure did not have the desired effect of having Dave leave Denise alone. Dave's determination to resurrect their relationship turned into a blind obsession that would prove to be deadly.

On Friday, December 15, 2000, a determined Dave went to Denise's midtown office in Manhattan. Many thought it to be a crime of passion, but it was more like a well-thought-out execution. Earlier that morning, Dave had been asked to leave the building at 15 West 39th Street where Denise and her new boyfriend worked. "He was causing a commotion trying to convince [Denise] Stevens . . . to get back together with him."[3]

Later, Dave confronted Denise and her new boyfriend, Lance, outside of the building. Like a hunter targeting its prey, Dave rushed out of a horde of tourists and shoppers. He pulled out his .38 caliber handgun as he spied Denise and Lance going on a lunch date.

Dave "aimed first at Lance shooting him once under the right arm, with the bullet traveling into his chest. As Denise started screaming, 'No! No! No!' Lance ran into the nearest building and collapsed face down in the lobby."[4]

Then Dave "shot Denise in the leg and face before chasing her through the holiday crowds out into an alleyway just around the corner from Lord & Taylor's windows."[5]

One can only imagine the feeling of utter terror and helplessness that Denise experienced during the last few moments of her life. After being wounded, Dave cornered her as she pleaded for mercy and for her life while Dave placed the gun to her head. "As she begged for her life, he killed her with a bullet to the forehead."[6]

Dave then turned the gun on himself, but the gun either misfired or jammed. He ran into the throng of shoppers, disappeared, and made his escape. Despite a massive manhunt that day, the police did not find Dave, but he did find them.

At about 1:00 a.m. on Saturday, Dave approached two detectives in the darkness of the early morning hours on the steps of a Bronx precinct saying, "'Excuse me, officers. I have a gun and I'm going to shoot myself.' . . . The stunned cops told him not to do anything—but he whipped out a pistol and shot himself."[7]

Dave died on Sunday from the self-inflicted wound to his head.

Dave Castor was a bespectacled, diminutive, and seemingly thoughtful and respectful man in his late forties when I first met him in the beginning of 1997. He served as the liaison between the Brooklyn Felony Domestic Violence Court and the initial batterers' intervention program (BIP) it utilized. Dave was an employee of the BIP. He worked as a counselor for men accused or convicted of domestic violence.

A condition of bail set for every defendant at arraignment in my court, other than those charged with some sort of elder abuse or those involved in a same-sex relationship, was attendance at a BIP. (These programs are now often called Domestic Violence Accountability Programs.) I employed the BIP as a monitoring device and to promote defendant accountability. The participants, under the tutelage of a group leader, are sensitized and discuss issues of power and control and their feelings, as well as the behavior of male entitlement, anger management, societal biases, and other domestic violence topics.

Every defendant-participant in the BIP is mandated to attend the program once a week for twenty-six weeks. The defendants appeared before me in court for monitoring every three weeks. I received an updated report from the BIP for each defendant. This procedure helped reinforce to the defendants that I was watching them.

In 1997, there was only one BIP in New York that would have met the proposed state certification standards. That BIP was outside New York City. No certification standards have yet been promulgated by any governmental agency. Although now there are proposed standards, the state, perhaps correctly, did not and does not wish to license or certify any program because it may imply to the general public and to victims alike that BIPs are effective in protecting victims. The government does not desire to appear to endorse the use of these programs to promote victim safety.

The literature in this nascent area seems to support this view. The studies thus far indicate that a person who attends a BIP or alternative-to-violence program is less likely to batter his domestic partner only while going or shortly after concluding a BIP course. The literature also suggests that there are no long-term salutary effects.[8] Thus attendance at a BIP does not mean that incidents of battering will be reduced over time.

Beginning in 1997, Dave appeared religiously before me every Tuesday, which was the arraignment and update day. Almost all the time, he arrived punctually at the announced 9:30 a.m. starting time. He would report to me orally on the participation, attitude, and attendance of those defendants who had made bail and submit a written summary for the court file and defense counsel. Dave would also meet with those defendants who were arraigned and who realistically appeared to be able to make bail. He would explain to them their obligations in attending the BIP.

Dave was a workhorse and diligently attended to all his duties. Although he had no real formal educational training, Dave ran many group classes each night and on weekends for men who were either accused or convicted of battering. Dave also took on many administrative responsibilities, as the head of the BIP spent much time living in his home in New England.

Dave and I, along with the assistant prosecutor, defense attorney, and court resource coordinator, would often conference a case dealing with a defendant who might not be taking his BIP seriously. I remember Dave more than once saying, while shaking his head in a disapproving and perplexed manner at a defendant who had exhibited a poor attitude in trying to grasp the issues of power and control necessary to his understanding of the dynamics of domestic violence, "This knucklehead just doesn't get it."

The court's resource coordinator on a few occasions encouraged Dave to go back to school to obtain the requisite credentials he needed to become a more effective counselor and to better himself.

After less than two years, certain inadequacies became apparent in the reporting practices of the BIP where Dave worked. If Dave were ever out because of illness at the same time that the head of the BIP was out of state, which was often, there was no one in authority at the office to convey to the court dependable information. The BIP was simply understaffed, and those who were employed there were overworked. The updated reports were shown to be inaccurate in more and more instances and with increasing frequency than one would desire in felony domestic violence cases.

A decision was made to start up batterers' groups with two other BIPs who were prior to that point in time reluctant to run alternative-to-violence programs for those accused or convicted of felonies. Less and less defendants were being sent to Dave's BIP. By the middle of 1999, no new defendants were being referred.

I remain appreciative of that first BIP. It met a monitoring need and performed it relatively well for almost two years despite the fact that it received no outside funding or grants. All of its revenue was derived wholly from payments received from the participants, a mainly indigent inner-city population who paid on a sliding scale.

I had virtually no contact with Dave after early 1999. I was aware that two or three times a day, six days a week he was still heading counseling groups for batterers. Dave had been immersed in the domestic violence field for at least five years. If anyone were to be sensitive to domestic violence and its attendant issues, it had to be Dave. He appeared to be thoughtful, respectful, soft-spoken, and aware of the pitfalls of domestic violence. He definitely and frequently "talked the talk." I thought that if anyone would "walk the walk," it would be Dave.

Dave's tragic story was carried in all the local papers over a period of days in December of 2000. Some of what I read seemed to depict Dave perfectly while much seemed unbelievable. Dave was described by his neighbors as "polite and helpful . . . always willing to offer cold drinks on a summer day to laborers or to help a neighbor carry her baby up five flights. . . . He was a music aficionado and a meticulous housekeeper, and he usually wore a necktie. . . . He was just a normal guy. . . . No matter how many times I saw him it was always the same thing, he would be outgoing and friendly."[9] "[A] very nice guy . . . well spoken, kept to himself, beautiful person . . . just seemed like a gentleman."[10] "Well dressed and well spoken."[11] "He always kept to himself. He was a very quiet man . . . not overly friendly, not the outgoing type."[12]

The police described another Dave with a history that neither his neighbors nor the courthouse staff knew. Dave had been arrested nine times between 1968 and 1989[13] and served four years for a robbery conviction and five to six years for attempted murder.[14]

One salutary benefit of state certification of BIPs would be mandated governmental background and fingerprint checks of domestic violence counselors. After the tragic episode involving Dave, I believe that the BIPs in New York City have increased their scrutiny of any employees they may consider hiring.

Others who also knew Dave expressed shock at this tragedy. My thoughts were best mirrored by Ted Bunch, who had run a well-respected domestic violence accountability program at Safe Horizons for batterers and who "knew Dave Castor from their work together at domestic violence task force meetings. . . . He sees Dave's actions as a cautionary tale. 'My reaction was disbelief, of course. At the same time I thought: It's not what you know, it's the choices that you make. He chose to work out whatever he had to work out with his ex-partner this way. I was shocked, but at the same time, I really wasn't surprised that men who don't take responsibility or don't have responsibility placed on them would continue to think that they're not ultimately responsible for their own behavior.'"[15]

Dave made the wrong choices, and three people are now dead. It was unforeseeable and unfathomable. What did I learn from this episode? I learned that my knowledge and predictability of who would commit crimes of intimate partner violence was lacking and that no one could have predicted this. It shook my world and my basic notions about domestic violence to the very core. I will never again look at the domestic violence universe the same way.

Chapter Seven

Boris the Bully

Nina remained dazed from the last blow delivered to her chin. She slowly started to clear the cobwebs from her head and attempted to rise, steadying herself by grasping the chair next to her. Nina's rubbery legs collapsed before she was able to stand. Boris had beaten and kicked her before, but he had never punched her so hard. Sitting on the floor, Nina felt the side of her face, guiding her hand gently along the contour of her misshapen mandible. When her fingers reached her temple, her deformed head was foreign to her touch. Her ear was throbbing, and the hinge where the upper jaw meets the lower was so swollen that Nina was unable to open or close her mouth. When she concentrated to move her jaws toward or away from each other, the pain was so excruciating that she passed out.

Prior to losing consciousness, Nina was undergoing an out-of-body experience. She was wondering how she had reached the abyss in her relationship with Boris. Then as the pain became more and more intense, her mind became more and more clear. Nina remembered their first encounter. She had been a teenager. She cursed that there was ever a second one . . .

It was the summer of 1989. Nina sat with one of her friends at a table in a restaurant in Urmala, Latvia. Men and women alike stared at her, so striking was her beauty. It had been this way ever since Nina was fourteen years old, the age she started to mature into a woman. She was flattered but never felt quite comfortable with the gazes of strangers affixed upon her. Nina was now seventeen years old with long golden hair braided down her back that complimented the brightest light blue eyes. She was statuesque—five foot ten with an athletic figure.

Nina was talking with her friend when Boris summoned her to his table. With a gesture of his hand, Boris motioned toward her and said, "Beautiful, come here with your friend and sit with us."

Nina ignored the very large man whom she later learned to be fifteen years her senior. Boris was six feet five inches tall and weighed at least two hundred eighty pounds. He was sitting with three other rather huge men, but none so big as the man who demanded her presence.

When it became apparent to Boris that Nina was not coming over to his table, Boris arose and walked over to Nina's table, grabbed her and her friend by their arms, escorted them to his table, and ordered her to sit down. "You shall stay where I tell you to stay."

Nina always walked on center stage because all recognized her presence and beauty and ceded the spotlight to her. Boris, on the other hand, seized the limelight, oftentimes with threats and force.

Boris and his friends began arguing with other patrons at the restaurant who were angry that Boris's table was monopolizing the waiter they shared. In the tumult, Nina and her friend were able to run out of the restaurant unnoticed. They were walking in the street when ten minutes later, Boris and his three comrades pulled alongside Nina and her friend in an expensive-looking American car.

"Get in the car," Boris commanded.

After driving for a while, Boris stopped the car and allowed Nina's friend to leave. Boris then drove to a friend's house in Riga where he raped Nina. Boris did not hit or threaten Nina, but he clearly took her with the unspoken threat of force. Thus began Nina's tortured relationship with Boris that lasted nearly ten years and spanned two continents.

After the breakup of the Soviet Union in 1991, the Balkan states of Latvia, Lithuania, and Estonia were reestablished as sovereign entities as they had been before World War II. In 1989, however, Latvia had not yet achieved independence from Mother Russia. Nina shared a small apartment in the city of Riga in the Latvian part of the Soviet Union with her mother and younger brother. Nina was a manager/salesperson earning a good salary at her friend's store.

From the time that Boris had forced himself upon Nina in the summer of 1989 until he immigrated to America three years later, he would come to Nina's apartment at all hours of the night, often uninvited and frequently intoxicated. Late in the summer, Nina discovered that Boris was married and had a teenage son only a couple of years younger than she.

She called Boris on the telephone. "I don't want to see you again." Nina continued, now mocking him, "Go back to your wife and child."

Boris immediately drove over to Nina's apartment infuriated at being dismissed by his lover simply because he was a married man. His response was swift, violent, and cruel. He attacked her with his hands and fist. Boris was sober and fully realized what he was doing when he slapped her in the face and struck her in the nose before leaving as quickly as he came. Nina was bleeding from her lower lip and nose.

Boris apparently thought that he had gone too easy on Nina or perhaps that the episode of the previous night did not have its desired effect. The next morning, he came to Nina's place of work with his fifteen-year-old son. Boris commanded Nina to leave work with them. His tone was serious, dead serious. Nina acceded to his demand. They drove to a secluded woodland area near Riga. Boris then proceeded to beat Nina in front of his son.

He shouted as he hit her, "You'll never leave me! You can't leave me! You dare not even say that you will leave me! You will stay with me and no one else. Who the hell told you that I was married? And here is one for calling my house. Don't you ever do that again."

"Now tell me that you love me," he commanded as he struck her still.

"I don't love you, and I never will. How can I love someone who hits me so?" Nina responded.

This only frustrated Boris more. He directed his son to beat Nina. His son refused. Boris's rage intensified. He continued to hit Nina more violently after he had first struck his son a few times.

Bloodied and barely conscious, Nina struggled to form the words with her lips. "I do love you. I love you. I promise to stay with you always."

Nina suffered bruises and swelling about the eyes, nose, and face. She was dizzy and nauseated for days. The beating was not done with the purpose to injure, but with the goal to intimidate and to crush any resistance in the future. Boris achieved his desired effect.

Nina passed out from the pain. Boris carried her from the woods and loaded her into his car trunk like a piece of luggage. Later Nina woke up in a friend's house, not knowing how she had arrived there. Fearing her next beating, Nina never reported this mindless assault to the authorities nor did she seek medical attention. Nina also thought the police and government to be corrupt and not to be trusted.

While Nina hadn't forgotten her sylvan assault, she and Boris had somehow made their peace. Late one fall night, Nina's mother, Anna, was awakened by her daughter's screaming. Thinking that Nina was having a terrible nightmare, Anna put on her robe, walked to Nina's bedroom, and knocked on the door. Anna was startled when she saw Boris in Nina's room.

"What is going on here?" Anna demanded to know.

Anna cringed when she saw Nina cowering in the corner of the room with a sheet pulled over her head as if she were able to hide the shame and humiliation that she surely felt.

"I'm going to call the police!" Anna shouted.

"If you call the police, I will kill you both." Boris stood up and replied with the conviction of a man that meant what he said.

Smelling vodka on his breath, Anna was uncertain as to what Boris might do. Hesitantly, Anna left to return to her bedroom. She did not call the police.

Nina asked Boris for permission to speak to her mother to ensure that she would not call the police. Nina knew that if she were to appeal to his sensibilities as a son or father, her entreaty would most probably be unsuccessful. When Nina directed her request to his self-interest, she realized that he would be responsive.

Boris acquiesced in a mocking tone, "Go speak to the witch. Tell her there is a sale on brooms tomorrow in the market."

Nina walked down the hall to her mother's bedroom in an attempt to reassure her. Nina's face was red as though she were aflame.

Through her tears, she told Anna, "I'm okay. Don't worry, Momma; everything will be all right."

The crimson color in Nina's face was not the consequence of her emotional turmoil. What Nina had neglected to tell her mother was that Boris had covered her with the bedsheet and had hit her about her body and face until she was forced to cry out. Upon reflection, Nina was relieved that her mother had intervened. The threat of calling the police seemed to have halted Boris's attack. Boris thought that the local police could be bought and sold, but he was nonetheless wary of them.

Nina did not seek medical attention. When the immediate danger had been eliminated, Nina never thought to report the beating she had received.

Two weeks later, Nina came home late after teaching an aerobics class. She was unaware that Boris was waiting for her. Unfathomably annoyed by her lateness, Boris dragged Nina into her bedroom and ripped her blouse open.

Boris continually berated her with nonsensical orders. "Don't you ever come home fucking late again! Do you understand what I'm saying?"

Once again Anna attempted to rescue Nina. She opened the door and walked into Nina's bedroom. She gasped as she saw Nina standing next to Boris with her blouse ripped diagonally downward from the neck to below her breast.

"Get the hell out of here before I give you some of the same," Boris barked.

Anna glanced at her daughter, who nodded, indicating that her mother should follow Boris's direction. Anna turned to leave, and after she took two steps, she heard Boris slam the door shut.

Throughout the various assaults by Boris upon Nina in Latvia, Anna had never actually witnessed Boris thumping Nina. She had observed firsthand the outcomes of these predatory assaults—the black eyes and bruises to her lovely Nina. She often wondered how Boris could do such terrible things to her treasure. Any man would be lucky to have Nina as his wife. Anna also wondered why a beauty like her daughter would put up with such a beastly man.

Then she bit her lip so hard that the blood started to squirt out of the fissure that she had created with her teeth. Anna had hoped that Nina was not emulating her. Anna's husband and Nina's father had died of a diseased liver when Nina was only eight. Her husband was an abusive alcoholic.

Secretly each year Anna would thank God on the anniversary of her husband's death. He was a frightful man who was only slightly crueler when he drank than when he was sober. He would verbally abuse Anna and swear at her and would not hesitate to strike her for any reason or no reason at all. He was opinionated and overbearing. He was often stubborn and almost as often wrong, which were awful characteristics when working in tandem.

All this she may have endured, but not after he cursed Nina for not being a boy child. For this she would never forgive him even in death. For this she never wanted his soul to rest in peace. Yes, Anna was happy he died. Anna feared that her husband, with her unwilling help, had made possible, almost as a legacy, Nina's acceptance of a man like Boris.

For the next three years, Nina and Boris's relationship continued despite the beatings and drunken episodes. On the only occasion that Nina threatened to leave him, Boris shaved her head. There was no second time.

In a strange way, Nina was fortunate that Boris was married. Boris was unable to devote his full time and energies toward Nina's subjugation. On the other hand, when he was around and not being a pig, Boris always seemed to have a lot of money to spend and to go on vacation with Nina. She enjoyed when he bought gifts for her and took her to new and interesting places. Yet she was also growing wary of Boris's mercurial twists of temperament. After each crazy episode of violence, which would sometimes last for days, he would ask her for forgiveness, promise not to repeat his behavior, and then buy Nina expensive presents or take her on vacation.

Nina thought that the time was ripe for extricating Boris from her life, but she did not know how to go about it. Then a miracle happened. All Nina's prayers seemed to have been answered and she did not have to do anything.

In early 1992, Boris secured papers for his wife and children and immigrated to the United States. Before he left, Boris instructed Nina that he wanted her to come to America too. He even helped her fill out an application and instructed Nina how to answer certain questions to have a better chance of being accepted into America. Boris had instructed her to request political asylum in America as a Jew even though she was not Jewish. Driven by the fear of Boris's past assaults even across an ocean and a continent away, Nina misrepresented her religion on her immigration papers. The Baltic peoples recognized all too well that their reputation for anti-Semitism was known throughout the world. The specter of czarist anti-Semitism that had earlier permeated Latvia, Lithuania, and Estonia and was symbolized by pogroms and the dreaded Cossacks burned brightly once again after the fall of the Berlin Wall.

In her heart, Nina thought that Boris might forget about her once he settled in the States with his family. A few months later, the economy took a drastic downturn in Latvia and Nina lost her job. There were tanks in the cities. The government was in crisis because of a food shortage and high unemployment and inflation rates.

Nina moved to Poland to work. One weekend while shopping at a bazaar in Warsaw, Nina was approached by a couple of men.

One of the men asked her in Russian, "Does Boris know you are in Warsaw? Did he give you permission to go to Poland?"

Then the man directed her, "I think you should return to Latvia."

Nina realized that Boris had not forgotten her at all. Taking this visit as a threat, Nina gave two weeks' notice at her job and returned to Latvia. After nearly four more months, the immigration papers that Boris procured for Nina were ready to be processed. She was denied political asylum but received authorization to work.

Nina arrived in Brooklyn in June of 1996. Boris met her at the airport in New York with flowers, smiles, and a promise to change his ways. He took her to a second-floor apartment in a private house located in the Brighton Beach section of Brooklyn, an enclave of Russian-speaking émigrés. Nina was hardly able to speak any English and was unable to work at first, but she was able to communicate with the merchants and her neighbors.

Their relationship flourished initially, but the violence followed shortly. Boris was a driver for a car service. Nina stayed at home, cleaned, washed, and so on. She did not work and did not leave the apartment very often as Boris refused to make a key for her. After one argument, Nina asked Boris to leave. This request precipitated a beating. Boris then took Nina's passport and hid her belongings. As before, the beating went unreported to the police and Nina failed to seek medical attention.

The next month, Nina also failed to make a police report or to seek hospital care when Boris banged her head against a table in a restaurant. What was Nina's crime? She was uncommonly beautiful. Another man looked at her in admiration. Boris became enraged. All Nina's efforts to calm Boris proved to be unsuccessful. His invective was now transferred from the voyeur to Nina, thus the head slam to the table.

Boris was staying more often with Nina even though he was still living with his wife and children. There was no denying that they shared some fun and good times in between the bumps and bruises. Boris took her to nice restaurants and exciting places like Atlantic City and to rock concerts that she really enjoyed. Still, Nina marveled that Boris had never broken any of her bones. She wondered if her luck would last.

During the summertime, two years after the incident in the restaurant, Nina and Boris had one of their typical disagreements. Nina had never fully learned to submit to Boris's authority. She was, in her own way, an independent woman. She hardly ever agreed with Boris when she truly held a differing opinion unless it was absolutely necessary. What she never came to realize was that if one were to disagree with Boris, one's health and safety were automatically placed in jeopardy.

Boris's reaction to Nina's failure to obey mindlessly his every direction was more violent than usual that evening. He hit Nina mightily and repeatedly in the face and ribs with his fists and stomped upon her with shod feet.

Nina remained dazed from the last blow delivered to her chin. She slowly started to clear the cobwebs from her head and attempted to rise, steadying herself by grasping the chair next to her. Nina's rubbery legs collapsed before she was able to stand. Boris had beaten and kicked her before, but he had never punched her so hard. Sitting on the floor, Nina felt the side of her face, guiding her hand gently along the contour of her misshapen mandible. When her fingers reached her temple, her deformed head was foreign to her touch. Her ear was throbbing and the hinge where the upper jaw meets the lower was so swollen that Nina was unable to open or close her mouth. When she concentrated to move her jaws toward or away from each other, the pain was so excruciating that she passed out.

Prior to losing consciousness, Nina had undergone an out-of-body experience. She was wondering how she reached the abyss in her relationship with Boris. Then as the pain became more and more intense, her mind became more and more clear. Nina remembered their first encounter. She had been a teenager. She cursed that there was ever a second one.

Then Nina passed out from the beating. The landlord came up to see what all the noise was about. Boris, now concerned that Nina was unconscious and fearing the worst for her, welcomed the landlord's help in taking Nina to the hospital.

When the landlord dropped a semiconscious Nina off at the hospital under the care of Boris, it was as though he had placed a fox in charge of the henhouse. Just as the police, prosecutors, and the courts had failed to investigate, prosecute, and adjudicate domestic violence cases properly, hospitals, until rather recently, had been likewise deficient in developing protocols for screening emergency room patients for possible domestic violence causation of injuries.

That evening, the emergency room doctors, residents, and nurses failed to separate Nina and Boris when interviewing her about how she was injured. It is not enough to draw a sheet to examine a woman in privacy; the significant other must be removed from the interview room and earshot so that candid discourse may occur. The proper questions must be asked. None of what should have happened came to pass that evening.

The examining physician asked Nina, "What happened to you?"

Boris was standing right alongside Nina's hospital bed, holding her hand. Nina was chilled from speaking the truth about what had transpired that evening. Nina, wincing in pain and muttering through contorted lips as she was unable to open her mouth, lied to the one who was trying to put the pieces of her body back together. "I tripped and fell down the stairs."

The young doctor must have been somewhat incredulous. After all, he had never seen a young fit person suffer a broken jaw from falling in one's apartment staircase. Yet her boyfriend seemed so concerned and caring. After all, he did bring her to the emergency room. Tears seemed to form in his eyes when they were both informed that surgery would be needed to mend her fractured jaw. Yes, as implausible as it seemed, the doctor believed the beautiful woman. He wanted to think that her injuries had occurred as she had reported even though his training and common sense should have told him otherwise.

Five days later, Nina was discharged from the hospital. With no family or friends to take care of her, speaking little English, she returned to live with Boris in their apartment.

Nina was completely dependent upon Boris for her care while she recuperated. Nina's reliance on Boris only exacerbated his controlling behavior. On the one hand, Boris liked being in command and the fact that Nina was at his mercy. On the other hand, he resented the fact that he had to shop, cook, and mash up and puree the food for her consumption. She was relegated to drinking her food in liquefied form through a straw.

"You need me. No one else would take care of you. Don't forget that."

Boris sadistically and scornfully told her a variation of this theme several times a day, always omitting that he was the one who had placed Nina in this predicament. He had removed Nina from her familial support and placed her in a new country where she was unable to speak the language easily and had no friends or acquaintances except for an extremely abusive boyfriend who was already married.

When Nina first began employment in New York, she sewed in a factory, as language was no impediment. Nina then secured a job for more money as a home attendant for an agency that dealt primarily with patients in the Russian-speaking community. She worked seven days a week and had actually requested overnight assignments to avoid spending evenings with Boris. Now he removed the one strand of independence that she possessed: economic. Nina was confined to their apartment and unable to work in her present condition.

In the weeks that followed, Boris exhibited his lack of remorse and compassion for what he had done and for what she was experiencing. One night while Nina was still convalescing at home, Boris beat Nina over some triviality.

With the stitches still fresh inside Nina's mouth, Boris pulled her face from side to side, causing intense pain, saying tauntingly, "Why can't you do anything? I don't understand why you are so weak. I need a strong woman who can keep up with me and satisfy me."

Boris then demanded sex from Nina. Fearing more anguish, she acquiesced.

The next morning, Nina sought medical attention for her mouth as she was bleeding and still in pain. Her stitches had been ripped open by Boris's sadistic tugging on her face the night before.

As the cycle of violence would wane, Boris like so many batterers would be full of "I'm sorrys" and promises of "never agains." This time the apology took the form of a holiday to Miami a month after the latest brutalization. Yet, even on vacation, Nina was not free from Boris's rage. One night after he drank too much vodka, Boris beat up Nina in their hotel room, re-injuring her jaw. In the morning under the sobering sun, Boris conveyed what can best be termed regrets without actually saying he was sorry. He thought that this incident, like all the others, was forgiven and forgotten. He was wrong. Nina remembered every time that Boris had hit her. While she may have submitted to his demands, it was because she had been coerced. The truth be told, she had never forgiven him.

Over the years, Nina suffered frequent beatings and other assorted abusive behavior by Boris. During these incidents, Boris would threaten and lambast Nina with verbal as well as physical abuse. He would sometimes say, "If you don't listen to me, I'll destroy you. If you disobey me, I will kill you. I've killed a lot of people." Another of his familiar refrains was "Tell me that you love me." If Nina were to refuse to recite those magic words, Boris would beat her more severely saying, "You'll beg me to stop. I'll make you become what I want you to be." It was never clear to Nina what it was that Boris wanted her to be. When exhausted from his attack, she would finally tell Boris that she loved him. He nonetheless would remain dissatisfied, responding, "Say it loud, bitch!"

Still at other times during beatings meted out by Boris, he would tell Nina, "You're not strong enough for me. I want to see you take my punch. Only a strong woman who can take my punch deserves to be with me."

The irony of their situation and Boris's explosive behavior were not lost on Nina when a few months after their return from Florida, Boris was shot three times in the chin and twice in the right arm in an unknown assassin's attempt to kill Boris in Staten Island. Boris was clearly involved in some sort of criminal activity that had gone bad, but he declined to cooperate with the police.

Boris had lost a lot of blood and was very weak. After spending three weeks in the hospital, he returned to the apartment that he shared with Nina to recuperate. Nina attended to his every need—dressing, feeding, bathing, and providing physical therapy for his arm. She continued to wait on him for an additional fourteen weeks after two more surgeries in Maimonides Hospital. During the time she nursed him back to health, Nina never reminded Boris of the cruel manner and words that he had employed in tending to her after causing her injuries.

In the winter of 1995, Nina was five months pregnant with Boris's child. He had apparently forgotten the care and concern that Nina had bestowed upon him in his time of need. In a sober fit of fury, he called Nina a whore again and again, sprinkling in other choice curse words for good measure. Not being sated with merely verbally abusing her, Boris began to hit Nina repeatedly and to pull her beautiful blond hair.

"Stop! Stop! Please stop!" she begged him while holding her arms across her belly in an effort to protect the unborn life within her.

Boris did not heed her words and continued to beat her. Fearing for her life and the health of her fetus, she ran out of the apartment and escaped to an acquaintance whom she had met at work and who was fast becoming her one friend in America. Nina remained there for a little over a week. Boris followed her from work one day and discovered where she was staying. He bought her flowers and implored her to come home with him with the usual excuses and promises. Boris was selling and Nina was considering whether to buy.

Nina, however, was hedging her bets. She was taking all kinds of vocational courses to prepare herself to become completely financially independent from Boris. Nina went to schools to become an EKG technician, a phlebotomist, a computer programmer, as well as a beautician.

The cycle of violence started again in early spring when in full ferocity Boris hit and kicked Nina, who was now in the beginning of her eighth month of pregnancy. He then proceeded to drag Nina by her hair across the apartment floor. She was able to break loose and run out of the apartment. Again she went to live with her friend for a couple of weeks. Like so many battered women, Nina later returned to Boris. She somehow rationalized in her mind that he would change once their baby was born. It would soon be clear to her how wrong she was.

Almost two months later, Nina gave birth to a baby girl. The couple had moved to a new residence in the same Brighton Beach neighborhood. Near the end of the summer when their girl was barely two months old, Boris held the baby out of the window in one of his notorious fits of madness. This was the most bizarre of all of Boris's episodes of mania that Nina had ever seen.

He taunted Nina saying, "I will kill your baby so that you will die a slow death!"

Four months later, Nina was celebrating her birthday with Boris and some of her friends at a Russian nightclub in Brighton Beach. Apparently Boris was put off by the attention exchanged between Nina and her friends. He exaggerated what he observed and became angry as he believed that some of Nina's girlfriends were being too affectionate to her. One of her friends had the temerity to hug and kiss Nina before offering a birthday toast.

Boris went into an inexplicable stormy diatribe, concluding, "You fucking lesbian! You kiss me and no one else."

The more Nina attempted to quiet Boris, the angrier he became until he punched Nina in front of her friends and a packed nightclub. Boris then grabbed a chair and tossed it at Nina. She ran into the bathroom.

One of the patrons helped Nina run out of the club before Boris could hit her. Nina was able to escape and to call 911. When the police arrived, Boris had already fled. He eluded arrest that night.

Later in the early hours of the next morning, Nina returned home to find Boris in the apartment. Boris, still irritated that Nina had called the police, started to punch and kick her again, calling her a cop because she had called the police.

In an effort to calm him down, Nina began kissing him, telling Boris, "You know I love you and only you."

This had the desired effect of stopping Boris's violence, but it also had the unintended consequence of arousing his passion. Boris demanded that Nina perform fellatio upon him. Nina, fearing that Boris would resume beating her again unless she complied, started to cry but nonetheless agreed. After Boris had fallen asleep, Nina cried in bed throughout the night.

In the fall of 1997, Boris found graduation pictures of Nina. Nina had hidden these photographs because she somehow knew, without being able to express the reason, that Boris would not like it that she had the snapshots taken. Boris refused to believe that it was customary to take photographs of the beautician and cosmetology vocational institution graduation ceremony, so he began to hit her.

Storming and ranting, he declared, "I will kill you if I ever find another photo taken of you without me! Now let's have sex."

Boris's anger over the graduation pictures had not abated. A few days later, he incomprehensibly erupted once again. He ripped up all the graduation snapshots that he found and began to hit her, saying, "If you ever go to school again, I will cut out your eyes with a knife and tear you into little pieces. If I have to, I will keep you chained in the house like a prisoner."

Days later Nina returned home after work. Boris screamed at her, "Whore, I hope you drop dead!"

Boris then sucker punched her, cracking her in the face as she entered the apartment. Nina's beautiful pearly whites were suddenly less than perfect. Her front left upper tooth was noticeably chipped.

Nina had experienced a constant barrage over the previous few days. Her anger caused by years of physical, mental, psychological, and emotional abuse exploded like a river cascading through a burst dam when Boris hit her in the face. She couldn't and wouldn't take any more. Nina, crying, called 911.

When the police arrived, Boris told the officers that Nina had been drinking and fell, causing her tooth to chip and crack.

Boris, ever the manipulator, said, "She's been drinking. Look how she looks. I am normal. I didn't hit her. If you want, I'll leave."

Nina was nervous and was unable to express herself in English as well as Boris. Nina was full of tears and appeared disheveled with her hair in a mess. She did appear to have been drinking even though she had not had a single cocktail.

The officers allowed Boris to dress and to leave the apartment despite the mandatory arrest provision in domestic violence cases. Although a police report was taken by the two officers, Boris apparently convinced them that they had no probable cause to arrest him as he had committed no crime. Nina washed up and went to bed disappointed, confused, yet undaunted. In her mind, she had her own plans.

Early the next morning, Nina undeterred went to the precinct and requested to speak to a Russian-speaking police officer. The officer filed a complaint report and a domestic violence incident report on Nina's behalf. He assured Nina that Boris would be arrested.

With the law on her side, Nina suddenly felt empowered. She had been reluctant to go to the police earlier, not only because of the usual reasons of domestic violence victims—love, fear, fear of fear, economic and health insurance concerns—but also for reasons peculiar to immigrants, especially those from former Communist countries. There was a natural distrust for the state in general and for the police in particular. In many of those countries, the police were the oppressors and the victimizers of the citizenry through corruption and other abuses of power.

Nina realized that this man who had terrorized her from their very first meeting was not the bogeyman with superpowers, but a brutal man who sought to control her for his own selfish purposes. Yet he too had his fears.

He was afraid of the police and of being locked up. Nina thought, and now knew, that she had an effective remedy, the order of protection, should he ever bother her again.

Soon after this incident, Nina moved with her little girl to a new apartment. Nina believed that Boris would not be able to find her new telephone number or address. She did not want to see Boris go to jail but did want him out of her life.

Boris was in fact arrested. The case was disposed of in criminal court with an "ACD." An "ACD" is an adjournment in contemplation of dismissal. If Boris were to stay out of trouble and adhere to the full stay-away order of protection that Nina secured from the court, the criminal case against him would be dismissed in six months' time. The protective order was to remain in effect for one year.

Although a protective order is only a piece of paper, should the public institutions and agencies step outside of their incorrectly perceived traditional roles, an order of protection can be given real teeth in helping to ensure a complainant's safety both pre- and post-trial. Nina was hoping that the court's order of protection would shield her from Boris's assaults for a sufficient amount of time for her to relocate.

From Nina's point of view, she would be able to disappear into the fabric of society in the year when Boris would be prohibited from having any contact with her. During that year, Boris was restrained from coming to her home, workplace, school, or any other place where she might be. He was also forbidden from calling her or writing her or contacting her directly or indirectly through family or friends. Boris was able to make an application for visitation with their baby girl only through the family court. Nina was not too concerned about that because Boris always chided her for having a girl instead of a boy child. Sometimes Boris would even tell her that he was not the father of their baby.

About four months later, in midwinter of 1998, Nina arrived home from her job. She had a message from her babysitter to call two phone numbers. When she called the first number, Nina was struck with abject panic when Boris answered the phone.

In a cold, steely voice, Boris informed Nina, "You cannot escape from me. I will find you, and when I do, I will kill you, your baby, and your mother. You will never know where I am or where I will come at you from."

Baffled as to how Boris was able to obtain her phone number and still reeling from the bluntness of his words, Nina hung up the telephone and called the police. A few minutes later, the doorbell rang. Nina, thinking the police were at the door responding to her complaint, answered but did not open the door.

"Who is it?" she asked.

She looked through the peephole in disbelief and saw Boris. She instantly ran to the phone to call the police again. As she was dialing, a voice all too familiarly brutal to her memory filled the chambers of her small apartment. "You will never escape from me. I will break your legs. The world is not big enough for you to hide. I will find you wherever you go. You will always belong to me!"

When the police had come, Boris had gone.

Two days later, Nina heard the phone ring. It rang with the same tone as always when a friend, the babysitter, or her mother would call, but this time she hesitated to pick up the phone. An unhealthy chill covered her body and beads of fear-induced sweat quickly matted her forehead as she lifted the receiver. Somehow she had an apparitional sense that it was Boris calling.

He threatened her once again. "You will meet with me. I will find you. If I don't, then I will kill your mother. You know I will always find you. If you change your address or phone number, I will find the new one. You know you are meant to be with me and only me."

Nina hung up on him and called the police. When the officers and the case detectives came to Nina's apartment in response to her call to 911, Boris phoned again. Following the officers' instructions, she agreed to meet Boris in front of her apartment building.

Nina was directed by the detectives not to go beyond the sidewalk in front of her apartment house. So when Boris drove his car slowly past her building, Nina stood fast on the sidewalk. A few minutes later Boris came by again and stopped his car. He beckoned Nina toward him with a wave of his hand. The police rushed Boris and surrounded his car. Boris grabbed a club in his car.

One of the detectives placed a gun to Boris's head. Through clenched teeth he ordered Boris, half hoping that Boris would disobey him, "Don't even think about it!"

Boris released his grip on the club, but his words were as defiant as ever. "Do you know who I am? You're messing with the wrong Russian. I am in the Russian Mafia. I will kill you and your whole family."

As Boris was rather forcefully removed from the car and rear handcuffed, the detective observed Boris spit at the uniformed sergeant. The detective wondered if he was dealing with a member of the Russian mob or with a blustering bully who stood six foot five and two hundred eighty pounds. The detective was more than a little worried about Boris's threat while the sergeant was plenty pissed off.

Nina and her child were immediately placed in the custody relocation program. The police and district attorney's office would perform a threat analysis, that is, assess the victim's allegations and the concomitant safety risk to the victim. The police moved Nina and her daughter to a hotel for the next three weeks until a more secure safety plan could be found for them. Later, a placement in another state was located in a shelter for victims of domestic violence.

Over the next four months, Nina struggled like a fish just removed from the water and placed on a wet slab of ice—not yet dead but not thriving either. Her inability to speak English with any facility posed a much greater obstacle in her new state than in Brighton Beach. Nina had no job, no driver's license or beautician certificate, no prospects of employment, no one to talk to while living in unfamiliar surroundings. There was no suitable child care in the unlikely event that she should find a job, and, most of all, she had no money.

Against all advice and the rules of the shelter, Nina returned to the familiarity, if not the safety, of Brighton Beach. There she lived with a friend, easily found a job in a beauty salon as well as affordable day care for her daughter, and resumed taking vocational courses. After a few months, Nina went to visit Boris who was still in jail awaiting trial. She wanted to assure herself that her daughter would always be safe. It was more like a confrontation than a visit.

"I cannot believe that you would kill our daughter or my mother." Nina angrily recounted the threats that Boris had previously made.

"You know I never would have done anything like that especially to my own daughter. You were driving me mad because you refused to let me see you. You know how much I love you." Boris answered as sweetly as he had ever talked to her.

"You have a funny way of expressing your love," Nina responded.

Boris apologized, "I am sorry." He continued, "You know how I feel about you and how I've always felt about you. Now you must do me a favor. Here is my lawyer's card. Call him and tell him that you want the case against me dismissed."

"It's a little late for that!" Nina abruptly declared and then arose to end their conversation as well as their meeting.

Upon leaving the prison, Nina instantly remembered Boris's long arms reaching her in Poland when he wanted her to come to America. She felt the chill of fear run through her body. The next day she gathered her belongings and made arrangements to return with her child to the shelter in the other state.

Ten weeks after her jailhouse visit, Boris's trial began. Boris's defense attorney was very capable in impeaching Nina's credibility during her trial testimony. He powerfully brought to the jury's attention that Nina had misrepresented her religion on her immigration application. As in many domestic violence trials, the defense was able to present that the complainant failed to report many prior incidents of abuse to the police, medical personnel, or her family. In this case, the defense attorney ably demonstrated that Nina informed the treating doctor and nurses at the hospital that her broken jaw was the result of a fall, not from a blow delivered by Boris. The defense lawyer also attempted to besmirch Nina's reputation by having her admit that she had danced for two months in scantily clad clothes and bikini bathing suits at a bar in New Jersey.

The prosecutor, Cynthia, a dedicated career veteran, regularly honed her combative skills in competitive basketball games with other like-minded women. Cynthia enjoyed the physical and mental exertion of both courts and only worried that soon her body would be unable to withstand the daily rigors of full-court basketball. She enjoyed the adversarial quality of courtroom work especially during trial. The physicality was absent, but the mental chess game invigorated her. She even enjoyed the innovative labors of searching for an exception to the rule against admitting hearsay and fitting the evidence sought to be admitted under that rule. Her scrappy spirit was only tempered by her obligation to do justice and to ensure that if she thought a defendant to be innocent, then a trial should not be had.

During redirect examination, Nina readily explained her dancing at the New Jersey bar. This was only one in a series of jobs that Nina had taken in order to make extra money to remove herself and her child from being financially dependent upon Boris. Only then could she leave him.

Although most think fear is the driving motive, economic considerations are probably the number one factor why women do not leave their abusers. The prosecutor then went to work on the immigration application. Nina testified that it was Boris who directed her to list her religion as Jewish and to seek political asylum. Boris had instructed her that this would ensure her admittance into the United States.

Finally, an expert on battered women's syndrome, now more commonly known as battering and its effects, was called to explain some of Nina's behavior and to explain the dynamics of an abusive domestic relationship.[1] The expert testified as to the classic model of domestic violence. In many battering relationships, each beating was followed by an apologetic stage where the abuser would beg the victim with emotional pleadings for forgiveness, bestowing upon her flowers and even lavish gifts and vacations. Most often these episodes of contrition, sometimes called the honeymoon periods, would be of fleeting duration, as they would invariably be followed by escalations of the violence and the severity of the beatings. I have since learned that one size does not fit all and batterers exhibit all kinds of behavior with one common goal—power and control or domination.

The expert was not permitted by the court to offer an opinion as to whether Nina was herself a victim of domestic violence. But after the expert had concluded her testimony, it was clear to the jury that Nina did not remember the precise dates and times of the assaults perpetrated upon her because of the frequency of the attacks. As with most battered women, only the most severe beatings stood out in Nina's mind. The expert informed the jurors that battered women, in many if not most instances, do not report these predatory attacks upon them to the police or to medical personnel or even to friends or family. Frequently, the batterers are the ones who administer the medical attention to the wounds that they have inflicted as the honeymoon phase commences after a severe beating. The expert also explained to the jury the possible reasons why a battered woman declines to leave or even returns to her abuser—fear, economic or financial concerns, love, a belief that the battering will stop or that the abuser will change, emotional dependency, including low self-esteem, and sometimes the need to know where the abuser is and where the next attack will be launched from. The expert on battered women's syndrome described how a victim undergoes an informal risk-benefit analysis in deciding when it is time to call the authorities—when the risk in not calling is greater than the risk she faces in contacting the police.[2]

Nina also had a plausible explanation for lying to the emergency room personnel and to the examining physician—Boris was present with her at all times and she rightly feared retribution. Unlike the doctor and nurses in the emergency room who had the benefit of viewing Nina's swollen jaw before wiring it shut, the jury understood why Nina did not finger Boris as her assailant. The jury did not believe Nina's original account of her injury—her broken jaw was caused by a fall down the stairs. The maxilla-facial oral surgeon who had performed the open reduction of the bilateral fracture on Nina's mandible explained the extent of the fractures and the considerable amount of force that must have been applied to cause such an injury.

Other witnesses testified about the various times that Boris had hit Nina, incidents either charged in the indictment or admitted as evidence of prior bad acts or uncharged crimes. These witnesses also depicted the injuries sustained by Nina. The jury heard about the times her face and nose were swollen, her eyes were bruised and discolored with shades of blue and crimson, and her front tooth was chipped.

Boris's attorney called only Boris's family members as defense witnesses at trial. In essence, their collective testimony indicated that Nina and Boris had a good relationship. Boris had cared for Nina with tender kindness when she had broken her jaw. Nina also tended to Boris after he was shot. Since that time Boris had lost much strength, mobility, and use of his right arm. The conclusion that they invited the jury to reach was that Boris was incapable of hitting much less hurting Nina with his right hand. Boris's ex-wife recounted how she and Nina had met in Latvia in 1990 while she was still married to

Boris. She told the jury that she and Boris remained good friends after their divorce. He was a good provider for his family and was always gentle and caring and never hit her.

The jury deliberated for almost two days as twenty-five counts were submitted for their consideration. Boris was found guilty of assault in the second degree for breaking Nina's jaw and for criminal contempt in the first degree for violating the criminal court's order of protection issued when Boris had chipped her tooth. I sentenced Boris to consecutive sentences for these two counts aggregating a total of four and one-half to ten years in jail. It was the most time that he could receive under the law. He deserved much more. I later learned that although Boris ordinarily could have been deported for his crimes, the United States had no reciprocal treaty with Latvia. Upon his release from jail, he would remain in America.

Nina persevered. She has become a successful hair colorist with her own business and, as I heard some years ago, is happily married.

What can we learn from this case? We know that in many instances domestic violence is learned behavior. When Boris's son witnessed Boris beating on Nina, was there an imprinting to perpetuate a next-generation batterer? There was a good chance of that.

We know now that the emergency room doctor should have examined Nina alone, in private and out of earshot of Boris, so that there would have been a chance that Nina would have related the true cause of her injuries. If Nina were to have told the doctor that Boris was battering her, an appropriate treatment would entail that Nina would not be released to her abuser. An interdiction would have occurred and the medical record would be so noted. Ordinarily the name of the perpetrator of a crime on a medical record is not admissible as necessary for diagnosis and treatment. However, in a domestic violence situation or in a scenario involving the physical or sexual abuse of a child, the identity of the perpetrator should be part of diagnosis and treatment as the patient/victim should not be returned to the cause of his or her abuse or injuries.[3] This medical exam in the emergency room was a missed opportunity to end the abuse and to perhaps extricate Nina from violence.

Boris's actions were typical of the paradigm of the cycle of violence. According to the cycle of violence, domestic abuse is not continual but follows a three-phase cyclical pattern. This cycle begins with minor battering incidents, progresses to an acute stage of battering, and ends with a period of nonviolence. The first phase can last for years. Battered women tend to minimize these incidents and place blame for the battering on their own failures or external situations. They attempt to keep the batterer calm and to control the situation by modifying their behavior and using techniques that have appeased him in the past. Although battered women initially have limited control over the situation, tension in the relationship builds as these incidents continue.

Phase two begins when the battered woman's attempts to calm the batterer lose all effect. This phase consists of acute battering characterized by uncontrollable violence. While the battering incidents in both phases one and two are unlawful assaults, the uncontrolled nature of phase two battering differentiates the two phases. Battered women isolate themselves after phase two and may wait several days to seek medical attention, even for broken bones. Additionally, they minimize the injuries they receive by refusing to acknowledge to themselves or others the severity of the abuse. At the beginning of phase three, the violence ceases and the batterer may be loving and contrite. He asks for his mate's forgiveness, promising not to abuse her again. Battered women are most likely to flee the abusive situation at the beginning of phase three and realize the need to escape the relationship; the batterer may convince them that he will change and stop the abuse. This nonviolent phase cements the batterer and the battered woman in the relationship. The theory of learned helplessness can also explain the battered woman syndrome. Learned helplessness is a term that has been applied to the psychological change that abuse causes in a battered woman. After a woman experiences repeated abusive episodes over which she believes she has no control, her ability to develop escape responses is lost, even when escape from the relationship is feasible. Repeated batterings decrease the battered woman's motivation to act, causing her to become passive in the situation; believing herself to be helpless, she becomes helpless and believes that no viable alternatives exist. Constant threatening situations can prevent her from thinking beyond the immediate situation. If avenues of escape are in fact available to her, she may not regard them as viable and may fail to see them at all. Consequently, the battered woman remains in a situation in which she inevitably experiences more abuse.[4]

Yet not all battering or intimate partner abuse is consistent with the cycle of violence or learned helplessness theories. Some researchers disagree with the learned helplessness theory and prefer a "survivor theory."[5] A study of six thousand women in Texas shelters indicated that battered women are, in fact, help seekers whose efforts to search for resources and support services increase with the severity of the beatings. This study further suggests that those same sources may not provide sufficient aid.[6]

Another researcher contends that a coercive control model is less limited than a violence model.[7] "The new definition recognizes that patterns of behavior and separate instances of control can add up to abuse—including instances of intimidation, isolation, depriving victims of their financial independence or material possessions and regulating their everyday behavior."[8]

In fact, this pattern of domination that includes tactics of isolation, degradation, exploitation, and control has been also called "psychological or emotional abuse, patriarchal or intimate terrorism."[9] This concept of coercive control has been included in the definition of domestic violence in England and has led France to create a criminal statute prohibiting psychological abuse.[10] Whether we describe the behavior in terms of the typical power and control model, the cycle of violence, the type of violence (coercive controlling violence, violent resistance, situational couple violence, or separation-instigated violence),[11] the types of abusive men,[12] or the degree of misbehavior ("[a] review and synthesis of the literature reveals three types of batterers common across current typology research—a low, moderate, and high risk offender"),[13] we must recognize that one size does not fit all. Once we realize this, the experts can develop policy and programs for abusive men that may be effective.

Chapter Eight

Predator Paul

Peaches was whispering inaudibly to her elderly neighbor. He could not hear what she was saying, let alone understand her. Peaches felt lucky that she had escaped from her room where Paul had held her captive for the previous seven days. She ran out of her room and up the stairs to the apartment door of the kindly older gentleman who had never failed to say hello to her whenever he saw her in the lobby. They both resided in the single-room occupancy hotel where many of the others there had barely escaped the streets or were on the way back to them. The older gentleman with the kind and open face would always have a good word for Peaches when she would meet him in the early morning upon her return from her work. Peaches was only sixteen years old, yet she was forced to labor throughout the night—her work ending very often with the advent of sunrise. She pounded on his door in desperation, seeking her very survival. When he opened the door, instead of the good-natured smile that was seemingly affixed upon his countenance, she palpably observed, in the midst of her distress, the stern visage of deep concern for her. It was unclear whether he noticed the swelling around her mouth or the bright hues of crimsons and shades of black and blue that she wore upon her face as a perverse reminder of the beating she had received. Yet it was apparent that he was frozen with fright, not for himself, but for her. Unable to talk because of the piercing pain, and in fear of opening her mouth lest more teeth fall out, Peaches quickly wrote out her requests, her instructions: "Call my mother! Call the police! I've been beaten and kidnapped."

Peaches had been a troubled teenager. In the summer of 1998, she was only fifteen and a half years old, but she looked and tried to act like a woman. Although Peaches completed her sophomore year of high school with passing grades, she hung out with a rough crowd. Her friends were not hard-core criminals but rather troublemakers who stayed out late, had difficulty in school, and rebelled against parental authority. Ellen, her mother, had difficulty coping with Peaches's late nights and her acquaintances.

Ellen was a hardworking, low-income single mother who was trying to hold it together. Ellen was too proud to take any handouts. She had never received food stamps or been on welfare. She worked as a saleswoman in a neighborhood department store and struggled to pay her rent and to make ends meet. She made sure that Peaches always had clean clothes to wear to school each morning.

In May of 1998, Ellen found herself feeling conquered where before she had never succumbed to life's pressures, which were in fact considerable. Ellen did not approve of Peaches's close association with a particular friend who was clearly a bad influence on her. Ellen would find cigarette butts in Peaches's room. Peaches would come home unusually late with a hint of alcohol on her breath. When confronted with Ellen's objections, Peaches would answer her mother very often in a fresh manner with words that she had certainly never heard at home. Ellen tried everything, including reasoning, banning Peaches's friend from the apartment, and punishment, as well as placing her on a curfew.

All of Ellen's endeavors in this regard were unsuccessful. Peaches remained defiantly uncooperative and unmanageable despite her mother's best efforts. It was a sad day indeed when Ellen felt compelled to place Peaches in a group home in a residential area of Brooklyn. It turned out to be a fateful decision for both of them.

The group home was a facility for troubled youth ages thirteen to eighteen. The teenagers were required to adhere to the strict rules of the home. Each resident was required to perform chores and received pocket money for doing so. A nightly nine o'clock curfew was imposed on all.

Peaches shared a room with two other young women, Susan and Jesse. Peaches liked these girls well enough, but she found the structure and discipline of the home too foreign and suffocating. She had broken various rules of the home in the short three months she had resided there by smoking in her bedroom and staying up after curfew. Peaches received seven demerits resulting in the loss of some of her pocket money as well as the assessment of a two-week kitchen duty penalty. She longed to leave but not necessarily to return to her mother.

Across the street from the group home resided a family in a private house. Peaches would see the various family members coming and going from time to time. The head of the family seemed to be a mother. There were also a number of grown-up children, both male and female, who lived there as well as a boy child who appeared to be about eleven years old. One of the children named James would come by almost daily to flirt with Jesse. It was clear that he liked her.

Paul, one of James's older brothers, would walk by the front porch of the group home on a few occasions within days of Peaches's arrival. Peaches noticed him right away. Peaches was unsure whether Paul lived with his family. She only saw him there every few days or so.

Paul had very smooth light brown skin with a fringe beard that ran from the left side of his jaw to the right along the chin line. Peaches thought that the dreadlock style in which he wore his hair made him a very sexy man. She loved the fact that he was always decked out in fancy clothes and big gold necklaces and rings, which she believed to be very expensive.

After a week, Paul discovered Peaches as well. He would at first return her coquettish smiles with a big Cheshire cat–like grin that displayed an open and seemingly happy face as well as two gold-capped front teeth. After a few times, Paul said hello and started talking to her. He told her that he found her attractive and exciting even after she told him that she was only fifteen years old.

Peaches enjoyed the fact that this twenty-eight-year-old man would talk to her. She looked like a young nineteen- or twenty-year-old woman. She was beautiful and busty with the waist and legs of an active fifteen-year-old. He was respectful but would invariably touch her shoulder sweetly or brush his hand lightly upon her arm.

Peaches knew that Paul liked her. She believed that he cared for her as much as she was starting to feel for him. Peaches craved and delighted in the attention that Paul bestowed upon her. Weeks later, she considered him her boyfriend. Several days each week, Paul would go to his mother's house. On those occasions, he would invariably seek Peaches out. The two of them would often talk about love and life.

One day in late August, Paul told Peaches that she was his girlfriend and that sometime soon they would live together. Peaches did not then realize how prophetic these words were and how soon they would become a reality. It was, however, not nearly what she had envisioned when these words were uttered.

Peaches had a boyfriend of sorts at the group home prior to her hooking up with Paul. His name was Ron. It was an appropriate, emerging, and flirtatious adolescent relationship with a lot of conversation and a little kissing. The counselors at the home provided close oversight. Even if Peaches and Ron were disposed to consummate their relationship, the vigilant supervision at the home would have thwarted any liaison. This was short-lived as Peaches and Paul had become an item sometime in June of 1998.

When Peaches first started to talk with Paul, she very quickly forgot about the ever present Ron. Yet Paul did not fail to remember Ron, who was not a realistic romantic rival. Whether Paul possessed some incomprehensible macho jealousy or had some Machiavellian plan to induce Peaches to live with him, one could only guess.

On the Saturday before Labor Day, Paul importuned some of his friends to jump Ron. He was not beat up badly, but he was more than roughed up, suffering some minor bruises and a black eye. The counselors incorrectly attributed this act of violence not solely to Paul but also to Peaches.

Peaches actually felt flattered that Paul was jealous of Ron. At the same time, she felt badly and almost guilty that Paul had chosen to demonstrate his interest for her by having Ron hurt. The incident, together with Peaches's previous infractions of the home's rules, resulted in the chief counselor asking Peaches to leave the premises on Labor Day. The group home alerted Peaches's mother.

Yet Peaches never went to her mother's home. Instead, Peaches packed her belongings in one suitcase and made a beeline to Paul's family home.

She remembered what Paul had told her only days ago: "One day soon we will live together."

She believed him then and was prepared to take him up on it now. As she approached the house where Paul's mother lived, Peaches saw Paul's brother James on the front lawn. She asked James whether Paul was at home. He told her that Paul would be coming home in a few hours.

James invited Peaches into the house and then into the backyard. James began playing with two dogs. She thought that the dogs were the family pets, but later Peaches would learn that they were Paul's dogs. They both had thick, muscled necks with powerful-looking jaws. They looked like some kind of pit bull hybrid. Although they seemed docile enough when James was playing with them, Peaches sensed that they could easily become vicious without much provocation or upon command.

After James tired of the dogs, they sat and talked awhile in the backyard before entering the house. James gave Peaches some lemonade that his mother had made the day before. She waited for Paul, who arrived approximately two hours later.

Peaches recounted how she was exiled from the group home. She told Paul that she did not wish to return to her mother's house. She also reminded him that only days before he had assured her that one day soon they would live together.

To clinch the deal, she recited the events that caused her to be put out of the group home: "After all, if your friends had not beaten up Ron, I would not now be looking for a place to stay."

Paul did not need as much convincing as Peaches thought. He feared taking her in because she was under age. Paul was not one to be ever motivated by conscience but always by self-preservation. He quickly performed the legal calculations and balanced the risk against the benefit.

His decision was quick and easy. "You can't stay at my mother's house. I will put you up in a hotel. You are my girlfriend and I will take care of you."

Later they ate at the house with Paul's mother and brothers and sisters. After dinner, Peaches held onto Paul's waist with willing arms as they rode off on one of his two flashy motorcycles. Paul parked the motorcycle at the Duchess Hotel in downtown Brooklyn just off of Atlantic Avenue.

The building was a single-room occupancy hotel. There were several long-term residents who paid monthly rent, but most of the persons who stayed there were transients—remaining only for a night or two. The police believed that just about on any night, several of the rooms were let by johns and women of the night. The location was known as a prostitution spot. Each room in the hotel had a sink, two single beds, and an old chest of drawers. There was one bathroom on each floor with a sink and a tub where one could either bathe or shower. The bathrooms on the odd floors were for men and on the even floors for women.

Paul introduced Peaches to a girl named Candy who appeared to be no older than she. Paul told Peaches that he was renting a room for her, which she would share with Candy. Paul rented a room on another floor.

Over the next few days, Paul lavished much attention on Peaches. They lunched at McDonalds, went to the movies, bowled or played pool, and then ate dinner at White Castle or Taco Bell. He complimented her at every opportunity.

At night they had sex, or as Peaches believed, they made love. Paul whispered all the right words in her ear when the lights were out. She thought that Paul was very sexy. He was a muscular one hundred and sixty-five pounds on a five-foot-eight-inch frame. She enjoyed touching his silky smooth skin as Paul led her to believe that he also loved to caress her body. She was certain that she was Paul's "one and only" girlfriend, his one and only love. Still she wondered, what was Candy's connection to Paul?

Then in an instant, Peaches's life would be forever altered. She was about to experience things that no woman should have to live through, yet alone a young girl. Her world would never look quite the same again.

When Peaches awoke on the fourth morning of her stay in the Duchess Hotel, she saw Paul standing over her bed. She mistakenly imagined that he was gazing at her lovingly while she was asleep.

Paul took Peaches and Candy for a breakfast of two eggs on a roll and a cup of coffee. Upon their return to the hotel, Paul brought Peaches and

Candy to a room on the second floor. There, Paul directed a woman named Wanda to give them haircuts and to style their hair. The style in which Wanda fashioned her hair made Peaches appear more grown up. Peaches reckoned that Paul wanted her to be more sophisticated. Peaches felt flattered all over again that Paul took such an active interest in her and in her appearance. Yet she pondered why Paul was doing the same things for Candy as for her.

Wanda talked to the two girls about making money and how women should always have their own private stash. Peaches considered this to be a good idea. She had observed that her own mother, who worked so hard, never seemed to have enough money to make ends meet, let alone to accumulate extra cash.

Paul then brought the two girls into his room. He explained to them that he wanted them to make some money for themselves and for him. He told them that he wanted them to have sex with men who would pay them a fee, which he would share with the girls.

Peaches protested, saying, "Am I your girl? Why do you want me to have sex with other men?"

Paul replied in his extra smooth voice, "Of course, you're my girl! I will love you all the more, if we can work to put some money together for our future."

This seemed to placate Peaches. She felt that she could do anything for Paul so long as he would continue to love her.

Paul, who was black, as was Peaches, recited the rules to Peaches and Candy. The girls would not have sex with black men. Paul explained to Peaches that their relationship would remain rock solid and be exclusive as long as she did not turn any tricks with other black men. Peaches did not really grasp the logic of Paul's fiat, but if it meant being his girl, she would go along with it.

There were other rules. Condoms had to be used at all times. She could not talk to any other men on the street who were not potential customers.

Paul was simply protecting his investment by not allowing any of his girls to talk to other pimps. Paul told them that he would collect the money from Peaches and Candy at the end of each night. He related that at the end of each week, he would divide the money up and give Peaches and Candy their shares. Paul informed them that he would decide how much to charge and where they would work on a particular night. Finally, he told them that they must call him "Daddy" from then on.

What Paul omitted was perhaps more important than what he stated. Paul's explanation of the rules failed to prepare Peaches for what was to come.

First, there were the clothes that she had to wear.

When Paul first showed them to Peaches, she said, "I can't wear them. They're nasty."

Each outfit was virtually sheer as well as skimpy. Paul sweet-talked her. He willed her into becoming a scantily clad woman of the night.

Candy was not so easily convinced. She finally felt the full burden of the life that she was soon to live. Candy simply told Paul that she would not wear those clothes nor would she give her body to men for money. She would not be so forthright with Paul ever again.

Peaches caught a glimpse of Paul's essence that had heretofore remained hidden from her but that she would soon see firsthand and close up again. Paul pulled a rather large-looking handgun from his waistband, which had been hidden from view by the dungaree jacket that hung just below Paul's hips.

In a controlled rage, he pointed it at Candy's head, saying, "If you don't do what I tell you, you won't do nothing."

Candy immediately acquiesced by showing pitiful obedience to him. "Yes, Paul, I was only kidding. Of course, I'll wear those clothes. I will do anything you want me to do."

Paul with a slightly twisted but wicked smile etched on his face replied, "That's right, bitch, and don't you forget it."

The long nights that followed over the next few months took Peaches and Candy on a journey that most tourists never see. Paul drove Peaches and Candy to work underneath the belly of the Fifty-ninth Street or Queensboro Bridge, which connects Manhattan to Queens; on Twenty-third Street in Queens; on street corners and parking lots in the Bay Ridge and Brighton Beach sections of Brooklyn; and in the Hunts Point area of the Bronx where city residents access the Willis Avenue Bridge into Manhattan upon returning from the northern suburbs and the upstate region.

Paul knew his business. There were many white males each night looking for some fun or to fulfill some sexual fantasy at these locations. Peaches would ply her trade mostly inside the "john's" car, but sometimes in a dark street corner or under a bridge. She felt dirty and cheap.

Often Peaches would finish work by two in the morning after starting at anywhere from nine to ten at night. Many times her work did not end until sunrise.

Paul had glossed over her work schedule when he had explained what he had expected of her. She was not permitted to cease her labors until she earned at least five hundred dollars each evening in the summer, spring, and fall as well on winter weekend nights.

On a winter weekday night, her quota was reduced to three hundred dollars. Even though the dollar amount requirement was greater, this was not too difficult in the spring, summer, and autumn weekends. She charged tricks fifty dollars for ten minutes of sexual intercourse and either more or less than that for other kinds of sex. Yet on the weekday evenings in the winter, Peaches would have to labor oftentimes until almost dawn in the cold, dark, and hard streets.

Paul was always nearby the "john's" car, which was usually the place where sex for a fee was offered and received. At first, Peaches thought that he wanted to be close by to protect her. This was partially true, but not because he loved her. He merely wished to safeguard his property, his investment. More pointedly, Paul wanted to be next to his money.

After the first week, when it was time to apportion the money among the three of them, the rules suddenly changed.

Paul simply declared, "I will keep the money and look after you. After all, I am your daddy."

Although Paul did make the payments for the rental of her room at the hotel and did oftentimes pay for her meals, his statement was very upsetting to Peaches and became a defining moment for her. The clincher was perhaps the abject humiliation that both girls suffered at the hands of Paul every early morning after the first week of work. He forced them to strip naked and jump up and down to show that they were not concealing any money from him in their private parts. The act of undressing and jumping made her feel dirtier than any of the sex acts that she had performed.

Although Peaches was not happy having sex with strangers, there were two reasons why she had agreed. One had to do with the strong emotional and physical attraction that she had for Paul. She was, however, coming to realize that any feeling that she imagined that he had for her was merely an illusion.

The second reason she consented to have relations with strange men was the money. She had never before had any money, let alone enough, for the things that she wanted while growing up. Prostitution was a way for her to obtain the material objects that she always wanted and that her mother was unable to provide for her. Her rationalization for becoming a prostitute was swiftly being exposed to be a great lie.

Paul would buy Peaches gifts with the money she earned by selling her body. Sometimes, but less and less often, they would have really good times. Paul became increasingly more difficult. He required Peaches and Candy to work seven days a week. He decided when and if they would have a day off.

Paul also became more and more abusive. Almost every other day he would thrash one of the girls. Paul would beat them with anything that was available—his hands, a belt buckle, or even a broomstick. Peaches was getting hit so often for minor and imagined infractions that she visualized herself as a punching bag.

In a four-month period from the end of September 1998 until the end of January 1999, Peaches was arrested five times for prostitution along with Candy. Each time they both entered pleas of guilty. Each time they were sentenced to jail for a period ranging from three to fifteen days. While in jail together, they promised each other that they would leave Paul and the life that he had thrust upon them. It was in prison, with nothing else to do and without Paul watching over everything they said and did, where Peaches learned Candy's true age, fourteen years old. Candy and Peaches were instructed by Paul to lie about their true ages to their johns and to the police should they be arrested.

On the first four occasions of their release from jail, they returned to Paul. Candy had contacted her mother on her fifth arrest. She quietly embraced Peaches to say good-bye as they exited the Anna Cross facility at Riker's Island. Neither Peaches nor Paul ever saw Candy again.

The irony of Candy's freedom was not lost on Peaches. Although she was relieved and happy that Candy had escaped the yoke of Paul's subjugation, her own plight seemed worse off than before. Paul would now bestow all his attention upon her. The beatings would now be directed toward her alone. There would be much more pressure for her to produce financially. She was sure that her dollar quota per night would soon be increased. Peaches only hoped that it would not be doubled.

All the indignities that Peaches had suffered—the degrading sexual acts performed by her on, and upon her, by strangers for money; the outfits that she was forced to wear; the hours spent in urine-smelling pens where she waited to go before a judge; and the financial, physical, and emotional control exerted upon her by Paul—did not foretell the ferocious violence that she would soon undergo.

In the early afternoon of February 12, Peaches awoke after a particularly long and cold wintry night on the streets. Paul had allowed her to cease her labors the night before by 1:00 a.m. even though she had not made her cash quota for the evening. There was very little traffic out by the Willis Avenue Bridge, so Paul decided to shift their base of operations to Bay Ridge at around 10:00 p.m. That area was equally quiet. Except for a few early encounters, there was very little action after eleven o'clock. Paul and Peaches stopped for coffee and then went back to the hotel.

Peaches will always remember that Lincoln's birthday falls on February 12. The incongruity of what Lincoln stood for and what she suffered on his birthday in 1999 was not lost on her.

Paul entered Peaches's room shortly after she had risen from bed that day. He was smiling, seemingly happy and playfully swinging a baseball bat. Suddenly the smile evaporated from his face.

In a very angry but cold and controlled tone of voice, Paul said, "'Fess up. Why did you talk to that no good Snake Eyes?"

Peaches had inadvertently broken a fundamental rule of the street and a particular rule of Paul's—never talk to another pimp. Peaches briefly reflected that one of the other street walkers must have ratted on her because of some petty argument, private pique, or trivial jealousy.

As she attempted to explain to Paul that she only asked Snake Eyes for a cigarette, he was on her in an instant with the metal baseball bat gripped firmly in his right hand. He tried to strike her, but Peaches succeeded in placing the mattress over her and between herself and Paul. With a powerful tug, Paul yanked the mattress from her hands. He swung the bat mightily right at Peaches's head. He connected.

The impact of the baseball bat upon her mouth was of such extraordinary force that Paul's hands stung as the metal bat vibrated. It was as though he had hit his first hardball on a cold spring day that seemed more like winter. Immediately the top four teeth in the front of her mouth and the left upper cuspid were knocked out. Numerous other teeth were loosened with some in imminent danger of falling out. Peaches felt immense pain to her upper and lower jaws, which she later learned were both broken. Still Paul did not stop.

He proceeded to hit her with the bat about her body. When Peaches was lying prostrate on the floor, he began kicking her legs. His attack, though brief, was merciless. In less than five minutes, Peaches was a bruised, battered, and bloody mess. As suddenly as the onslaught began, it abruptly ended. Perhaps Paul thought that Peaches had learned her lesson. In reality, Peaches's brain was a pile of mush. She was groggy, and her head was spinning.

Paul underwent a complete metamorphosis. He attended to her wounds to the mouth and face and to the bruises on her body and legs. He applied ice to her mouth and face in an effort to keep the swelling down. At first the area around Peaches's mouth was numb. She did not open her mouth to speak, eat, drink, or even spit because she feared that any movement would result in more teeth falling out. When the anesthetic effect of the numbness wore off after almost an hour, Peaches experienced the intense pain that accompanies fractures to upper and lower jaws, swollen gums, broken teeth, and bodily bruises.

Peaches asked Paul to take her to the hospital. He not only refused to provide medical attention for her injuries; he laid down a new set of rules—she was not allowed to leave her room or to open the door. Paul kept Peaches in virtual captivity.

Paul never left her alone except when he went to the store to buy soup. That was all Peaches could consume and that was what sustained her. Unwilling to open her mouth, she drank soup through a straw. Unable to speak, Peaches had to write down all her needs to Paul. When she had to leave the room to use the bathroom on the floor, Paul would accompany her and wait outside to ensure that she would not write or tell anyone what had occurred. Her imprisonment went on for a week. Lincoln, who freed the slaves, was born on the February 12, the day her personal enslavement began.

On the morning of February 19, Paul, who now mistakenly believed that his control over Peaches was nearly absolute, departed to "attend to his business."

As he was leaving, he told her, "Remember, don't leave the room or open the door."

Peaches remained in her bed as though Paul might return to check up on her. She was prescient. Two minutes later, Paul opened the door and smiled when he saw her in bed.

Confidently, he said, "You're a good girl. I'll be right back."

This time Peaches sat in her bed for almost ten minutes. Then in a frantic rush of adrenaline, she pushed open the door and flew up the stairs. She balled up her fist to beat on the door of the kindly older gentleman who never failed to say hello to her whenever they would meet. She pounded in desperation, seeking her very survival.

When he opened the door, instead of the good-natured smile that was seemingly affixed upon his countenance, she palpably observed, in the midst of her distress, the stern visage of deep concern for her. It was unclear whether he noticed the swelling around her mouth or the bright hues of crimsons and shades of black and blue that she wore upon her face and legs as a perverse reminder of the beating she received.

Yet it was apparent that he was frozen with fright, not for himself, but for her. Peaches whispered inaudibly to her elderly neighbor. He could not hear what she was trying to say, much less understand the words she muttered. Unable to talk because of the piercing pain and in fear of opening her mouth lest more teeth fall out, Peaches quickly wrote out her requests, her instructions: "Call my mother! Call the police! I've been beaten and kidnapped."

Four police officers responded to the 911 call that was placed by the kind elderly gentleman. They immediately noticed the week-old injury to Peaches's mouth. Despite the fact that her face was still very swollen, the trained eyes of the officers recognized that Peaches's wounds were infected and not fresh. She had dried blood caked about her mouth. Her lips were enlarged and unhealed. She was disheveled from her week of captivity and from not changing her clothes during this period.

She was obviously upset, but she was unable to speak. Peaches wrote out the room where she lived. She had also written a description of Paul.

Two of the police officers went to look for Paul in Peaches's room. When they entered the room, they saw many spots and a large oblong shape of dried dark red blood. These two officers had seen much evidence of violence at crime scenes. They thought that they had seen it all. They were wrong.

Nothing before prepared them for the sickening sight of Peaches's teeth marks imprinted on the metal bat. The officers secured the room and seized the bat as evidence. The officers questioned Peaches further about Paul. With greatly impaired speech, she told the officers where Paul's mother lived and that Paul owned a white four-door new model Acura with tinted windows and two motorcycles. That day the police staked out the house of Paul's mother as well as the Duchess Hotel.

The other two officers took Peaches to Long Island College Hospital. Later, a maxillofacial oral surgeon readied Peaches for the first of many reconstructive operations to repair her broken upper and lower jaws and to secure her loosened teeth.

The next morning, Paul was observed in the front of his mother's house. When the police officers approached, he ran into the house. One detective ran to the back of the house, while a uniformed officer covered the front.

In an instant, Paul came running onto the back porch, into the backyard, and off into the street. The detective attempted to follow but was deterred by the barking and jumping of the two aggressive-looking pit bull hybrids who were roaming the backyard, seemingly daring the detective to enter. The officer was brave but certainly not foolish. There would be another opportunity to catch Paul and perhaps in a setting that was not so dangerous.

The next morning, two plainclothes detectives in an unmarked car drove by the Duchess Hotel and spied Paul's Acura double-parked about forty-five feet from the main entrance. The detectives exited their vehicle and went to see the manager on duty. They asked the day manager where Paul was located. The manager feared Paul, but he was more concerned that the police would make things difficult for him should he fail to cooperate. The manager directed the officers to a room in the rear of the third floor.

Two uniformed officers arrived at the hotel in response to the detectives' request for backup. The two detectives and the two police officers proceeded to Paul's room. One of the detectives knocked on the door. A young scantily clad female opened the door.

The detective asked, "Is Paul here?"

The young lady replied while pointing with her right index finger to a closet in the back of the room, "No, he is not here."

The detective opened the closet door and peered in. It was dark and it was very difficult to see what was behind the coats. The detective reached back and felt a muscular arm, which he grabbed and explosively pulled out of the closet. Paul was pushed to the ground face down. His arms were pulled behind his back and he was handcuffed. He was made to stand up, frisked, and brought to the Eighty-fourth Precinct were his arrest was processed.

At midnight, Paul was arraigned in the criminal court. Bail was set at twenty-five thousand dollars cash. Paul was free on bail the following afternoon when his mother posted the bail in cash.

Peaches was released from the hospital after her jaws were wired shut. Peaches never thought that she would be relieved and even grateful for the opportunity to return home to live with her mother.

In late September 1999, the case against Paul proceeded to trial before me in the Supreme Court, Domestic Violence Part. On the Monday after the Friday when jury selection was concluded, Paul failed to appear in court for the scheduled opening statements to the jury.

Paul's mother presented a note from a doctor at one of the Brooklyn hospitals. Apparently Paul was treated the night before in the emergency room. He had run a fever of one hundred and one. The note left more questions unanswered than it resolved. Was Paul admitted? Had he been discharged after his admission? Did he still have a fever? If so, what was its cause and when would he be discharged and be able to come to court?

The hospital's attorneys were contacted and served via facsimile with a subpoena for Paul's emergency room records. Within ninety minutes, an inspection of the ER records was faxed to my chambers. A review of the records revealed that Paul was discharged from the hospital two hours after he had arrived. His temperature went down to ninety-nine point eight prior to his release from the hospital. The documentation of Paul's purported illness was genuine but was utilized by Paul and his family to perpetrate a ruse—a gross misrepresentation and exaggeration for the reason why he had failed to appear for the commencement of his trial.

The jury was sent home for the day while the district attorney's office conducted the required investigation to demonstrate that Paul had voluntarily absented himself, thus forfeiting and/or waiving his right to be present and to confront the witnesses against him at his criminal trial. The prosecutor's office provided Paul's pedigree information as to height, weight, eye and hair color, race, sex, date of birth, and social security number to the city morgue as well as to the hospitals in Brooklyn and many other hospitals in the other boroughs in an effort to find him. The Department of Corrections and the Central Booking precinct in each borough were furnished with his date of birth and New York State inmate identification number to determine whether Paul had been rearrested and whether he was presently incarcerated.

The institutions reported that Paul was neither dead nor injured and in a hospital, nor incarcerated in the criminal justice system. The next morning, the trial began in his absence. Peaches was unnerved that Paul could not be found by the authorities. She was dismayed by the prospect that Paul would hold her accountable if he were to be convicted. After all, he had often beaten her for perceived wrongs that were of much less consequence. She was extremely frightened.

Peaches testified quite credibly at trial. The defense attorney did score some points when Peaches conceded that one of the reasons she acquiesced to become a prostitute was to make money for herself. Additionally, Peaches admitted that she was a teenager who had given her mother problems. She stated that her mother "kicked her out of the house."

The medical expert testimony and hospital records were quite compelling. The oral surgeon communicated to the jury the scope of the injuries suffered by Peaches. The maxilla bone beneath her nose had been shattered by the blow received from the metal bat. The doctor talked about the fractured upper and lower jaws, the missing and cracked teeth, and the two reconstructive surgeries with the certainty of more operations to follow.

When the prosecution completed its case by calling various police officers, detectives, and hotel staff, Paul's defense counsel, a former assistant district attorney, not only cross-examined the prosecution's witnesses effectively and made appropriate and timely objections but also decided to put on a defense in Paul's absence.

Two of Paul's sisters testified on his behalf. One of his sisters, Julia, came from down south. She had graduated from Virginia State in 1993. Julia had on a conservative blue business suit. Her hair was pushed back into a ponytail. She wore a pair of wire-rimmed eyeglasses that made her appear more like a professor or school librarian rather than an account supervisor, which she was for a firm in North Carolina. She did not add too much to the facts of the incidents in question but was proffered as a witness to demonstrate to the jury that Paul was from a good family.

The second sister, Agnes, was twenty-two years old and lived in Brooklyn with Paul's mother and his other siblings. She testified that she had visited Peaches and Paul after the incident of February 12. Agnes had not observed anything wrong with Peaches's mouth, nor did she ever see Paul feed Peaches soup through a straw. The implication was that Peaches had not been telling the truth and that she was injured by someone other than Paul in plying her trade as a prostitute.

The third witness was a woman/girl nineteen years of age named Tanya. She testified that she first met Paul in 1995 in their old neighborhood of Crown Heights. She became a friend of Paul and a few years later became his girlfriend.

Tanya stated that Peaches and she were both prostitutes working on their own and not for Paul. She swore that Paul had never hit her or Peaches. She also maintained that Paul had never slept with Peaches. Tanya claimed that Peaches was obsessed with Paul. She and Peaches had words many times over Peaches's obvious interest in Paul.

In mid-February, she and Peaches had a tremendous verbal argument that soon turned physical. They were punching each other, pulling one another's hair, and scratching the other's face and body. Tanya contended that she was getting the worst of it in her battle with Peaches. Tanya stated that she retreated out of Peaches's room, went to her own room, and retrieved an aluminum baseball bat. Tanya came back to Peaches's room and, without a word, promptly and forcefully struck Peaches with the metal bat. That was the defense in a nutshell—Tanya was the perpetrator. The motive was jealousy. Paul's sisters were merely window dressing at the trial.

Paul's mother and a third grown sister as well as another attractive woman in her early twenties attended all the proceedings from jury selection until the rendition of the jury's verdict. It appeared that the third woman was Paul's current girlfriend. She and Paul had held hands and acted affectionately both in the hall and in the courtroom while the panel of prospective jurors was being summoned and during breaks in the jury selection process.

Paul had skipped out just before opening statements. During almost every break in the trial, it was reported by court personnel that either Paul's mother or sister used the pay phone down the hall from the courtroom. It is possible that they had phone calls to make during each recess. Most probably they were calling Paul to keep him informed about what was transpiring at his trial.

The summations by defense counsel and the prosecutor were both effective in drawing on the evidence presented at trial. Paul's attorney not only reiterated the theory of the defense, but also drew attention to the fact that Peaches had never before made a complaint to the police or sought medical attention for any of the beatings allegedly perpetrated by Paul. The assistant district attorney, a supervisor in the Domestic Violence Bureau with many years of trial experience, reminded the jury that a woman working as a prostitute for a pimp could not easily seek medical attention or go to the police when it was the pimp who had caused her injuries.

The jury was given the case in late morning. The jury requested that I read back a portion of Peaches's testimony regarding the incident in question. They also requested to see certain of the exhibits received into evidence, including Peaches's hospital records. At about eleven at night, the jury submitted a final note written in very neat print: "We have reached a verdict."

Paul was convicted of assault in the first degree, kidnapping in the second degree, and several counts of statutory rape.

Peaches made a statement to the court when I sentenced Paul in absentia a few weeks later to twenty-two years in prison. Now all the authorities had to do was to find Paul.

Peaches felt free, but she was still very scared. Peaches's state of alarm reached critical proportions when she thought she observed Paul riding on a motorcycle days after his conviction. She was mystified how he could escape capture by the authorities when she saw him on the street. She had no peace of mind knowing that Paul was out there somewhere lurking and waiting to hurt her once again.

Although she was frightened, she was determined to help the authorities in any way she could to apprehend Paul. Six weeks after the conclusion of the trial, she told a reporter that she was prepared to go on midnight runs with the police in an effort to catch Paul.[1]

Paul was listed as one of the most wanted fugitives by the FBI. It was not a dragnet, stakeout, or manhunt that resulted in his capture. Rather, it was something much more mundane. Peaches's living nightmare ended when Paul was stopped for a traffic offense in Virginia some six months after the conclusion of his trial. Paul was extradited to New York when the fugitive warrant appeared on a run of his name and date of birth. He was produced in my courtroom for the execution of his sentence, which he is now serving.

Peaches carries on, but she will never be able to recapture her lost youth and the remnants of her innocence. The scars on her face and in her psyche will never disappear despite numerous reconstructive surgeries and all the kisses and hugs her mother may give her.

The story of Peaches is just one example of the dangers a young person faces when she leaves her parents. Whether she ran away from home because her home life was too strict, or whether she was put out because her family could no longer tolerate her behavior and did not want her there, Peaches was left with no one to support her. At that point she became exceedingly vulnerable to human trafficking.

New York's New Abolitionists, a partnership of organizations formed to combat human trafficking, reports: "Serial predators, traffickers seek out victims rendered vulnerable by such factors as youth, poverty, and a history of abuse. Traffickers brutalize their victims until they are too broken to be lucrative commodities and then move on to new prey."[2] This partnership cites, among others, the following statistics: "On any given night in New York State, more than 4,000 underage youth are the victims of sex trafficking. In the United States, women and girls from racial minorities are disproportionately recruited by sex traffickers. The average age that a pimp recruits a girl into prostitution is between 13 and 14. 5.5 million children worldwide are victims of human trafficking each year. The National Human Trafficking Resource Center hotline received 3,598 reports of human trafficking in 2014. 83% of victims in federal investigations of confirmed sex trafficking incidents were identified as American citizens."[3] Thus it is clear that young American teens are particularly vulnerable to human trafficking.

What can we do to help fight this problem? We can encourage the passage of laws similar to the recently enacted New York legislation entitled Trafficking Victims Protection and Justice Act.[4] This sweeping reform of New York's anti-trafficking laws does, among other things, the following:

1. Ensures that buyers of prostituted children will now face the same penalty as perpetrators of statutory rape.
2. Provides sex trafficking as an affirmative defense to prostitution; a defendant can now argue that her or his participation in the crime was a result of having been the victim of human trafficking.
3. Increases the penalties by making trafficking a violent crime by creating the felony sex offense of "aggravated patronizing a minor" or where the trafficker caused physical injury, serious physical injury, or death.
4. Enhances penalties for patronizers who frequent school zones.
5. Allows victims of sex and labor trafficking and compelling prostitution to commence a civil action for damages against her or his trafficker within ten years after the victim is no longer subject to the victimization.
6. Removes the term "prostitute' from the penal law and substitutes the gender-neutral term "person for prostitution."

Laws like these would encourage defense attorneys to investigate their clients' experiences and to bring trafficking concerns to the attention of prosecutors and the courts. Police and prosecutors should target for prosecution the pimps, other traffickers, and purchasers of sex rather than concentrate their efforts on "persons for prostitution." We should recognize that human trafficking and the promoters of prostitution engage in human slavery. We should educate our community—places of worship, work place, schools, and so forth—about human trafficking and its perilous ramifications.

Victims of human trafficking and coerced prostitution, like victims of domestic violence, are often in plain sight. When we suspect someone is being victimized, we should try to intervene and to obtain help for that person. A referral should be made to the police, the local prosecutor, or U.S. Attorney's office. If a victim refuses help and we believe that she or he is in immediate danger, we should call 911 and report what we know. This is a societal issue, and if we are all not part of the solution, then we are part of the problem.

Chapter Nine

Same-Sex Savagery

What truly and exactly did happen the night when Joe fatally stabbed Stanley in the chest, we may never know. The homicide detectives and the crime scene unit described the floor of the living room as being strewn with used condoms. Joe claimed that Stanley called a male prostitute service and had sex numerous times with different males, while charging the bill to Joe's credit card. There was no doubt that a male escort service or two delivered prostitutes to Joe's apartment. The payment was in fact made from Joe's credit card. There were no witnesses to the altercation between Joe and Stanley. Was it murder or was it justifiable self-defense?

Domestic violence is not limited to traditional husband-wife and boyfriend-girlfriend and elder abuse. Approximately thirty felonies arose from same-sex intimate relationships during the first eleven and one-half years of the Domestic Violence Court's existence. Same-sex and transgender domestic violence cases are more underreported than the conventional domestic violence cases. The victims perceive, sometimes correctly, that the police will not take their complaints seriously. The victims are often more fearful of being "outed." They may not wish their employers and coworkers, and even their families, to know that they are gay.

There are two cases that stand out in my memory, not only because of the underlying crimes, but also on account of the dynamics of the relationship between the partners. They both involved the classic features of domestic violence: power and control.

Sheila was a registered nurse with a good job at a prestigious Manhattan hospital. She owned her own cooperative apartment in Brooklyn by the circle where Prospect Park meets Grand Army Plaza. On the surface, she was a respectable professional woman in her late thirties. No one knew she had physically and emotionally abused a series of gay partners, some live in, over the past few years.

Nancy was a quiet twenty-eight-year-old woman from a conservative churchgoing family. She lived with her parents in their home. Nancy was shy, quiet, and modest. She worked as a librarian in Brooklyn. Although Nancy realized that she was gay, she never openly admitted her sexual preference for women. She had only one or two relationships. She had broken off both of them when her partner wanted Nancy to go public. Nancy was troubled about how being outed would be handled by the people in her life. She was afraid of her parents' reaction and fearful of being ostracized by her church where she was a lay deacon.

Sheila had courted Nancy with great care over a period of six months. Sheila took her to expensive dinners, concerts, and parties. She also implored Nancy to move into an apartment with her. For Nancy, this was a huge step. She had never lived with anyone other than her family. In the end, Sheila wore Nancy down with kindness, a showing of love, and the belief that they would be a couple whose relationship would endure.

Within months, there was a drastic change in their relationship. Sheila started to inflict verbal abuse on Nancy in the privacy of the apartment they shared. Soon thereafter, Sheila began to denigrate Nancy publicly. After a few drinks, Sheila's range of language would change from salty to downright vulgar. The object of Sheila's curses was Nancy.

What had Nancy done to deserve this? She had merely been the fly entrapped in the spider's web. Nancy had left behind the foundation of her life, her family and church, to live with the one she loved. Sheila was allowing her true personality to show, now that Nancy had abandoned her support groups and was indeed isolated. Nancy was completely at Sheila's mercy.

The verbal abuse became physical, first pushing and then slapping. Perceived to be shunned by her parents and church, Nancy had nowhere to seek refuge from the onslaught that was only beginning. Nancy was chilled from seeking help from the authorities. She was uncertain of how her complaint would be received. Nancy believed that the police would ridicule claims of domestic abuse coming from one woman against another. She felt trapped.

One night the physical abuse took an ugly turn into the realm of criminal violence. Sheila and Nancy had been out drinking at a bar in Park Slope. Nancy had one beer and a few diet Cokes. Sheila started with a couple of gin and tonics followed by at least eight beers.

After a few hours, Sheila was nearly wasted but not too debilitated to refuse Nancy's entreaties to go home. Nancy was finally successful in prodding Sheila off of her bar stool and onto the sidewalk. They continued to argue throughout the twenty-five-minute walk to their apartment.

When they neared their house, Sheila became downright abusive and slapped Nancy twice across the cheek.

"Don't tell me what to do, don't tell me how much to drink, and don't tell me when you don't like my cursing. You're my little bitch. You live with me in my house. I should tell you what to do! You're lucky I don't give you the beating that you deserve." Sheila threatened as much as instructed.

Nancy cried out, "You can't talk to me like that! I gave up everything for you. You've changed. Where is all this coming from?"

Sheila answered with venom, "I'll show you where this is coming from, you little twit. I'll show you right now."

Sheila speedily pulled a scalpel from her jacket pocket and slashed Nancy's neck from under the left ear clear across to the underside of the right ear. Instantly a thin line of red appeared as though drawn with a fine marker. Then the blood began to flow down Nancy's neck, saturating the upper front of her blouse and dyeing it to a dark crimson.

Nancy, holding her neck with both hands, ran down the street, screaming, "Help me! Help me! I'm bleeding! I've been stabbed! Call the police; I'm going to die!"

Sheila paid no attention to the import of what had just occurred. She calmly shifted the scalpel from her right hand into her left and with her right hand removed the keys from her pocket, walked up the steps of her stoop, opened the front door, and proceeded down the hallway to her first-floor apartment. Upon entering her apartment, she slammed the door, threw her coat onto the sofa, and plopped into her bed. Sheila fell asleep still holding the scalpel.

Nancy stumbled around for less than a minute, when a patrol car stopped to assist her. The officers decided not to wait for an ambulance. A towel was placed tightly around Nancy's neck in an effort to stem the hemorrhaging, and they drove her to the hospital with turret lights flashing and siren blaring. Nancy was stabilized after being on the verge of shock.

The police officers then questioned Nancy. She told them what had happened. The officers called for another patrol car to back them up and proceeded to Sheila's apartment.

More than two hours after the assault upon Nancy, the police came, first knocking, then banging on Sheila's front door. Sheila remained sleeping during the cacophony. The police, fearing an ongoing exigency, possibly a suicide, called for the emergency services unit to break down the door. Before ESU arrived, Sheila awoke and opened the door.

The police asked Sheila to identify herself. She stated her name and told the officers that she had identification in her bedroom. Two of the officers accompanied her into the bedroom where they observed the bloody scalpel lying on top of the bedsheet in plain view. Sheila was arrested for assault in the first and second degrees.

Sheila was counting on Nancy chickening out of following through to trial. The more than one hundred stitches provided Nancy with the necessary resolve to testify in an open court. She was reunited with her parents, who now realized that Nancy was their daughter whom they loved unequivocally. They accepted her and her sexual preference.

Sheila stood on her respectable profession of nursing and alleged some kind of self-defense. She was nonetheless convicted of assault with a dangerous instrument.

The story of Nancy and Sheila paralleled that of Joe and Stanley. Joe was thirty-two years old, introverted and soft-spoken. He was lean but muscular and had served a four-year stint in the Marines. Stanley, a year younger than Joe, was much more outgoing and a take-charge kind of guy. They met while they were both volunteering in the Gay Men's Health Crises Center.

The truth of what actually happened during that fateful evening in 1997 may never be divulged. The facts that were revealed in the aftermath of the investigation were the subject of a murder indictment.

Stanley was stabbed by Joe; the knife penetrated nearly five inches into Stanley's chest. As a result of his injuries, Stanley died. Joe's statements to the police indicated that he was claiming justification for his acts or self-defense.

Joe's attorney successfully requested that I extend battered women's syndrome, a post-traumatic stress disorder, to a male who claims to have been the subject of battering at the hands of his same-sex partner. In the application petitioning the court to allow Joe to call an expert witness on battered women's syndrome or the effects of same-sex battering, Joe's attorney alleged the existence of facts that indicated that the classical aspects and dynamics of power and control were present in same-sex relationships and similar, if not identical, to those in heterosexual partner domestic violence. This all was presented as part of the justification defense. The picture that was painted could have been taken from a domestic violence training manual or a textbook on Domestic Violence 101.

Within weeks of their meeting, Stanley and Joe started a relationship that soon became sexual in nature. After three more weeks, Stanley moved into Joe's apartment. Stanley became very possessive. Stanley interfered with the friendships that Joe had and would not permit Joe to meet new people. He would follow Joe and curse him out as well as anyone with whom he was talking.

When Joe was able to work, Stanley would dole out fifty cents a day to Joe besides carfare. This was ironic, as Joe was the only one of them earning a salary. Stanley required Joe to carry a beeper to work each day so that Stanley would always be able to reach him. One day Joe returned Stanley's call after the work day and outside of his job site. Stanley was furious at Joe for being able to call him back on a pay phone because Stanley knew that Joe had exhausted the fifty cents given to him that day. Stanley wanted to know where Joe had obtained the extra quarter. Joe lost two jobs due to Stanley's obsessive jealousy. On both occasions, Stanley went to where Joe worked to spy on him. When he observed Joe talking to a male coworker, he ran out of the shadows and shouted obscenities at both Joe and his coworker. Both times he created such a scene that Joe's employer was forced to fire him. Stanley made it impossible for Joe to find a new job. When Joe received his unemployment insurance proceeds, Stanley took control of that money too.

After three weeks of Stanley moving in, Joe was no longer in possession of all the keys to his apartment. Stanley gave Joe the key to only the bottom lock. Stanley controlled the keys to the top lock and to the mailbox. Stanley would read the mail and take any checks belonging to Joe. Joe also claimed that even though Stanley was extremely possessive and jealous, on a single night Stanley would sometimes invite a series of lovers and prostitutes into Joe's apartment for trysts. Joe claimed that he would have left if he had sufficient assets to find a new apartment. He lamented that there were no shelters for battered gay men. He had attempted to find one.

What truly and exactly did happen the night when Joe fatally stabbed Stanley in the chest, we may never know. The homicide detectives and the crime scene unit described the floor of the living room as being strewn with used condoms. Joe claimed that Stanley called a male prostitute service and had sex numerous times with different males, while charging the bill to Joe's credit card. There was no doubt that a male escort service or two delivered prostitutes to Joe's apartment. The payment was in fact made from Joe's credit card. There were no witnesses to the altercation between Joe and Stanley. Was it murder or was it justifiable self-defense?

A jury never had to decide that issue. I ruled that if Joe were able to make out a justification defense, then he would be permitted to have an expert testify on battered person syndrome and battering and its effects.[1] The prosecution offered Joe a plea to manslaughter in the first degree with a promised sentence of eight to sixteen years in jail. Joe accepted the plea offer. As no one knew exactly what transpired during the actual incident causing Stanley's death, I believed that the plea bargain was appropriate.

Although shelters are available for women, men who are the victims of same-sex violence have no place to go. There is the societal perception that only women are the victims of domestic violence. Recent studies show that not to be the case:

The National Violence Against Women survey found that 21.5 percent of men and 35.4 percent of women living with a same-sex partner experienced intimate-partner physical violence in their lifetimes, compared with 7.1 percent and 20.4 percent for men and women, respectively, with a history of only opposite-sex cohabitation. Transgender respondents had an incidence of 34.6 percent over a lifetime according to a Massachusetts survey.

The CDC's 2010 National Intimate Partner and Sexual Violence Survey, released again in 2013 with new analysis, reports in its first-ever study focusing on victimization by sexual orientation that the lifetime prevalence of rape, physical violence, or stalking by an intimate partner was 43.8 percent for lesbians, 61.1 percent for bisexual women, and 35 percent for heterosexual women, while it was 26 percent for gay men, 37.3 percent for bisexual men, and 29 percent for heterosexual men (this study did not include gender identity or expression).

These studies refute the myths that only straight women get battered, that men are never victims, and that women never batter—in other words, that domestic violence is not an LGBT issue. In fact, it is one of our most serious health risks, affecting significant numbers within our communities.[2]

Law enforcement, government agencies, and the general public recognize that domestic violence is a serious societal issue. The most commonly understood type of abuse involves partners of the opposite sex engaging in conduct that is physically and often mentally harmful, with the victim being the female. Less recognized is same-sex domestic violence.

Opposite and same-sex domestic violence share many common characteristics:

1. The pattern of abuse includes a vicious cycle of physical, emotional, and psychological mistreatment, leaving the victim with feelings of isolation, fear, and guilt.
2. Abusers often have severe mental illnesses and were themselves abused as children.
3. Psychological abuse is the most common form of abuse and physical batterers often blackmail their partners into silence.
4. Physical and sexual abuses often co-occur.
5. No race, ethnicity, or socio-economic status is exempt.
6. Abusers can threaten to take away the children.[3]

But domestic violence in same-sex relationships is distinctive in many ways from domestic violence in heterosexual relationships:

1. Gay or lesbian batterers will threaten "outing" their victims to work colleagues, family, and friends. This threat is amplified by the sense of extreme isolation among gay and lesbian victims since some are still clos-

eted from friends and family, have fewer civil rights protections, and lack access to the legal system.

2. Lesbian and gay victims are more reluctant to report abuse to legal authorities. Survivors may not contact law enforcement agencies because doing so would force them to reveal their sexual orientation or gender identity.

3. Gay and lesbian victims are also reluctant to seek help out of fear of showing a lack of solidarity among the gay and lesbian community. Similarly, many gay men and women hide their abuse out of a heightened fear that society will perceive same-sex relationships as inherently dysfunctional.

4. Gay and lesbian victims are more likely to fight back than are heterosexual women. This can lead law enforcement to conclude that the fighting was mutual, overlooking the larger context of domestic violence and the history of power and control in the relationship.[4]

As same-sex marriage is now permitted under the law in the United States and some other countries, gay and lesbian victims of domestic abuse are more likely to report the incidents of same-sex violence as the general public has become increasingly more accepting of same-sex relationships. Thus, it follows that the definition of domestic violence should include same-sex abuse in all jurisdictions and LGBT persons should gain access to the family courts. Law enforcement should be educated as to same-sex domestic violence and sensitized as to issues confronting LGBT people. Same-sex domestic violence programs should be established in the community. Survivors of same-sex domestic violence deserve the same protections afforded to those survivors of opposite-gender abuse. Laws can help to change attitudes, but this process is slow. We must recognize that members of the LGBT community face more hardships and lack the same resources that are available, yet still insufficient, to those victims of opposite-sex intimate-partner abuse.

Chapter Ten

Alvin's Allowance

Miriam's death was officially listed by her physician as "heart failure induced by cancer." The death certificate could have easily and accurately read as the cause of death "aggravation hastened by a broken heart." Aside from the traditional domestic violence cases that come before the Domestic Violence Court, namely, spousal or domestic partner abuse, the court also handles elder abuse, most commonly committed by a grown-up child against a parent. Most of the elder abuse cases involve serious crimes including patricides and matricides, also killing of grandparents, all unthinkable crimes. Many of the defendants in these types of cases have mental health/illness issues. Here is the story of Miriam and her son, Alvin. This case was not about a homicide or an attempted murder. The story about Alvin and Miriam was chosen, not as an example of the violence inflicted by a child against a parent, but rather as an illustration of the complexity of the emotions and issues involved in elder abuse . . .

Alvin was born into a nurturing Brooklyn home in 1955. His parents, Max and Miriam, were hardworking people who provided Alvin and his older sister, Stephanie, with love and affection as well as much care and attention. Although Max labored many hours as the proprietor of a hardware store, he regularly spent time with Alvin in the early morning before work. Max always made sure that he was home for dinner at 6:45 p.m. sharp to spend quality time with his children.

Miriam was ever ready to listen to her children's problems and to lend a helping hand with their homework. Her work as a French teacher at a nearby public high school enabled her to be home each day shortly after Alvin and Stephanie arrived from school.

Alvin was a difficult child. In his teenage years, his parents attributed his stubborn behavior to adolescence. They were soon to learn that his being difficult had little to do with his growing pains. On one occasion, Alvin punched his mother in the face. Max and Miriam felt this was an aberration. They did not know that this was merely a preview of the main show that was yet to come.

During his late teens, Alvin had continuous personality clashes with both of his parents. He had decided to immigrate to Israel months prior to his nineteenth birthday. This was a spiritual journey for Alvin. He was religious in his own odd sort of way. He chose to observe some of the Jewish laws—those that fit into his personalized form of religion. He obviously paid no heed to the fifth commandment, "Honor thy father and thy mother."

When Alvin would return to his home in Brooklyn from his travels abroad, his visits would be more akin to acts of terrorism. Many times he threatened to set the family house on fire. He told Miriam on several occasions that he would take a contract out on her life. One time, he kicked in the bathroom door while his mother was inside.

These arguments and threats later turned into physical assaults perpetrated by Alvin upon his elderly father and mother. On numerous occasions, Alvin struck his father on the head and face, many times causing bruises and black eyes. Miriam and Stephanie often witnessed these attacks by Alvin. They attempted, albeit unsuccessfully, to intercede upon Max's behalf.

Miriam was not spared from Alvin's rage. He had several times knocked his mother's glasses off of her face and hit her on the head and arm. Alvin was not physically impressive. He was rather thin and of ordinary height. He had pale blue eyes and dirty blonde hair. His imposition of fear upon his family was based on his rage coupled with an iron-fisted will to have his own way about almost anything that he deemed to be important. Unfortunately, Alvin thought that everything that he wanted to do was critical, especially any issue where his parents' opinion would differ from his own.

In August of 1981, Alvin was arrested for smashing a glass bowl over his father's head, causing lacerations. Max, who was seventy-six years old at the time, was treated at Coney Island Hospital for his injuries. Alvin's Criminal Court case was adjourned for six months (now the law would require a one-year period of "wait and see") in contemplation of dismissal with the condition that he receive psychiatric care. His parents were given a full order of protection requiring Alvin to stay away from them for one year.

The mental health care was doable as well. Yet Freud himself would not have been able to exorcize the demons within Alvin in only six months. Staying away was not so difficult for Alvin to do. He lived abroad much of the time, subsidized in part by the generosity of two abused parents who still loved him.

During the time that Alvin spent in Israel and in Europe, his parents regularly sent him money. After Max passed away in 1985, Miriam continued to dispatch funds to her son. Many times, Alvin would demand more money than what was given. He would call Miriam and threaten her. He would tell her that he knew when she left the house and that he was going to come home and kill her and Stephanie.

Miriam took these threats very seriously. She had observed the beatings that Alvin had inflicted upon Max. She had also experienced Alvin's terror and violence firsthand. Alvin's menacing words had the ring of truth, as he once before was able to obtain money from other sources to return home when Miriam refused him. Based on their prior history, Miriam believed that Alvin would come back home to carry out his threats against her and Stephanie. Alvin had sufficiently scared Miriam into sending him more and more money because of these threats and his past conduct.

While living in Israel, Alvin was reportedly convicted of numerous crimes and offenses between 1979 and 1992—sexual assault (two times), assault (four times), threats (four times), insulting a public servant (two times), rape by deception and trafficking in weapons (knife), indecent acts by means of compulsion, and trespassing (three times). Alvin was incarcerated for three and one-half years and had also been committed to a psychiatric hospital.

When Alvin was not in Israel or back in Brooklyn terrifying his mother, he was bumming around Europe. In 1996, he was sentenced in Switzerland to fourteen days in prison for an offense under the Swiss Foreigner Law. Alvin reportedly altered a passport.

Alvin returned to the United States in August 1996 to live with his mother after his deportation from Switzerland based on his latest conviction. He took over his mother's household and continued his reign of terror as though never interrupted by the years that he lived abroad.

Alvin refused to work. He would sleep and watch television all day. He would go out to clubs and drink at night. On the weekends, he would order his mother to stay in her bedroom every Saturday and Sunday morning until 8:00 a.m. in the unlikely event that he would bring a woman home with him at his 5:00 a.m. standard arrival time.

Miriam did almost all of the shopping for the house, and she paid for everything, including his bar and club hopping. On the few occasions when Miriam would attempt to refuse Alvin's demands for money, he would either physically menace or verbally threaten her.

For the ten-month period from the time of his return home until June of 1997, Alvin, then forty-two years old, demanded an allowance from his mother. To secure this money, Alvin threatened his mother's life and physically intimidated her.

In June of 1997, Miriam procured a mental hygiene warrant against Alvin based upon the suggestion of the New York City Police Department.

Grounded on the warrant and his history of mental illness, Alvin was admitted into a psychiatric ward of Coney Island Hospital for observation. Miriam then obtained an order of protection from the Family Court in Kings County. Service of this protective order was made in the hospital, albeit in violation of rules for service of process on alleged incompetents.

Between late June and early July 1997, while under observation in the psychiatric ward pursuant to the warrant, Alvin made several phone calls to his mother threatening to pay someone to kill her and informing her that he wanted her to disappear off the face of the earth.

Shortly after the Fourth of July, Alvin called Miriam. She informed him that he was in violation of the Family Court order of protection.

Alvin replied, "I am not concerned about the order of protection. I do not have to accept or abide by any order of protection until a court declares me mentally competent."

Alvin may have had an uncanny understanding of this area of the law. A few days later, he called Miriam again.

He stated with great clarity, "I don't care about any court or any judge. If I do not get out of this hospital soon and you do not allow me to live in the house, you will experience a catastrophe."

During the second week of July, Miriam, still the loving mother, visited Alvin in the hospital. He reiterated his past threats.

He went on, "I am sane. I want to leave the country. My plan is to have back packers stay in our house and pay rent which I will keep. I will use the money for transportation. When I leave, I will accept allowances by the week. You know that you owe me three weeks back allowance."

Miriam was alarmed as Alvin was dead serious. She tried unsuccessfully several times to sidestep any inquiries relating to this theme. Feeling agitated and upset, she abruptly said good-bye and went home.

Over the next two days, apparently in response to his mother's reaction, Alvin called his mother at home.

He threatened, "If you do not let me back home, I will once again resort to a life of crime by supporting myself as a drug dealer. If you do not take me back and give me my allowance, I will take care of Stephanie with my bare hands."

He repeatedly made similar threatening phone calls over the next several days. One of the phone calls was particularly distressing to Miriam.

Alvin warned Miriam, "If you don't withdraw the mental hygiene commitment, there will be ruinous consequences for you and me."

Miriam surmised, probably correctly, that her son meant that he would kill her and then commit suicide.

Alvin was charged in a thirty-four-count indictment with various crimes, including grand larceny by extortion, aggravated harassment, and attempted coercion and menacing. He was later released from the hospital psychiatric ward and incarcerated as he could not make the bail set by the court.

Miriam, now seventy-eight years old and ravaged with terminal cancer that had spread from her breast to several vital organs of her body, remained a concerned and forgiving mother. She barely was able to resist Alvin's appeals for her to bail him out of jail.

Miriam frequently contacted the prosecuting assistant district attorney and victim advocate to relate her concern for her son. She clearly did not want him to be incarcerated. She only wanted him to undergo appropriate psychiatric treatment and to be placed in a residential setting away from her home. Each time she spoke to the prosecutor, Miriam was firm in her resolve to spare her son from jail. Almost forgotten were her past fears caused by Alvin's terrorist tactics, verbal abuse, and physical menace. These heavyhearted memories were distant when juxtaposed with the love, care, and concern of a dying mother for her troubled son.

These worries were heard by the prosecutor and related to the court and defense counsel. Alvin was generously offered to enter a plea of guilty to grand larceny by extortion. The sentence he would receive would be probation, including a condition that he be required to undergo psychiatric treatment for five years as a condition of his felony probation.

In reality, Alvin was proffered this "deal" not out of respect to a mother's love and concern, but rather in deference to Miriam's illness. The prosecutor was aware that a trial would require Miriam to testify against her son. This would be quite traumatic to Miriam in that she would be asked to relive the anguish of her life with her son and particularly the events charged in the indictment. There would be pre-trial preparation as well as her actual trial testimony. All this would take a toll on Miriam emotionally and would certainly drain the little remaining strength she had and that she so badly needed to combat the scourge of cancer ravaging her entire body. I was certainly willing to go along with the plea agreement, especially since Alvin had spent nearly a year being confined under the mental hygiene warrant as well as being incarcerated while awaiting trial.

No matter what Alvin had earlier perpetrated upon his family, no one was prepared for his response to the very generous plea offer. This was an opportunity for him to right many past wrongs. He would be able to spare his mother from further emotional pain and the physically draining prospect of testifying against him at trial. Alvin would also personally benefit by avoiding trial and a possible state prison sentence by accepting the plea offer. Most significantly, Alvin would receive much needed and extended psychiatric care to be monitored by the court through probation.

Alvin, however, was adamant. There would be no guilty plea.

Alvin declared defiantly in open court, "I am innocent. I am going to trial."

Alvin was quite fortunate that he was living outside the United States for much of the time during the previous twenty-three years. Many of the crimes for which he had been convicted would have certainly constituted felonies in the United States, and several may have been the equivalent to violent felonies under New York law, subjecting Alvin to mandated enhanced punishment as a violent felony offender. However, as he was a "foreign felon," any sentence received would not be increased due to his convictions abroad.

When Miriam testified at Alvin's trial about the incidents that were the subject of the indictment, the pain expressed in her face and the anguish heard in her voice was palpably felt by all who were present in the courtroom. Yet when Miriam recounted her relationship with her son for the jury, there was love trumpeting through the hurt. There were tears in everyone's eyes, including the prosecutor. This was one of the most emotionally moving moments experienced during any trial in which I presided.

Alvin was stridently unsympathetic to his mother's emotional turmoil. By refusing a fair and beneficial plea, he forced her to testify against the son she still loved. Alvin was also plainly indifferent to his mother's health, which was fast deteriorating.

He maintained at trial that Miriam was using the police to evict him after the expiration of the mental hygiene warrant and his release from Coney Island Hospital. Alvin also contended that first his parents, and then his mother, consistently supported him financially for his entire life, such was the nature of their relationship. He maintained that he never threatened his mother to give him money or an allowance, but rather, Miriam did so voluntarily.

The three counts of the indictment relating to violating the Family Court's protective order were dismissed earlier in the proceedings due to improper service. The court charged the jury to consider seventeen counts. Alvin was convicted of grand larceny by extortion, menacing, and two counts of aggravated harassment.

Miriam, in a noticeably weakened condition, spoke passionately at Alvin's sentencing proceeding. She was barely able to stand, supporting herself by leaning on the prosecutor's table. In a very shaky voice that wobbled more pronouncedly with the emotion she conveyed, she asked me to show leniency for her son.

She only wanted Alvin to be provided with psychiatric attention. Unfortunately, Alvin demonstrated no remorse. He exhibited an absolute zero concern for his mother. He was sentenced to one and one-third to four years' incarceration, the maximum for the nonviolent E felony of grand larceny in the fourth degree, the most serious charge.

Miriam died a few weeks after Alvin had been sentenced. She continued to cradle him from her grave. Although she drew up a new last will and testament while Alvin stood accused of the charges for which he was convicted, she nonetheless bequeathed him half of her estate, the other half going to her daughter, Stephanie. Despite all he put her through, a mother's love shone brightly.

After about three years, Alvin was discharged from jail. One of the conditions of his parole mandated him to report to me, the sentencing judge in the Domestic Violence Court, upon his release. There I explained to him all of the other conditions that he must keep. These included the psychiatric care that Miriam so desperately wanted him to receive. There was a protective order barring him from having any verbal or physical contact with his sister, Stephanie.

I reminded him that I was still watching him even though he had been released from jail. I then told him how extraordinary it had been for his mother to leave him half of her estate after all he had done. I proceeded to tell him that she must have loved him dearly and that I hoped that someday he would learn to appreciate her.

Alvin stood in front of me expressionless and motionless. It was as though I had told him that it might rain the next day. Then I realized that he was unreachable, maybe heartless. I was only relieved in a sad sort of way that he could not break Miriam's heart anymore.

The Administration of Aging of the U.S. Department of Health and Human Services defines elder abuse as physical abuse (inflicting physical pain or injury on a senior, e.g., slapping, bruising, or restraining by physical or chemical means), sexual abuse (nonconsensual sexual contact of any kind), neglect (the failure by those responsible to provide food, shelter, health care, or protection for a vulnerable elder), exploitation (the illegal taking, misuse, or concealment of funds, property, or assets of a senior for someone else's benefit), emotional abuse (inflicting of mental pain, anguish, or distress on an elder person through verbal or nonverbal acts, e.g., humiliating, intimidating, or threatening), abandonment (desertion of a vulnerable elder by anyone who has assumed the responsibility for care or custody of that person), and self-neglect (characterized as the failure to perform essential self-care tasks and that such failure threatens his or her own health or safety).[1] All except self-neglect are inflicted by another on the elderly.

Elder abuse differs from intimate-partner violence in that in most cases it is the children, grandchildren, or caretaker who is the abuser. There are exceptions. Where an intimate partner was abusive or violent before becoming a senior, the violence and abuse will continue when the couple becomes elderly.

Miriam, unlike many victims of elder abuse, was able to articulate the abusive conduct and report her abuser to the law enforcement authorities. Some of our elderly have dementia, are uncommunicative, or suffer in silence. As elder abuse is a violation of human rights and a major cause of illness, injury, loss of productivity, isolation, and despair, what can we do to recognize its presence in order to rectify an abusive situation?

We can look at the signs of elder abuse such as bruises, broken bones, abrasions, burns (signs of physical abuse); withdrawal from normal activities, sudden depression (indicative of emotional abuse); bruising around the genital area (signs of sexual abuse); drastic and sudden change in assets (indicative of exploitation); change in medical condition, poor hygiene, bedsores, dramatic weight loss (indicative of neglect); threats or belittling, tense relationship or power and control exhibited by caregivers, children, or partners (signs of verbal and emotional abuse).[2]

We should be alert and observe our elderly carefully. As stated earlier, many of our elderly are either unable to articulate the abuse or suffer in silence. If we should notice a change, especially a dramatic change, in an elder's behavior or personality, we should question her or him as to what is happening in the elder's life situation. If the elderly person cannot converse or is reluctant to do so, then unannounced visits should occur or a surveillance camera should be introduced into our loved one's environment. If we see or hear hitting, shouting, or other abuse, we should contact the local agency for Adult Protective Services. Of course, if an elderly person is in immediate peril, the police should be immediately called.

Many defendants who had come before Alvin, especially those accused of elder abuse, had mental illness issues. For example, one woman who professed great love for her grandmother killed her by stabbing her more than two hundred times. She also cut her eyes out.

My colleague, Judge Matthew D'Emic, and I became greatly aware of mental illness issues. Judge D'Emic subsequently was assigned to preside over the much-heralded Mental Health Court because of his experience and expertise gained in the Domestic Violence Court.

Chapter Eleven

Jeremiah Jonah

Darren dialed the phone number that Jeremiah had given him in jail. The deal was clear. Darren was to call Jeremiah's brother who was to give Darren one thousand dollars, a Rolex watch, two TVs, and a gun that Jeremiah had stashed in a car. The money, the watch, and the televisions were payment for the deed. The revolver was the means to accomplish it. Jeremiah's brother was the middle man. The phone rang and rang. Darren now only had to make contact with Jeremiah's brother to effectuate his mission—the killing of Marlene, Jeremiah's ex-girlfriend and the mother of his child . . .

Jeremiah's mother was a religious Baptist who loved the Old Testament. The family name was Jonah. Most people remember the story of Jonah, a minor prophet, being swallowed by a big fish or a whale. Jeremiah's mother recalled a more profound story about Jonah. According to the Bible, Jonah, although initially resistant, did preach to the people of Ninevah that their wickedness would lead to their destruction should they fail to repent. Repent they did and they were spared.

She also loved the story of Jeremiah. This prophet lectured the people of Jerusalem that unless they turned away from idolatry and returned to study the Bible and the ways of God, the city and the holy temple would be destroyed. Unlike the people of Ninevah, the people of Jerusalem failed to heed Jeremiah's warnings. The temple and the city were both demolished by Nebuchadnezzar, the king of the Babylonians. She named her first son after Jeremiah. She reasoned that he would twice be reminded to follow God's ways and to return to morality were he ever to stray.

Jeremiah was called "JJ" by his friends at a very early age. The only ones who called him Jeremiah were his mother and Marlene, his girlfriend. Nothing really turned out for Jeremiah as his mother had planned.

It was a mystery to all who knew them why Marlene would take up with Jeremiah. He was a knock-around guy who would often do things the "easy way," which most often turned out to be the hard and wrong way. He was a hothead and irresponsible. Marlene was thoughtful, smart, and trustworthy. She was introverted while Jeremiah was extroverted. He had entered a plea of guilty and served state jail time for a street robbery in 1992 where he used a knife to threaten the victim during the crime. Marlene was someone who would think twice about doing anything wrong no matter how small. Although he did graduate from high school, Jeremiah always had trouble with his studies. Marlene, on the other hand, had a stellar academic record. She had graduated from college and had an MS in computer science. She owned her own computer consulting business servicing many of the larger hospitals in Brooklyn.

They began dating in July 1994. Jeremiah was unlike anyone Marlene had dated and was her opposite in almost every way. Despite their obvious differences in background, temperament, and education, Marlene liked Jeremiah and his outgoing personality. In April of 1995, Marlene allowed Jeremiah to move in with her and her child.

They had some good moments together, but much of their time was spent arguing, mostly about nothing. It was not the substance of their arguments that was so baffling to Marlene; it was the process. They could never talk through their differences calmly, logically, and without a great expenditure of emotional energy. Jeremiah's voice volume level would immediately rise, and Marlene's loudness would soon rival but never equal his. Jeremiah would never admit that he might be wrong. The odds were that Marlene had to be right at least some of the times when they would disagree. The best that Jeremiah would ever be able to say was "Let's agree to disagree." This was even more frustrating to Marlene, as there was never any resolution of the issue at hand nor any improvement in their manner of disagreement.

After a little more than two months of living together, they had an awful quarrel once again about something insignificant: Jeremiah's failure to do his part in keeping the house clean and neat. Jeremiah became so upset that he resorted to physical violence against Marlene for the very first time. He punched Marlene twice in the face. Marlene failed to report this incident to the police or to receive medical attention for the bruises on her head.

She did not leave Jeremiah. But soon after the dispute had cooled down, she told him, "If you ever put your hands on me again, I will leave your sorry ass."

Although their arguments persisted, Jeremiah kept his anger in check and never hit Marlene again while they lived together. Yet in late November 1995, after a particularly contentious Thanksgiving holiday, Marlene, now pregnant with Jeremiah's child, broke up with him and moved back into her mother's apartment.

Marlene's stress from the volatile relationship that she shared with Jeremiah was alleviated somewhat by their separation. Other pressures reared up in its place. Marlene was now facing the prospect of bringing a baby into this world without a partner. After the initial threat of a miscarriage in February, she was ordered to bed for rest.

Marlene was the sole proprietor and worker in her computer consulting business. If she were unable to work, she earned no money. There were no sick days, unused vacation time, or disability benefits to be paid. The financial strain and the resulting emotional turmoil weighed heavily on her. It was almost as though she were once again an adolescent. She lived in her mother's house and relied on her for both financial and emotional sustenance. She felt guilty that her mother supported her at a time when her mother should be winding down and readying herself for retirement.

In late July, Jeremiah went to the house of Marlene's mother. He asked Marlene's mom whether he could see Marlene. Jeremiah requested admission in a respectful manner. He was courteous and well dressed. Neither his appearance nor demeanor signaled what was soon to transpire.

Upon entering Marlene's room, he took out a handgun, pointed it at her, and threatened to kill her. When Marlene's mother looked into the room, she screamed and yelled while running toward the kitchen phone, "Police! Police! Help!"

Jeremiah was startled and bolted from the room and dashed out the front door of the house. Marlene prevailed upon her mother not to call the police.

The stress that Marlene had been experiencing, together with the painful event with Jeremiah at her house, resulted in her baby girl's premature birth two days later. Marlene was in labor, but unknown to all, the baby's umbilical cord was wrapped twice around her neck. The baby was unable to come down the birth canal even though Marlene was fully dilated. The monitoring devices attached to Marlene's extended belly indicated that the baby was in distress. An emergency C-section was performed.

The surgery was successful. Marlene and the baby both lived. If the gynecologist had not recognized the peril to the baby, the newborn would have been strangled by her cord in the very act of her mother giving birth.

The complications attendant to the baby's traumatic and early birth caused the baby to remain in an incubator for an additional fifteen days after Marlene's discharge from the hospital. Marlene was required to stay in the hospital for five days to recover from her Cesarean surgery. Her health insurance carrier was not pleased that the doctor authorized such an extended stay as a medical emergency.

Three days into her recovery from the emergency C-section, Marlene was knitting a blanket in her room in the maternity ward for the newborn now named Tina. Jeremiah unexpectedly appeared, seemingly in a happy mood. Marlene did not know what to think. Was he happy that he was now the father of a baby girl?

After exchanging pleasantries, Jeremiah's facial expression abruptly changed. He curled his lips, puffed his cheeks, and wrinkled his brow into a menacing look. He then closed his fist and delivered a forceful punch to Marlene's nose.

She cried out in agony, "Ah! Ah!"

The floor nurse on duty in the maternity ward was in the hallway outside of Marlene's room in the process of making her rounds. When she heard the shrieks of pain, she ran into Marlene's room. She observed Marlene holding her nose, which had blood freely flowing from it. The nurse measured Jeremiah's body language and immediately knew that he was the one who caused Marlene to cry out.

The nurse said in a loud, firm voice, "Get out of here right now or I will have you arrested."

Jeremiah looked at her for an instant, weighing the cost and benefit of escalating the confrontation, and walked quickly out of the room, down the stairs and out of the hospital. When the nurse determined that Marlene's nose was bruised, battered, swollen, but not broken, they both decided to call the police.

Marlene filed a complaint. Jeremiah was arrested and charged with assault and menacing, both misdemeanors. The judge in the criminal court issued an order of protection directing Jeremiah to "stay away from Marlene, [her] home, place of business, school, or any other place where she may be." He was also commanded to "refrain from harassing, annoying, assaulting, menacing, intimidating, coercing or stalking" Marlene and from conducting acts of "reckless endangerment or disorderly conduct" directed at her.

Jeremiah made the bail that had been set. The judge was constrained to fix bail in an amount necessary to ensure Jeremiah's return to court. The severity of any sentence imposed should Jeremiah be convicted was not likely to cause him to flee. He had no history of bench warrants in any of his prior cases.

The judge was hamstrung by the rules in setting bail. She was upset by the fact that in New York, unlike in other state jurisdictions and the federal courts, a judge at the initial arraignment cannot consider criteria in determining bail other than those that impact on whether a defendant will return to court to face the accusations against him. She was cognizant that the public and the press often criticized the judiciary on bail issues especially in domestic violence cases when all that was needed were changes in the law passed by the legislature, not in the appointment or election of different judges implementing insufficient criteria. In a domestic violence case in New York at that time, the arraignment court could not consider the safety of the victim in fixing bail.[1]

In early 1997, a few months after the attack, Jeremiah entered a plea of guilty to assaulting Marlene. Based on his prior felony conviction and the heinous act of punching a woman only three days after she had given birth to his child, Jeremiah was sentenced to the maximum allowed for a misdemeanor, one year in jail. Marlene received a final order of protection mandating Jeremiah "to stay away" from and to refrain from communicating with her in any manner for three years.

Jeremiah's incarceration should have marked the conclusion of his involvement with Marlene. Yet in some way it was merely the beginning of a new and more tangled and almost lethal drama.

Jeremiah began a letter-writing campaign from jail in violation of the order of protection. He wrote Marlene almost fifty letters in a period of less than a year. Some letters were of a threatening nature.

Close to the time when he was due to be released from prison on his assault conviction, Jeremiah was indicted on more than fifty counts of both felony and misdemeanor criminal contempt. Bail was set in an appropriately high amount that reflected Jeremiah's violation of the protective order issued by the court in the assault case. Unable to post bail, Jeremiah remained incarcerated as he awaited a disposition on the allegations of contempt. Even after Jeremiah had been indicted, inexplicably he continued to write Marlene in violation of the court's mandate.

For a defendant who has been convicted of a crime and sentenced to state prison time, namely, incarceration for more than one year, the State Department of Correctional Services will enforce the court's protective order by prohibiting the inmate from writing or calling the victim as long as the sentencing judge attaches a copy of the order of protection to the order committing the defendant to a state penal institution. I began to do that after I learned that the State Department of Correctional Services had no idea that a defendant was convicted of assault or another crime involving an intimate partner without having the protective order. The New York City Department of Corrections houses accused persons awaiting trial as well as convicted persons who are sentenced to prison for up to one year in jail. The City Department of Corrections now attempts to prevent violations of orders of protection by monitoring outgoing mail and calls of convicted inmates. When Jeremiah's case was pending, the city jails were not monitoring the calls and letters for violations of court orders of protection for those awaiting trial. Yet Jeremiah was both serving a one-year sentence for a conviction of a crime and also awaiting trial for other crimes.

Jeremiah was facing a maximum sentence of ten to twenty years in jail as a predicate felon if he were to be convicted of five of the fifty-plus felony contempt charges. The prosecution was prepared to offer Jeremiah a sentence of two to four years in jail for the many letters written. The letters that were sent after the indictment was filed were also to be covered in the plea agreement.

Jeremiah was resolute in not taking any plea bargain. He was not doing any more state time in jail. He was determined to take the case to trial. Jeremiah thought that he had figured out a rather unusual way to win.

Although some of the prisoners in Riker's Island were serving their sentences of imprisonment of one year or less,[2] almost all of the inmates were awaiting a trial or disposition of their cases and were unable to post bail. The TV room was a place where one inmate could feel free to speak to another without fear that someone would think that he was too nosy or talkative. They all played along with the quiz shows such as *Wheel of Fortune* or *Family Feud*. Many watched the evening and daytime soaps, sports, and news. Commentary and conversation naturally began under such conditions, especially in a crowded prison such as Riker's Island.

Darren was one of the prisoners with whom Jeremiah would talk in the TV room on his floor of the C-95 facility. Darren had entries on both sides of the ledger. He did have a criminal record. His liabilities consisted of serving a sentence of fourteen days for misdemeanor assault in 1991. In 1994, he was sentenced to thirty days in jail for the felony of attempted possession of a weapon in the third degree. He also received three days of community service for his conviction of disorderly conduct, which is a violation and not a crime. Darren presently was serving a sentence of ninety days for his misdemeanor conviction based on possession of a forged instrument, namely, a credit card. He had been released on four hundred dollars' bail but failed to return when he claimed he had a military obligation. The judge then remanded him until his case had concluded.

Darren also had some admirable aspects of his character. He lived with his two-year-old boy and her mother. He supported them both emotionally and financially. He had served in the army for three years and received an honorable discharge in 1993. He was a reservist in the National Guard, but his status was uncertain due to his felony conviction.

When Darren had been re-incarcerated for failing to return to court on the forged instrument charges, he had struck up a relationship of sorts with Jeremiah. They both lived in Brooklyn. Jeremiah seemed to have taken a liking to Darren and was especially interested in the fact that Darren resided in the neighborhood of Jeremiah's girlfriend, Marlene. Although Darren did not know Marlene, he recognized the names of some of her friends.

A few days prior to Darren's scheduled release date, Jeremiah asked to speak to him in the TV room.

"Sweetness, let's go over there where we can talk," Jeremiah said while motioning to a rear corner of the television room where there was some degree of privacy.

Darren was known in prison as "Too Sweet" because of his remarkably good looks. Jeremiah, who for some reason loved the Chicago Bears football team, simply called him "Sweetness" after the great running back Walter Payton.

Instead of talking to him in their usual seats by the television set, Jeremiah had beckoned Darren to the far corner of the room where no one ever sat because it was nearly impossible to see the screen from there. Darren knew something was up and that this was not going to be one of their normal conversations.

"I need you to do me a real big favor. I want you to do Marlene, my girlfriend," Jeremiah implored.

"To do" had two very different meanings in jailhouse lingo. To do could mean to have sex with or to kill. Either way, Darren thought that Jeremiah was kidding, but there was no laughter in his voice or smile on his face. Jeremiah's demeanor obviated the need for Darren to inquire as to what "to do" Jeremiah intended.

Jeremiah quickly resumed, "I want you to waste her so she cannot testify against me."

Darren was almost speechless. He sought to buy himself some time in order to put Jeremiah off until his release in three days.

Ineffectually, he replied by means of an inquiry, "JJ, there is no way you can pay me for doing something like this. I would have to be paid to do this to her. The heat will be down on the entire 'hood. This is not like busting a cap. This is serious shit."

Jeremiah answered, "You know the 'hood and some of her friends. I will see that you are paid."

Darren was prepared with a reply that he believed would extricate himself once and for all from the topic of conversation. "I cannot do something like this on a promise, JJ. And even if you do pay me, I have no gun. How will I get a piece to do her?"

This apparently put Jeremiah off, but only momentarily. "I will have all the answers for you tomorrow. We will meet back here at one in the afternoon."

That evening Darren had a very difficult time sleeping. He lay on his cot tossing and turning endlessly. Darren was hopeful that the plan would dissolve because Jeremiah would recognize its absurdity and the impracticality of accomplishing his goal, the dismissal of all charges against him. Did

Jeremiah not realize that if he were to succeed in this venture, he would be facing far more serious charges, including murder?

Perhaps Jeremiah would be unable to secure the weapon and the payment for the proposed murder of his girlfriend. Darren knew that upon his discharge from jail, he would be free from any pressure to do Jeremiah's bidding. Darren fantasized that in the morning Jeremiah would forget about the entire scheme or say to him, "I was only kidding."

Darren was scared. He was in way over his head. Darren lied to himself that everything would be all right. He was finally able to doze off at about three thirty in the morning.

Upon waking from his restless sleep a few hours later, Darren's apprehension returned with the opening of his eyelids. He tasted nothing of his breakfast or lunch. In fact, Darren did not remember what he had eaten. Darren was dreading the advent of his appointment with Jeremiah. At first, Darren thought that his prayers were answered.

Jeremiah told him, "Sweetness, all I want you to do is to confirm Marlene's location. Here is her address. Don't do anything until I call you."

Darren gave Jeremiah his phone number. They shook hands and agreed that Jeremiah would call within a week of Darren's release from jail.

The days went by one by one without Darren receiving a telephone call from Jeremiah. Yet Darren's anxiety about Jeremiah's proposition had not diminished. Darren simply believed that Jeremiah had forsaken his harebrained plan. Darren preferred to be in a state of denial and to dismiss Jeremiah from his mind.

On the eleventh day after Darren's liberation from prison, the phone rang.

A familiar but unwelcome voice was heard. "Hey, Sweetness, how are you doing?"

Darren unsuccessfully tried to still the pounding in his heart and head and attempted to answer in a calm manner.

He simply said, "Okay, and how you making out, JJ?"

Jeremiah replied, "I'm doing all right. Have you located Marlene?"

"No, but I have made several attempts," Darren lied.

"That's good. I will call in a few days. I have it all scoped out. I may want you to visit me in the Queens house. Don't do anything more until I speak to you again," JJ ordered.

They exchanged good-byes, and Darren wiped the sweat from his forehead as he replaced the telephone upon the receiver. Darren sat quietly in a chair by the dining room table. He cradled his chin with his right arm resting his elbow on his thigh.

The call had enervated him. It was a cold day in early December. The landlord was never generous with the heat even on the bitterest of winter days.

Despite the fact that Darren could almost see the steam of his breath in the cool air, his face and neck were drenched in an unhealthy sweat. He was so spent emotionally that he was hardly able to move, yet his mind was racing.

After a few deep breaths, Darren was able to calm his nerves, slow his heart rate, and control his thoughts. At first, he contemplated ignoring Jeremiah's entreaties by not answering the phone. Upon reflection, Darren deduced that when it was clear to JJ that Darren would not follow through on this, JJ would simply have someone else do the deed. Darren was troubled that he might be blamed for Marlene's death even if he had withdrawn from the plot. Darren was also concerned for his own safety should he decline to do JJ's bidding.

Darren knew that he had made mistakes in his life and was no choir boy, but he was a soldier and soldiers only killed in battle. He realized that it would not be right to stand by idly while Marlene was going to be murdered. But what could he possibly do to stop it from happening?

For the better part of the next hour, Darren sat and sat and thought and thought. He then came up with a solution that would satisfy all his concerns.

Three days later, Jeremiah called again. This time Darren was calm and composed.

After greetings were exchanged, Jeremiah came directly to the point.

"I want you to come see me. Sweetness, I have everything worked out!"

Darren answered, "That's great. I have a real bad dude that I recruited to help me with our little project. We both will be there soon."

Jeremiah replied, "Are you sure this guy is okay? How do you know him?"

Darren reassured JJ, "I know this bro since we were both knee highs. He is as mean and as tough as they come and he has done this more than once before."

Jeremiah concluded, "If you are down with him, he is all right with me."

Five days later, Darren with two associates in tow arrived at the Queens House of Detention. Emptying their pockets of all metallic objects and placing them and other belongings in a locker, they were searched. They were then brought to the visiting room, where each was searched again before gaining entry to the visiting area.

Jeremiah came in the room and gave Darren a big handshake and a huge, heavy hug.

"That's the man?" Jeremiah said in a tone resembling a question more than a statement.

 Darren nodded yes.

JJ first warily eyed Cecil, the male who accompanied Darren. Then he ignored him.

Cecil was hard to ignore. He was big, thick, heavily muscled, and mean looking. He had a shaved head that seemed to sprout directly out of his shoulders, bypassing the need for a neck. He was a black version of "Mr. Clean." But instead of a hooped earring, he wore a perpetual scowl on his face that made him even more menacing.

Jeremiah then asked, "Sweetness, who is this lovely lady?"

As guarded as JJ appeared toward Cecil, he was totally infatuated with Karen, who he thought was gorgeous. She was tall and stately if not regal. She had a sunny smile and endless legs that transformed men into boys. Her clothes, a red V-neck sweater and blue jeans, fit snugly, accentuating her womanly figure. She had a real presence and personal magnetism.

Jeremiah was completely under her spell. He pretty much neglected Darren, forgetting the reason for the meeting and the business at hand.

Jeremiah devoted all of his attention to Karen. Although Karen did react coquettishly toward Jeremiah's entreaties by shooting her dazzling eyes and radiant smile in his direction, Jeremiah was clearly the instigator and more interested party. He constantly would place his hands on Karen's waist and arms in his many futile but insistent attempts to hug her. Jeremiah incessantly whispered "sweet nothings" in Karen's ear, calling her "black Venus." She would smile at him, but nothing more. Yet it was enough to encourage him and to keep him interested.

Darren repeatedly and unsuccessfully attempted to get Jeremiah to concentrate on the purpose of their visit.

Near the end, Jeremiah told Darren: "I have a .32 caliber Beretta stashed in a car. This piece will more than do the job."

Darren asked, "How will I get paid?"

JJ replied, "My brother Matthew will call you and take care of you and get you the gun. But, Sweetness, who's going to do Marlene, you or Mr. T here?"

JJ clearly meant Cecil.

Darren informed Jeremiah, "This is a two-man contract. In case she runs or resists, we have her covered."

JJ seemed satisfied and returned his attention to Karen. The visiting hour was coming to a close, and Darren, Cecil, and Karen made their way out of the prison.

On their way to the car, Darren thought what a formidable assassin Cecil would be, if he were not a cop. Darren had contacted his local precinct when he had realized that Jeremiah would have proceeded with his murderous plan even had Darren withdrawn.

The commander of the local precinct notified the commander of the neighborhood precinct where Marlene resided. That commander, Adam Franks, an inspector in rank, had been a captain in the army during the war in Vietnam and afterward a colonel in the reserves. During the Gulf War against Saddam Hussein in 1990, his unit was activated. Cecil had been a first lieutenant serving under Colonel Franks in Kuwait and Iraq.

Cecil Hargrave had proven to be invaluable to Adam and the entire unit while in Kuwait. Cecil was cool under pressure and had been trained in counterintelligence by the CIA in Langley, Virginia.

Cecil had been effective in interrogating Iraqi prisoners. His methods were based on finesse with subtle pressure rather than on naked violence. His mere presence raised the specter of the future use of force if needed. He would inform a prisoner that another captive had already told Cecil certain facts about the placement of strategic arms and munitions. Then Cecil would throw in a wild claim, credibly delivered, that the prisoner before him had killed a friend of Cecil. Cecil would then add that he had heard that the prisoner had bragged to other Iraqi soldiers that he was sad that Cecil's friend had died so quickly, depriving the prisoner of the pleasure of torturing an American.

At this point, the prisoner was terrified that Cecil would kill him. Not only would the prisoner declare Cecil's outrageous allegations to be untrue, but invariably, to prove the veracity of his denials, he would offer information either correcting Cecil's misapprehension while supplying accurate coordinates or corroborating Cecil's belief where the strategic weapons were located. Without actually questioning the prisoner, Cecil was able to obtain the desired information very quickly. The details garnered were instrumental in helping to locate and to destroy advanced weapon rocketry that had been purchased from Russia only years before. Many American soldiers' lives were saved.

Adam Franks, upon returning to the States and being relieved from active military duty, reentered the ranks of the New York Police Department. After the Gulf War, Police Captain Franks requested headquarters to assign Detective Sergeant Cecil Hargrave to serve with him. When Adam was promoted to inspector and placed in charge of one of the largest precincts in Brooklyn, it was a given that Cecil would follow to take charge of the precinct's detective squad.

When Inspector Franks was contacted by the precinct commander where Darren resided, he immediately called in Cecil. After pulling the complaint report filed by Marlene in the precinct, Cecil contacted the assistant district attorney assigned to the case.

Arlene, the assigned assistant, like all the prosecutors in the Domestic Violence Bureau, was extremely dedicated to protecting victims and to punishing their assailants even though many times the women whom they were trying to help were uncooperative. She and Cecil decided that they would wire Darren with a recording device and send him along with Cecil and a detective investigator from the district attorney's office to visit Jeremiah in jail.

Karen, the detective investigator, was as smart and as tough as she was attractive. Karen was one of many female investigators, social workers, and paralegals who served in the Domestic Violence Bureau. The presence of these women, along with the prosecutors, all helped to ensure that each complainant felt comfortable in discussing the facts of her case.

Cecil also wore a recording device under his clothing. The prison officials were notified that the three of them would be coming. This was a necessary precaution to ensure that the guards would not blow their cover and that there would be no intrusion at the jailhouse conference. It was imperative that the wires would not be noticed, removed, or tampered with when the two undercover agents and Darren underwent a routine search upon entering the jail.

Although the safeguards had proven to be effective, there was a very serious problem. The tapes were both ninety-minute microcassettes. Out of necessity, the tapes had to be turned on prior to Darren, Cecil, and Karen's entry into the prison.

The three were only searched in a perfunctory fashion. Yet more than twenty-five minutes elapsed before they were admitted into the waiting area and ten more minutes went by before Jeremiah was produced from his cell for the visit. This was not an inordinate amount of time to wait. Unfortunately more than fifty-five minutes had passed since the tape was turned on. There was less than thirty-five minutes remaining on the tape when the visit began. Jeremiah's infatuation with Karen relegated the incriminating dialogue to the last ten minutes of the hour visit. The tape had already run out by then. They had no proof of the incriminating statements made by JJ independent of their own testimony despite the great efforts that were made.

It was decided by Arlene and Cecil that more proof was needed to convince a jury that Jeremiah intended to kill Marlene. With Darren's consent, a recording device was hooked up to his home telephone.

Several days later, Matthew, Jeremiah's brother, called Darren: "JJ wants to squash it. Forget about it."

There was no reply. There was no sound on the other end of the phone. Matthew hung up as suddenly as he had called.

Immediately and with a great sense of relief, Darren called Cecil at the precinct: "Jeremiah wants to cancel the hit."

Cecil inquired, "Are you sure? How do you know?"

"Jeremiah's brother called me only minutes ago. He told me that JJ said, 'Squash it; forget it,'" Darren argued.

Cecil suggested, "If you don't mind, we will keep the tap on your phone for a few weeks more just in case."

Cecil must have been clairvoyant. Five days later, Jeremiah phoned Darren: "What's happening, Sweetness?"

Darren answered, "Nothing much. I got your message."

"What message?" Jeremiah asked.

Darren told him about Matthew's phone call taking him off the job.

"What? No, no, no!" JJ exclaimed. "I'll fix that sorry ass brother of mine! The deal is on. He'll call you in a few days. He'll know what to do."

Darren called Cecil to inform him of the latest developments.

Cecil reinforced Darren's resolve. "In a few more days this will all be over. Hang in there! Let me know when Matthew calls. In the meantime, we will collect today's tape."

A few days later Matthew contacted Darren: "Sorry about the mess up. Our wires got crossed and there was a miscommunication."

"Okay. So what's up?" Darren grunted.

"I have one thousand dollars, a Rolex watch, and two brand new Sony twenty-one-inch television sets for you," Matthew informed.

Darren replied, "That's fine for payment, but what about the piece?"

Matthew answered, "I've got no gun. I don't know anything about a gun. You better speak to JJ."

With that Matthew was gone.

Cecil was not in his office at the detective squad in the precinct that day. When Darren called him, he was informed that it was Cecil's regular day off. Darren worried that Matthew would call him again to pick up a gun and that in Cecil's absence Darren would not know what to do.

The next day, Cecil phoned Darren. Apparently Cecil had either listened to the tape of Darren's discussion with Matthew or the substance of the conversation had been relayed to him by the officers assigned to the eavesdropping detail. In any event, Cecil was fully apprised of what Matthew had talked about with Darren the day before.

After evaluating the latest discourse with Arlene, the assistant district attorney assigned to the case, Cecil decided that Jeremiah would be arrested for the conspiracy to murder Marlene. Cecil and Arlene both thought that Matthew would be involved up to a point but apparently would not supply the weapon, the means for the murder, nor explicitly mention it to Darren on tape. They now believed that they had ample evidence to arrest, indict, and convict Jeremiah for conspiracy.

At the trial, Jeremiah's defense counsel tried with some success to impeach Darren based on his criminal record and especially his credit card fraud conviction, which directly went to his credibility and his truthfulness. Cecil and Karen were excellent witnesses and made Darren's testimony more believable. Marlene provided relevant background about their relationship and the prior assaults perpetrated upon her by Jeremiah. The most telling and damaging evidence were the tapes of Darren's conversations with Jeremiah and Matthew. There was no way for Jeremiah to wiggle his way out of their incriminating nature.

Jeremiah had wrongfully and mistakenly believed that Marlene's life was worth less than his remaining in prison for two to four years. This mistaken notion and his subsequent criminal acts proved very costly to him.

After the jury returned a guilty verdict, I sentenced Jeremiah as a second felony offender to a period of incarceration of twelve to twenty-four years for conspiracy to commit murder followed by a period of two to four years in jail for criminal contempt in the first degree. His attitude of entitlement and lack of regard for the life of the mother of his child will cause him to spend at least fourteen years of his life behind bars.

Will others learn from this story? Hopefully, but perhaps not until the societal norm will be communicated to the unenlightened. Domestic violence is caused mainly by an attitude of entitlement by men. If sex and dinner on demand or abject subjugation are not forthcoming, then some men react with violence. Some rappers, music, commercial advertisements, and movies promote this feeling of entitlement by romanticizing and featuring graphic violence against women. There is currently a greater incidence of teen dating violence because of the cultural exposure of our youth to violence against women. Until the proper message that violence against any and all classes of persons is disfavored and never a positive thing, society will not effectively relay the message that domestic violence is not to be sanctioned in any form. We need our teachers, clergy, coaches, and parents to teach, preach, instruct, and reinforce to children at an early age respect for women.

As I recommend in the chapter "What Can We Do to Protect Abused Women and to Aid Them to Help Themselves?" there should be more school-based programs and educational programs in youth centers to alert youngsters of teen dating violence. High schools should develop a curriculum of instruction concerning teen dating violence and what is not acceptable behavior. College orientation should require every student to attend a program on sexual assault, including a clear message that no means no and yes must be stated and not simply implied by failing to say no. Until then, the criminal justice system and specialized domestic violence courts have to do their jobs in protecting those oppressed and in punishing their tormentors. As former Chief Judge Jonathan Lippman once said, "The courts are the emergency rooms treating the ills of society." We along with houses of worship and other institutions of morality should speak out, educate, and sensitize society.

Chapter Twelve

Fatal Frankie

Rosa, an eleven-year-old girl with a beautiful dark complexion that went with the biggest saucer-shaped black eyes that one can imagine, was frightened to disobey her father. He had ordered her to stay in her room with her little sister, Carmen, until he returned to the house. Her father informed her that he would be back in about fifteen minutes. Thirty minutes passed. Three-year-old Carmen had been pleading with Rosa for the last ten minutes to take her to the bathroom. Rosa yielded to her sister's pleas. She figured that she would be able to accompany Carmen to the bathroom and return to their room before her father could come home. She knew that her father expected strict obedience from her, but she also believed he would not be upset if she simply took Carmen to the bathroom. She grabbed Carmen's hand. Upon exiting the bedroom, it was necessary to pass through the kitchen in order to get to the bathroom. As the two girls entered the kitchen, they came upon their mother slumped in the corner and bleeding from her head. There were two metallic screws protruding from the end of a table leg that was lying close to their mother's motionless body. Rosa called out to her mother, "Mommy, Mommy!" There was no response. Rosa, sobbing, immediately dialed 911 from a kitchen phone. She screamed, "My father hit my mother with a piece of wood! She is bleeding from her head! Please come quickly!"

Frankie was thirty years old and had never been married when he first set his gaze on Migdalia in Prospect Park on a warm summer day almost thirteen years ago. He was Rollerblading, wearing a tight tank top shirt that accentuated his pumped-up biceps and a massive chest developed from years of weight training. Frankie's thigh and calf muscles also bulged. He had good looks to match. He had a full head of wavy hair, flawless features, including high cheekbones and a strong chin, with near-perfect bright white teeth that lit up his face when he smiled.

Frankie stopped skating around the park when he spied Migdalia tossing a Frisbee with her five-year-old son. She was a vision of feminine pulchritude. She wore short-shorts that displayed long, firmly toned legs. Her T-shirt revealed a tight, bare midriff that bore no hint of childbirth. She was a great-looking woman with straight, shiny black hair, dark eyes as big as coal, an olive complexion, and a terrific figure.

Under the thinly veiled guise of a water break, Frankie started to speak to her. They talked about nothing really, perhaps the weather or how crowded it was in the park. There was instant chemistry between the two that was noticeable to those around them. Small talk led to an exchange of phone numbers and to an inevitable date.

Migdalia thoroughly enjoyed Frankie's company. It was effortless to be with him, and he was a lot of fun. He certainly was easy on the eyes. These things were necessary to Migdalia but not sufficient. What really won her heart over was the fact that her five-year-old son, Gilberto, worshipped Frankie. Gilberto's adoration was repaid by Frankie with much attention and what seemed to be genuine affection.

After about six months of dating, Frankie moved in with Migdalia. Things were going well for them. Frankie's business was picking up. He was an adjuster for an insurance company. Three other companies approached him about adjusting their claims in the Brooklyn-Queens area. Frankie received permission from his primary company to perform services for the new carriers. Migdalia had a steady job as a secretary in a small law firm in downtown Manhattan.

They discussed marriage, but Migdalia was hesitant to formalize their relationship because of her first failed union. Frankie and Migdalia, nonetheless, decided to start a family together. With their financial prospects rosy and their income increasing, they began to look to rent a larger apartment a few months after it was discovered that Migdalia was pregnant.

They moved into a three-bedroom apartment in the Williamsburg section of Brooklyn two months before their baby was born. Migdalia wanted everything to be perfect. When Migdalia was told that the baby would be a girl, she had Frankie paint the baby's room a pale yellow. With an artist's loving hand, he placed flowers on the side walls. Migdalia decorated the baby's room with teddy bears and dolls. She was ready for their baby.

When Rosa was born, Migdalia thought how her life had become complete. She was truly contented. She nurtured Rosa and enjoyed her every giggle, sound, and movement. She loved her man. Frankie remained a guiding force and playmate to Gilberto. Her apartment was spacious and comfortable, a real family home. The partners at the law firm where she worked told her to take her time coming back. They provided her with three months' paid maternity leave and stated that they would hold her job for one year. Her life seemed trouble free, and it nearly was for a long time, at least for the next eight years, until shortly after her youngest, Carmen, was born.

Business had been good for Frankie. Migdalia did not need to return to work. She had enjoyed being an executive secretary at the law firm. She knew all of the partners and the work was anything but mundane. Migdalia met many of the firm's clients. More than a few were recognizable personalities. But she really relished being a mother. She delighted in picking up Gilberto and then Rosa from school. Migdalia, unlike most of the other mothers, always wanted the children's play dates to be in her house. It was as though she was also a participant in the activities. She felt good having her babies near her.

Shortly after Carmen's birth, things began to change. Frankie lost many of his accounts due to an invoice mistake where one carrier thought that he was overbilling. The insurance industry being close-knit, Frankie was dropped as an adjuster by all the companies save one. His income decreased dramatically. This placed pressure on Migdalia and consequently on their marriage.

Migdalia was forced to return to work. She was fortunate that her law firm took her back after an absence of more than eight years. Previously she had looked forward to going to work. Now she worked because she had no choice. Migdalia viewed her labor as a barrier preventing her from welcoming home Rosa from school and keeping her from spending the day with her baby, Carmen. She would come home to her kids exhausted from her day.

Migdalia felt bitter that she was shortchanging her babies of her time, which she equated with her love. She envied the mothers who remained home with their children every day. Migdalia resented the obligation of having to support their family; she began to resent Frankie too.

Frankie was also changing. His manliness, which was once so attractive to Migdalia, had been transformed into a virulent machismo. While Frankie accepted his wife's financial contribution, he hated her for it and started to loathe himself.

Frankie was underemployed. He worked each day and tried to hustle business, but he was not making the same money as before. He now had to do the food shopping and cleaning during his work day, chores that he viewed as belonging to a woman. There was little money left over for entertainment as a babysitter had to be paid to stay home with Carmen and to pick up Rosa from school on the days that Frankie hustled for work. For Frankie, it was the worst of all worlds.

Frankie's patience was the first to go. He was short with the kids, especially Gilberto. He would regularly be sharp, judgmental, and hypercritical when talking to the children. This did not go unnoticed by Migdalia.

Frankie was busy doing household duties and attempting to rebuild his business. He now had very little time for the kids. The one who felt his absence so acutely was Gilberto, the boy who used to idolize Frankie.

Gilberto was now a thirteen-year-old whose hormones were starting to kick in and who needed more fatherly companionship and supervision, not less. No longer were Frankie and Gilberto able to manage a baseball catch or share a chocolate shake at the corner coffee shop or discuss the basketball playoffs. The relationship between Frankie and Gilberto became estranged and then dysfunctional. The edge to Frankie's tone frequently brought a teenager's angry response.

"Gilberto, what did you do with my favorite Yankee baseball cap now? I can't find it. Where is it?" Frankie grumbled.

"How the hell should I know!" shouted Gilberto.

Migdalia and Frankie would bicker often. After several months, these skirmishes quickly turned into full-fledged battles. Migdalia perceived, perhaps incorrectly, that Frankie was treating Gilberto worse than the girls because he was not Gilberto's father. This along with their financial difficulties only exacerbated the friction and bad feelings.

Their home, instead of being a symbol of security and peace, became a place associated with tension and unpleasantness. Migdalia anxiously awaited the end of each weekend so that she could flee the confines of her home, which now seemed to suffocate her whenever Frankie was present.

Although she enjoyed time spent alone with her children, Frankie often interfered with her tranquility. He constantly challenged her decisions regarding almost anything having to do with the kids. Frankie became dictatorial and pedantic. It was difficult to spend any time with him and impossible to live with him.

Migdalia made one last effort to save their relationship. She was willing to spend the remainder of their savings for a trip with Frankie to visit her relatives in Costa Rica. They could not afford to bring the children. She would leave them with her sister who lived nearby. Migdalia figured that she and Frankie would stay with her parents for two days and then vacation together in hopes of resurrecting their union.

In a few weeks time, they flew to Costa Rica. The two days that she was with her parents were uneventful as Migdalia spent much of that time visiting other relatives. Frankie went fishing with one of her cousins. Migdalia had little time alone with Frankie.

On the third day, Migdalia and Frankie drove off to a beach for the day. At the beach Migdalia inadvertently kicked sand on Frankie, who was lying down on a large towel. His reaction was unexpected and extreme.

"You fucking bitch. What the hell are you doing?" Frankie screamed as he sat up, releasing and misdirecting months of pent-up emotions, mostly anger.

"You know that was an accident. How can you possibly think that I did that on purpose?" Migdalia asked.

Frankie leaped to his feet. He drew his hand back readying to strike.

Migdalia was frozen in shock and disbelief. As bad as their relationship had become, Frankie had never hit her nor ever threatened to hit her. She stood motionless thinking that he would pull up before making contact. She was badly mistaken. Frankie hit her with a powerful open-handed slap on the left side of her face.

She was unsure which stung more sharply—the pain in her face or the betrayal in her heart. One thing was now certain. Migdalia would not live with Frankie for a minute more. She did not cry.

With cold, steely eyes mirroring her will, she told him, "I want you to fly home today. You can no longer live with us. Find a place to live and move your clothes and stuff by the time I come home."

Frankie knew that he had finally stepped over a line from whence he could not return. He recognized Migdalia said what she meant and meant what she said. Frankie slowly turned away. Later that evening he flew back to the States.

Frankie moved in with a friend. He did keep a few things at the family apartment. After a couple of weeks, Migdalia and Frankie worked out a visitation arrangement where Frankie would have the kids every other weekend and for dinner two nights a week. He did not have sufficient space in the apartment he shared, so he was unable to keep the kids overnight. To his credit, Frankie also asked to be able to have Gilberto on the days that he had Rosa and Carmen. Gilberto would go to dinner on the weekday nights, but he rarely went with his sisters on the weekends.

For a while there was relative peace between Frankie and Migdalia. They were cordial with one another and most cooperative in planning the children's schedules and providing for their needs. Then one warm weekday night in the spring, Frankie had the kids over for dinner. They all decided to go out for ice cream.

While walking to the store a few blocks away, Frankie spied Migdalia dining with a man at a sidewalk café across the street. His intellect left him, and his negative emotions took over his body and mind.

Suddenly and silently he ran up to where Migdalia was sitting, and without warning he punched her in the eye. Migdalia was dazed but conscious. Gilberto had followed Frankie across the street when he realized where Frankie was heading. Gilberto grabbed Frankie and pushed him away from Migdalia.

Frankie seemed as though he were in a trance. When Gilberto separated him from Migdalia, Frankie's senses reappeared and he felt fear. He left the children by the restaurant and ran away.

Migdalia's dinner companion was stunned by the violent interruption of the evening's repose. As he applied an ice pack to Migdalia's raw left eye, he attempted to convince her to file a complaint with the local precinct. She was uncertain whether to have Frankie arrested.

Gilberto saw his mother in pain with a swollen eye that had not yet started to blacken. "Look at yourself. See what that asshole did to you! Have him locked up! Call the cops!"

Rosa, confused and scared for both of her parents, pleaded with her mother, "Don't send Daddy to jail! Please, Mommy!"

Rosa touched Migdalia's heart and soul. The mother felt the anguish in her daughter's heart more acutely than the pain in her eye. Migdalia resolved that she would never see Frankie again. Yet she also decided not to have him arrested.

The next day, Migdalia stayed home from work nursing her wound. The ice packs placed on her eye, a half hour on and a half hour off, helped reduce the swelling. She soon realized that the puffiness was not the main issue in keeping what had occurred concealed. Her upper lid and the skin below the orbital were becoming a dark blue that was fast approaching the blackness of a moonless night in the country. If she were to return to her job the next day or any day that week, she would definitely need the camouflage of sunglasses to keep her secret, her shame, hidden from her coworkers.

With the children at school, Migdalia's day at home was a luxury. She contemplated the events of the past few months and in particular what had unfolded the previous night. She concluded that she would never reunite with Frankie, nor spend time with him together with the children as a family.

Her resolve softened somewhat. Migdalia had been prepared the night before to tell Frankie that he no longer would be able to see his children. If he were to have resisted this ultimatum, she would have informed him that she would make a complaint to the police about the assault. That evening when the children were all tucked in bed, Migdalia called Frankie.

"You may see the children on certain days and every other weekend. If you wish to see them at any other time, you must call in advance and ask whether it is convenient and mutually agreeable. Under no conditions are you to set a foot in this apartment again. The kids will always meet you in front of the house," Migdalia stated in a tone more directive rather than for merely informational purposes.

Frankie meekly assented in an unusually hushed voice, "Okay."

A few weeks later, Frankie, entered the apartment unannounced with the keys that he had retained. No one was at home. Migdalia had been at a party with Rosa and Carmen. Gilberto was sleeping at a friend's house. When she came home, Frankie was in the apartment.

Migdalia was visibly upset. She sent Carmen and Rosa to their room to watch television. Rosa thought that her parents' voices were so loud, especially Frankie's. Rosa arose to shut the door to the bedroom. Still their parents' voices could be heard from the kitchen through the closed door and over the sound of the television show.

After the cartoon program was over, the sisters noticed that the house had become quiet. A few minutes later, their father came into their bedroom. Frankie told Rosa and Carmen that he would be leaving the apartment and would be back in about fifteen minutes. He ordered Rosa to remain in her room with her little sister, Carmen, until he returned to the house. He told them to be quiet so that they would not awaken their mother, who was asleep.

Thirty minutes passed. Rosa, an eleven-year-old girl with a beautiful dark complexion that went with the biggest saucer-shaped black eyes that one can imagine, was frightened to disobey her father. Three-year-old Carmen had been pleading with Rosa for the last ten minutes to take her to the bathroom. Rosa yielded to her sister's pleas. She figured that she would be able to accompany Carmen to the bathroom and return to her room before her father came home. She knew that her father expected strict obedience from her, but she also believed he would not be upset if she simply took Carmen to the bathroom.

She grabbed Carmen's hand. Upon exiting the bedroom, it was necessary to pass through the kitchen in order to get to the bathroom. As the two girls entered the kitchen, they came upon their mother, who lay motionless slumped in the corner and bleeding from her head. There were two metallic screws protruding from the end of a table leg that was lying close to her mother's motionless body.

Rosa called out to her mother, "Mommy, Mommy!"

There was no response. Rosa, sobbing, immediately dialed 911 from a kitchen phone.

Rosa screamed, "My father hit my mother with a piece of wood! She is bleeding from her head! Come quickly!"

When the police and the Emergency Service Unit arrived, Migdalia lay still on the kitchen floor. Her legs were stretched out toward the middle of the room. Migdalia's head was bent downward toward her chest with her hands resting on her lap. She was dead and probably had been when Rosa had called the 911 operator.

One of the senior detectives of the crime scene unit became physically ill when he viewed pieces of bone and drops of blood sprayed upon the two corner walls where Migdalia lay. Another detective almost threw up his dinner when he vouchered the table leg as evidence. He saw blood, hair, and a skull fragment attached to both of the metallic screws that jutted out of the end of the table leg.

The detective immediately realized the degree of force that was needed to puncture a hole in a human skull. He remembered his days a long time ago as an amateur boxer when before each fight and sparring session, each hand would be wrapped in more than a yard of cloth bandages kept together with medical tape and covered with sixteen-ounce boxing gloves. Yet his fists would still sting when he would hit his opponent on the top of the head. His hands would ache even days after a bout. He knew that the person who hit this beautiful woman was determined to crack her head open and to kill her.

After interviewing Rosa, the detectives ordered the patrolmen responding to the scene to conduct a canvass of the area to search for Frankie. Their initial efforts were futile. He was not found in the street or in the apartment where he lived.

After a few days, the case detective got lucky. A tough veteran had inculcated in the then neophyte detective that "luck is a result of preparation and perspiration." The detective, now a veteran himself, thought how this advice usually panned out for him. He conducted a detailed investigation, which included gathering a list of all of Frankie's relatives and friends as well as all the places where Frankie had worked.

The detective finally hit pay dirt. He visited the restaurant where Frankie would sometimes hang out. The owner of the establishment had been a good friend of Frankie for the past ten years. Frankie had worked there, first as a waiter and then as a cook, before going into the insurance adjusting business.

The owner informed the detective that on the night of the murder, Frankie came over to the restaurant at ten and asked for two hundred dollars. The owner reported that he did not have that much money on hand, but he did loan Frankie eighty dollars. Frankie had never before asked for any money despite their long-standing relationship.

The detective's hard work led to more results. He interviewed Jimmy Gonzalez, who had been Frankie's friend for the past seven years. Gonzalez, who was evasive at first when questioned, quickly cooperated when informed that Frankie was the prime suspect in the murder of his wife. Jimmy was fearful that he would be targeted as an accomplice, coconspirator, or facilitator of Migdalia's murder.

Jimmy informed the detective, "Frankie came over to my house at about ten-thirty that night. My girlfriend let him in. He asked me to drive him to the Port Authority bus terminal in Manhattan. I told Frankie that I could not drive because I had too many beers. Frankie tried to shame me into driving him, by ragging on me and calling me a wuss. I wouldn't bite. I already had one DWI conviction. If I would have another, it would mean a felony for me and state prison time. I wasn't going to risk that shit for anyone."

The detective, following up, asked, "So what did Frankie do when you told him that you wouldn't drive him?"

Jimmy took a big gulp of air and explained, "I told him I would get him a cab. I then asked him, 'Where are you going and what's the rush?'

"Just then my girlfriend Mona came back into the room. Frankie said, 'I had a fight with Migdalia. I hit her with a stick. I think I killed the bitch.'

"Mona also knew Migdalia. She told Frankie, 'Maybe she's not dead. I'll call the hospital.'

"That can't be. The bitch ain't dead? I hit her so hard; I must have cracked her head wide open. She has to be dead.'"

After a minute of silence where the detective finished writing what was just said in a scratch DD-5, the detective asked, "What did Frankie do then?"

"He went to the Port Authority in a cab that I called for him," Jimmy replied.

"Has he called you?" the detective inquired with a certain "I mean business" tone of voice that was matched with an intimidating expression affixed to his face.

"Yes, but I don't know where he is," Jimmy said pleadingly in an effort to convince the detective that he was telling the truth.

"Did he say that he would call again?" the detective quickly followed.

"No," Jimmy answered.

"If he should call again, press star fifty-seven. I can then lock in where he is calling from," the detective commanded.

About three days later, Jimmy called the detective at the phone number of the precinct, printed on the card that the detective had left behind. Frankie had called Jimmy again to find out if the police were looking for him. Jimmy pressed star fifty-seven and then called the detective.

The police determined that Frankie was calling from a house in Hialeah, Florida. The detective and two of his colleagues flew down in hopes of apprehending Frankie. They were met at the airport by two members of the Hialeah Police Department. They all proceeded to the house where Frankie had made the call to Jimmy.

The police knocked. Frankie opened the door.

When he saw standing before him the three New York City detectives with their shields attached to metal chains hanging around their necks, Frankie said in a rather nonchalant manner, "I know why you are here. I know what this is about."

The Florida police officers handcuffed Frankie and then transported him to the Hialeah Police Department station house. The New York detective assigned to the investigation gave Frankie Miranda warnings first in English and then in Spanish. Frankie answered yes to all the questions indicating that he was aware that if he were to talk to the police he would be giving up certain of his constitutional rights, including the right against self-incrimination and the right to counsel. Frankie indicated that he wished to answer the case detective's questions.

The detective now remembered another lesson taught to him by his mentor many years ago. Be prepared to be tough and persistent when interrogating a suspect. He put his mean, serious, and determined game face on. When he had barely finished introducing himself, Frankie started to sob uncontrollably.

Frankie muttered in a barely audible voice, "I wish it were me and not her."

The case detective started to follow up, but Frankie continued to cry, holding his lowered head in his hands. Any hopes of questioning Frankie would have to wait for a while, thought the detective. He also remembered the corollary to the tough cop rule. When a suspect is vulnerable and wants to unload his soul, be his priest, not his inquisitor.

After forty-five minutes, the detectives all returned. Frankie asked for a cigarette. He was given a lit cigarette while the Miranda warnings were re-read. Frankie made an oral and written statement:

> I went to our house to talk with Migdalia about getting back together. I had no intention of harming her. She was not there so I waited for her and the kids to come home. When they arrived, I guess she was mad that I let myself in with the key. We went into the kitchen and Migdalia started to argue with me. She then turned violent. She snatched a knife with a red handle and came at me as if to cut me. I grabbed a table leg lying nearby to defend myself. I swung it at her to keep her from stabbing me. I didn't think that I hit her so hard. I never was in trouble with the law before. I was scared. I panicked and came down to Florida.

Frankie waived extradition proceedings and was sent back to New York to stand trial. Frankie put on a good face. He wore a suit or sport jacket and tie every day. He never lost his cool throughout the proceedings. The demeanor that he displayed for the consumption of the jury was that of a calm businessman, not a jealous man way out of control. His court-appointed attorney tried to establish a justification defense, better known as self-defense.

There were two fatal flaws in Frankie's justification defense. First, the police officers who initially secured the apartment as well as the detectives in the crime scene unit all testified that they conducted an exhaustive search of the apartment for evidence. No knife was found in the kitchen, the place where Migdalia had been assaulted, other than in the silverware drawer, or in the living room, the place where the argument commenced. There was no red-handled knife recovered from the entire apartment. Secondly, there were no defensive wounds or any wounds at all on Frankie's body.

The evidence refuting Frankie's version of the incident was compelling. The prosecutor was permitted to introduce evidence that Frankie had hit Migdalia in the eye weeks prior to her murder as probative of who was the initial aggressor. The owner of the restaurant informed the jury that he had given Frankie eighty dollars the night of the murder. Jimmy and Mona testified how Frankie told them that he thought he had killed Migdalia and how he had asked for a ride to the bus terminal on that fateful evening. The investigating detectives informed the jury that Frankie was arrested two weeks after the incident in Hialeah, Florida. The fact that he left New York right after the incident indicated Frankie's consciousness of guilt. The medical examiner, a forensic pathologist, related that the wound in Migdalia's head consisted of a gaping hole six and one-half inches long by two and one-half inches wide. The doctor testified that she observed pieces of bone on Migdalia's face and how her brain was exposed. She explained that the blow that was delivered to inflict this wound must have been delivered with considerable force. The veteran crime scene unit detectives gave their account of how they observed pieces of skull fragments and hair affixed to the metal screws protruding from the table leg that was believed to be the murder weapon. The energy used in hitting Migdalia with the table leg was significant in discerning Frankie's criminal intent.

The prosecutor's case was sufficient to negate Frankie's justification defense beyond a reasonable doubt. The jury rejected his testimony, his charm, and his version of the events and his reason for fleeing to Florida. After five and one-half hours of deliberation, the jury returned a verdict of guilty to murder in the second degree and criminal possession of a weapon in the fourth degree.

Frankie never finished his sentence of twenty-five years to life in jail. He had only barely completed four months in an upstate prison when an argument with another inmate turned very ugly.

In an ironic but perhaps fitting ending to his life, I later found out that Frankie was stabbed in the neck with a jail-made weapon. The knife-like object cut his carotid artery. Despite the valiant efforts of the state corrections officers, Frankie bled to death on the floor of the prison laundry room.

Intimate-partner violence is not of one type. One commentator opines that based on a growing body of research "domestic violence can be differentiated with respect to partner dynamics, context and consequences. Four patterns of violence are described: Coercive Controlling Violence, Violent Resistance, Situational Couple Violence and Separation-Instigated Violence."[1]

Coercive controlling violence is used to describe a pattern of emotionally abusive intimidation, coercion, and control along with physical violence perpetrated against an intimate partner.[2] "Abuse is a repetitive pattern of behaviors to maintain power and control over an intimate partner. These are behaviors that physically harm, arouse fear, prevent a partner from doing what they wish or force them to behave in ways they do not want. Abuse includes the use of physical and sexual violence, threats and intimidation, emotional abuse and economic deprivation."[3] This is what most people call "wife beating, battering, spousal abuse or domestic violence."[4]

Violent resistance or female resistance or self-defense is a violent reaction to a coercively controlling partner. This term recognizes that both men and women may attempt to stop the violence by reacting violently to the partners who have perpetrated coercive control.[5]

"Situational Couple Violence results from situations or arguments between partners that can escalate on occasion into physical violence."[6] It occurs less frequently and the power and control model is not implicated.

Separation-instigated violence describes violence that occurs when couples are separating or divorcing or preparing to do so. This type of violence may occur even when a partner has never exhibited violence toward his or her partner on a prior occasion. This may occur when one spouse is served with divorce papers or discovers that a partner is having an affair.[7]

Frankie at first exhibited situational couple violence. Although his slapping of Migdalia was a violent act, it was not born of the classic power and control or coercive control model. His argumentative and bad behavior stemmed from his losing his employment and the concomitant loss of self-esteem. While I am not excusing his behavior, all reports seemed to indicate that Frankie was not violent toward Migdalia prior to losing his job. However, once they were separated and he observed her dating, he exhibited separation-instigated violence, first by hitting her and then by acting in the extreme by murdering Migdalia.

Nothing that Migdalia could have done would have averted Frankie's criminal conduct. Frankie, like many other men whose cases I had presided over, was unable to move on with his life. A theme that I had seen all too often was unfortunately present: "If I can't have her, no one can."

Chapter Thirteen

Classic Carl

Heather could not believe what was happening. Carl told her that she reminded him of his girlfriend, Sherrie. He said that she looked somewhat like her and they both had boyfriends from Trinidad. Carl proceeded to tell Heather how much he did for his girlfriend, how much he cared for her, and how she callously left him for a younger man, one her own age. He told Heather about his design for Sherrie. He showed her the "Tech 9" semiautomatic pistol that he planned to use to kill Sherrie and then himself. Heather was terrified for a woman whom she had not even met. Heather wondered where she fit in this mad design. Fear overcame her again, not for some stranger, but for her own survival . . .

Carl was born and raised in Jamaica. He was married and divorced and left five children behind in his native land. Carl was a responsible father who supported his children financially even though they were separated from him by sixteen hundred miles.

Carl came to the United States in 1990 and had become quickly established. He located initially in the Crown Heights section of Brooklyn, where there was a large Caribbean population. He enjoyed the people as well as the supermarkets and restaurants. It made him feel almost at home. He did miss the ocean and the year-round warm weather along with the sea breeze.

Carl was an industrious man. He worked his way up from busboy to waiter to manager of a popular West Indian restaurant called the Caribbean Palace, located near where he lived. He proved himself to be a hardworking and trustworthy employee who would work six days a week closing up each evening or opening up in the early morning and making the cash drop in the local bank's night deposit box. Carl treated the restaurant as though it were his own business.

Carl attributed his work ethic to his father's indoctrination. His father had a lot of sayings when Carl was growing up: "A day's work for a day's pay. Hard work never killed anyone. If it wasn't hard, they would call it play, not work." Unfortunately, this penchant for dedication to duty was not the sole legacy left to Carl. His father, like Carl, was a stern man. Carl's father not only ruled Carl and his three siblings with an iron hand, but he controlled the important family decisions with very little input from Carl's mother. His father routinely asked not only the children but also their mother about their daily activities—not in an interested sort of way but rather as an interrogator. This was Carl's role model for his future interpersonal relationships, especially with women with whom he would become romantically involved.

Carl, then thirty-one years old, was introduced to Sherrie in the second June after his arrival in New York. Carl had rented an apartment in Brooklyn from Sherrie's relatives upon arriving in the States. Carl had impressed Sherrie's aunt and her husband with his immaculate housekeeping and with his industriousness.

Sherrie was a lovely woman who was twelve years Carl's junior. He was instantly smitten by Sherrie's youthful joy, openness, and great smile, as well as her inner and outer beauty. Their dating shortly turned into a relationship. After four months, they decided that they would live together.

Carl wanted to move to Far Rockaway. Sherrie knew that she would have a big commute to her college in Brooklyn, but Carl said that he would drive her right to the front door of her school and even walk her to her classroom. Of course, she thought that he was kidding.

Sherrie also liked the idea of living in Queens near the ocean. She realized that Brooklyn had its share of communities near the shore too—Brighton, Coney Island, Manhattan Beach, Sea Gate, and Sheepshead Bay—but she had always lived in Brooklyn and fancied Queens as the suburbs. She also wanted to please Carl. They found a beautiful garden apartment, which was attached on one side with the Atlantic Ocean on the other. The blue water and its waves reminded Carl of his beloved Caribbean Sea. Far Rockaway was a perfect place for Carl to live.

Sherrie was slowly finding her way. After she had graduated from high school, where her grades were much more than average, she had drifted from job to job and even attended a vocational school for court stenography for a few months. She knew that being a court reporter was not for her. Yet her short exposure to legal steno school led her in the direction of the law. The spring before she met Carl, Sherrie decided to attend college and to major in legal assistance studies in order to become a paralegal and later perhaps an attorney.

Carl was a serious older man who had a good job and had taken a profound interest in every aspect of Sherrie's life. Sherrie thought how lucky she was to have a man like Carl. The other guys that she had dated were difficult to talk to and had not been concerned at all about things that were of interest to her. Carl, on the other hand, was involved in the very details of her life. He not only paid for her tuition at the college of the City University that she attended, but Carl helped Sherrie choose her classes. He pointed out to Sherrie that she ought to schedule early morning classes each day so that he could drive her to school in his Jeep and she would not need to wait around for class.

Carl also accompanied Sherrie when she purchased clothes for school because he wanted her to dress conservatively. He reasoned with her that this was the proper way to dress in the legal world. Sherrie wanted to dress in more lively colors and in sweaters and jeans, but she acceded to Carl's opinion; after all, he was interested in her success.

Despite his heavy work schedule, Carl was true to his word. Every morning he would drive from Far Rockaway to downtown Brooklyn to drop Sherrie off at school before going to work. He arranged for her to be driven to Crown Heights after her last class each day so that she could do her assignments while waiting for him to finish his work. If she needed to go to a library on the weekend, Carl would take her and wait for her to complete whatever project she was working on. Carl even gave her a cell phone so that they would be able to contact each other during the day. It was clear to Sherrie that Carl really cared for her.

Sherrie's four years in college passed quickly as she thoroughly enjoyed her academic experience. She especially loved the courses in her legal studies major—business law, constitutional law, criminal justice, and American jurisprudence. During this time, Sherrie thought that her relationship with Carl was near-perfect.

Carl was completely devoted to her and supported her in every way. She took great delight in the interest that Carl demonstrated in her studies and in her future professional career. He truly was not jealous of the time that she devoted to her schoolwork. Sherrie rightly treasured Carl. The fact that he paid her tuition was perceived by Sherrie as a sign of real commitment to their relationship. Sherrie also appreciated his thoughtfulness in driving her to school each day as well as the efforts that he made for someone to take her from school to his restaurant.

Sherrie did really well in college. After she obtained her degree, Sherrie applied for a job as a paralegal with several law firms. She received many offers of employment, some with large Wall Street firms. With Carl's help, Sherrie decided on a medium-sized well-respected establishment on the west side of midtown Manhattan. Carl accompanied and advised Sherrie when she went to purchase a "proper business wardrobe." He also paid for her clothes as a graduation gift.

Sherrie's enchantment with Carl quickly started to deteriorate shortly after she began to work in mid-July. Carl was all too eager to drive Sherrie to work in the morning. He moved up his hours at the restaurant so that he would be able to pick Sherrie up at about seven in the evening in order to drive her home. Carl would deposit Sherrie's salary each week and give her an allowance to live on. He started to call Sherrie frequently at work especially on the cell phone during her lunch break. Simply stated, Sherrie felt suffocated by Carl.

On the weekends, things were not much better. Carl worked more than a half day on Saturdays, and by the time he came home, it was almost five o'clock. As Sherrie was not required to work on most Saturdays, she felt a bit isolated in Far Rockaway as she was no longer busy with course work. She did not have a driver's license, so it was difficult for her to see her family and friends who lived for the most part in Brooklyn. Inexplicably Carl was not willing to drive her into Brooklyn on Saturdays. Sundays were sometimes spent together visiting both Sherrie's family and Carl's few relatives who lived in Brooklyn, but on most Sundays, Carl was too tired to do much of anything. They would often stay at home.

At about the time of her first anniversary at work, Sherrie started to feel not only smothered by Carl but also isolated from loved ones and friends. The event that truly changed Sherrie's feeling toward Carl was not so egregious. It was the final act in a course of conduct by Carl that Sherrie realized was not driven by loving and caring, but by a desire to control her schedule and contact with others.

At the beginning of her second September at the law firm, Carl took to making Sherrie lunch to bring to work each day, ostensibly to save some money. Sherrie now knew that it was clearly intended to limit her social interactions.

After a little more than a month had elapsed, Sherrie approached Carl about her uneasiness about what was happening to her and to their relationship. He pooh-poohed everything that she said. Carl gave no validity to any of Sherrie's feelings.

"You just don't get it, Carl!" she finally exclaimed in a sign of frustration as well as protest.

"No, you don't get it! I put you through college and cared for you when you needed me. I know what's best for us, what's best for you. Do it my way! It's the best way; it's the only way!" he shouted at her, very much annoyed, in a declaration that clearly indicated that this conversation was over and any further discussion would be fruitless and not tolerated.

Sherrie believed that she had never heard that volume or tone of voice before from Carl, at least not directed at her. Sometimes at the restaurant Carl would talk to a waiter or cook like that when a matter of concern had been discussed ad nauseam and only after Carl grew tired of the debate. At the restaurant Carl was in charge and always had the last word. This was not the restaurant. This was their lives, their relationship, and what she felt was their partnership.

Sherrie suddenly realized that this was Carl's show and his alone. He would not permit any give and take.

She thought, "How could I be so wrong?"

Her frustration turned into a feeling of defeat. Then Sherrie felt only one emotion permeate every pore of her body and deep into her soul—anger, which soon transformed into intense rage. Over the ensuing days, weeks, and months, she tried to will, to drive the fury out of her psyche. Her efforts were futile.

The fury spread from her body to her heart and soul. Although she still continued to have sexual relations with Carl when he initiated them, Sherrie was unable to love Carl. Somewhere deep inside of her stirred a strong and steady feeling that she would never be capable of loving him again. In her mind their relationship changed from one of lovers and intimates to that of parent and child. Only she was an unwilling and rebellious woman, not a child.

A few weeks before Thanksgiving during her second year at work and the sixth year of their relationship, Sherrie silently defied Carl. Although Sherrie brought her paper-bagged lunch each day, she went out with her coworkers to eat. Sherrie struck up a friendship with Lon, another paralegal in the law firm where she worked. After a few weeks of lunching with him in a group context, they started to dine only with each other.

Lon was originally from Trinidad and Tobago, another Caribbean island almost twelve hundred miles from Jamaica, where Carl was born. Yet Carl and Lon were so unlike in almost every other respect, especially their personalities. Lon was soft-spoken. He listened intently. Lon only offered his opinion on a subject when asked. He never told Sherrie how to dress or behave. He treated her as his equal, not a daughter or an ingénue that he was coaching or molding. Lon never lost his temper. Even when they disagreed about a particular topic, he very rarely raised his voice. When he did, it was hardly noticeable at all as his elevated voice was almost like another's normal talking voice.

It was shortly after Sherrie began to eat lunch with Lon that she realized that Carl was not the man with whom she wished to spend the rest of her life. She pondered how to tell Carl that she no longer loved him.

In early February, Sherrie gathered the courage to speak to Carl about leaving the apartment that they shared. It was not easy, and it became more difficult once they embarked on the discussion of ending their relationship.

"What do you mean you're leaving?" Carl roared.

He snarled, "After all that I gave you, all that I did for you, this is what I get in return?"

"Carl, it's not going to work. I didn't plan it this way. I wish I could make myself love you again, but I can't." Sherrie sobbed with tears streaming down her face, which made her checks look bruised from the bluish-purple dye of running mascara.

Carl howled, "You think I am going to take this lying down, you cunning little bitch? I paid for your college, told you what courses to take, taught you how to dress right, and set you up in a nice apartment and job. You're a real fucking cunt! You're lucky I don't kill you right now."

Sherrie had never before heard curse words from Carl. She continued to cry and whispered with hands covering her wet eyes, "I'm sorry, I'm sorry, I'm sorry." Sherrie did feel truly sorry as Carl did a lot for her, but she knew she could not live a life with him.

Sherrie's crying had some effect on Carl. His external anger seemed to dissipate to a certain extent. Yet he was still seething inside.

"I will be leaving for two hours. Pack up your shit and be out of here by the time I get back!" Carl growled as he grabbed his coat. He then opened and slammed the door behind him as he ran out.

Sherrie had no plan, but then realized that she had to get out of there quickly. She called her mom.

"Momma, I tried to get CC and Michael, but there was no answer. Get a hold of them, and tell them that they have to pick me up within two hours. Carl and I have broken up and I can't stay here any longer," Sherrie pleaded on the phone while weeping.

Sherrie's mother replied, understanding the immediacy of the situation, "Sugar, if I can't get your sister and brother to pick you up, I'll do it myself!"

Sherrie felt instant relief. When Sherrie was a little girl, her mother routinely made Sherrie's problems seem so small and easily solved. Her mom was always able to soothe her no matter how badly Sherrie felt. Her equanimity was shaken when Sherrie remembered that her mother did not drive a car.

Sherrie put the unpleasant prospect of not being picked up out of her mind and began packing her belongings. After almost ninety minutes, her sister, CC, Christine Carolyn, and her brother, Michael, arrived, helped place her belongings in the car, and drove Sherrie to her mother's home in Brooklyn.

After a few days, Sherrie realized that she had missed her period. She took a home pregnancy test, which came up with a positive result. She went to a doctor the next week and confirmed what she had thought. Sherrie was carrying Carl's baby.

Over the next few months, Carl called Sherrie often, both at her home and office. Sherrie consistently declined Carl's demands, and then requests, that she come back to live with him.

On three occasions that Sherrie was aware of during the spring, Carl came to Sherrie's place of business. Each time she refused to speak to him. Carl seemed to be familiar with her routine and schedule. Sherrie did not think that Carl went inside the building where she worked. Instead he would wait by the entrance outside the building, catching her twice at lunchtime. Carl became a stalker.

Carl approached her one time when Sherrie was on her way to lunch with Lon. On another occasion, she was returning to work with Lon. Sherrie vividly remembered that day because Lon had asked her over lunch to marry him. She had assented. A third time, Carl asked Sherrie to talk to him when she was departing for home at the end of the workday. On this last occasion, a sunny day in May, Sherrie did finally speak with him.

"Carl, I will listen to you, but I also have something to say. I'm pregnant and the baby is yours. I thought that you should know this and hear it from me," Sherrie informed him calmly and softly but directly.

Carl was slow to respond and appeared to forget what he had planned to say. His expression of bewilderment turned to one of joy, the first such feeling that he had felt since Sherrie had left him.

"That's terrific news! Terrific for you and me!" he exclaimed with a broad smile spreading over his face.

Carl went on, "Please come home. We can start a family. We are a good team."

This was a new variation on an old theme. He had asked Sherrie a number of times on the phone to come back before he knew she was pregnant.

"Carl, the only team that you are capable of being a member of is Carl's team. You once told me it's your way or no way. I believed you then. What has changed besides my being pregnant?" Sherrie told him, ending with what she believed to be a rhetorical question.

Carl desperately attempted to convince her. "I can change. I can do anything that you want. I'm more determined than ever to make it work."

A few months before, Sherrie would have given Carl an opportunity to show her how it would be different the second time around. She would have given him a chance to get it right. But now too much time had gone by. Sherrie cherished the feeling of not being subjugated by a benevolent despot. She enjoyed her freedom. No longer was someone telling her what to wear and eat and how to dress and behave.

Sherrie was also growing much closer to Lon. Carl suffered by the comparison. She had confided in Lon that she was pregnant with Carl's child.

Lon was not rattled or affected in any noticeable way. Weeks later they were engaged. Sherrie loved Lon for his complete acceptance of her. He did not need to control her nor to change her.

"Maybe you can make it work for you, but it can't work for me or for us," Sherrie answered after a pregnant pause.

"Is that an engagement ring you're wearing from that fucking guy who takes you to the movies every weekend?" Carl snapped back.

Sherrie with moistened eyes turned away. She had hoped that she had obtained some kind of closure, but instantly realized that Carl would always be in her life once she had the baby. As she proceeded to the subway station, Sherrie had firmly resolved that Carl would not be her husband or her life companion.

At about 5:15 p.m. on a Friday afternoon in mid-August, Carl, carrying a briefcase, approached Sherrie, who was walking from work toward the subway station, hand in hand with Lon.

"I want to speak to you!" Carl barked more in the form of a command than of a request.

Sherrie, alarmed that a fight might ensue between Carl and Lon, told Lon, "Honey, wait for me here a minute while I speak to him. It's fine. I'll be all right."

Sherrie walked up to Carl with the intention of requesting that he leave her and Lon alone and that Carl should respect her privacy. Instead their conversation was even briefer than she had anticipated.

"Look what I have here!" Carl exclaimed as he dialed the combination locks and opened the briefcase displaying its contents toward Sherrie.

Sherrie was in shock. She saw what appeared to her to be a machine or submachine gun. Carl had closed the case as soon as Sherrie had peered in. Its objective was to instill fear. The viewing had its desired effect. Sherrie immediately caught control of the panic about to overtake her. She successfully hid her emotions from Lon, who was standing nearby but who had no idea what Sherrie had just seen.

"Nice seeing you, Carl," Sherrie calmly stated as she casually walked toward Lon and away from Carl.

She grabbed Lon's arm but was careful not to clutch it with anxiety. Sherrie did not wish to set off any alarms for either Carl or Lon. She was concerned for not only her own safety but also for Lon's. As she walked, she debated with herself whether to inform Lon or the police about what Carl had just shown her.

Sherrie decided not to make a fuss. She believed that Carl was only attempting to act like a big boss man again, trying to intimidate her. Sherrie really did not believe that Carl would do anything to hurt her physically, but she couldn't be sure as she remembered the two times he did hit her out of anger.

Sherrie sought unsuccessfully to forget about the gun that she had seen. She was certain that she could never tell Lon. Sherrie did not want to test Lon's easy ways to see another side of him. Besides, she did not wish to jeopardize his safety in any way. He was going to be her husband and he would help her raise her baby.

After a few weeks, Sherrie was able to put the incident and Carl, if not out of, then clearly in the back of her mind. The same was not true of Carl. His fascination with Sherrie became a fixation now that he knew she was carrying his baby. Carl did not talk about Sherrie or their former relationship with others. When he was unoccupied or alone, there was no other thought going on in his brain.

On a particularly busy Wednesday following the Fourth of July weekend, a woman came into the Caribbean Palace looking for work as a waitress.

"Hi, my name is Heather. Nice to meet you," she told Carl.

Carl noticed how pretty she was. Her soft tone of voice, her body type, as well as her facial features reminded him of Sherrie. Carl wanted to talk to her, but he was much too busy to chat as he was doing double duty as the chef's helper had earlier called in sick. Carl also knew that in two weeks one of the waitresses was returning to the Bahamas for good.

"Have you ever been a waitress before?" Carl inquired.

"Both in New York and in Kingston. I'm going to college for my degree, but I need to work to support myself and to pay my tuition," Heather answered in an exaggerated Jamaican accent. Carl was interested as Heather was also Jamaican.

"Call me in a few weeks. I think there might be an opening," Carl informed her.

"Thanks! I'm in the process of moving, but after I'm finished I'll do that," she replied.

"I would like to speak to you more about your work experience, but as you can see, we are quite busy tonight. Look forward to hearing from you," Carl said with real sincerity as he turned to resume his work while Heather walked out of the restaurant.

About three weeks later, Heather called the Caribbean Palace to speak to Carl.

"Hello, this is Heather again. You told me to check back in a few weeks, so here I am. Do you have any waitress positions available?"

"As a matter of fact I do. One of the girls went back to her home country a few days ago, so I'm short on help. When can you start?"

"Tomorrow and thank you very much," Heather concluded.

"That's great!" Carl exclaimed with relief. He had been short-staffed the previous couple of days, and Heather would be a welcome addition.

The next day, Heather arrived at 10:30 in the morning, which was appropriately early for the first day of work. She had to set up for lunch, and most of the waitresses arrived at 11:15 for the noon opening. Carl had the only other waitress present show Heather her workstation and where the condiments were stored.

The waitress, a woman named Cindy from Freeport in the Bahamas, gave Heather a detailed explanation of her duties and the unique schedule of assignments that was peculiar to the Caribbean Palace. Three nights a week she would work through the late dinner shift, and three nights, including tonight, she would wait only until eight o'clock, and then she would clean and prepare her station for approximately an additional half hour.

The lunch traffic was moderate. It was noticed by everyone, including Carl, that Heather knew her away around a restaurant. She handled the customers as well as the chefs like a veteran, all without ruffling any of the other girls' feathers.

During the lull just after lunchtime and prior to preparation for dinner, Carl complimented Heather on her first meal performance. "You were terrific for a rookie. I bet none of the patrons knew this was your first day."

"Thanks. Cindy was real helpful in showing me the ropes. I wish everything were this easy," Heather mused wistfully.

"What's troubling you?" asked Carl.

"Remember the day I came looking for a job? I told you that I was moving. Well, I'm not happy with my apartment or the neighborhood. If you remember, keep an eye out for any available apartments that are not too pricey," she explained.

"You know, I live in Far Rockaway. There are lots apartments there right off or not far from the water. I think there are some up for rental right now," Carl informed her.

"Really?" Heather's could not hide her interest, and her reaction was truly spontaneous.

"I'm off tomorrow. I am hardly ever off on a Saturday. If you want, you can come with me after work tonight and you can see if anything is available. After, I will drive you home," Carl offered.

On the night before his day off at about nine o'clock, the owner would relieve Carl from closing in order to allow Carl to go home a little early. During the summer, Carl was able to negotiate about three Saturdays off, which, in effect, gave him three weekends to himself.

Heather felt awkward. It was her first day of work. Carl was her boss, and already she had come to him with a problem that wasn't even work related. He seemed like such a nice gentleman. She was certain that he wasn't interested in her as a boyfriend, which was a good thing. Heather already had a beau. Heather decided that she would soon work her boyfriend into their conversation when appropriate to be sure that Carl did not have any misconceptions. It was a big deal for Carl to drive her to Far Rockaway and then back to Brooklyn. After all these thoughts ran through her head in a matter of moments, she decided that she would take Carl up on his offer.

Heather noted her acceptance and gratitude. "I appreciate the gesture. It's so nice of you. That will be great."

After cleanup from dinner, Heather put on her civvies. As she came out of the small bathroom in the basement that also doubled as a changing room for the employees, Carl approached her. "I need a few more minutes to go over the day's receipts."

The surprisingly light traffic on the Belt Parkway as well as the conversation flowed easily on the drive to Far Rockaway. They talked about each other's interests, their respective hometowns and families. Carl mentioned without any specificity his relationship with Sherrie and the fact that it had ended rather recently. Heather had earlier intended to inject her boyfriend into their discussion. She thought that this was the appropriate time to lead into the subject.

"You know, my boyfriend is also from the islands." She knew that "islanders" always felt a certain affinity to a fellow Caribbean.

"Where exactly is he from?" Carl asked with a smile.

"A little town in Trinidad and Tobago," she answered.

Heather perceived a marked change in Carl's discourse and demeanor. It wasn't as though he became nasty or sarcastic, but the warmth in his voice evaporated, and the normal ebb and flow of conversation disappeared.

The awkwardness of their exchange mirrored how she felt when Carl's Jeep hit a pothole or bump. Carl had become sullen and, for the remainder of the trip, talked only when he was spoken to and even then he provided one-word or simple sentence answers. Yet when they arrived in Far Rockaway, Heather did not think it out of the ordinary when Carl suggested at twenty to ten that she see his apartment to obtain an idea of the type of rentals available and their comparable worth to apartments in the section of Brooklyn where she was currently living.

When they came to Carl's garden apartment, they walked around to the entrance, which was in the back. Heather went into the living room while Carl walked in the opposite direction. After a few minutes, Carl, from his bedroom, started to ask Heather about what kind of films she liked and what movies she had seen lately. After this subject had been exhausted, Carl continued to talk from afar.

"What do you like to drink?" he asked.

"I don't drink," answered Heather.

"Do you smoke?" Carl inquired.

"No."

Just as Heather replied, Carl entered the living room with what appeared to be a big black water gun.

Heather fidgeted uneasily while posing the question, "Is that a toy?"

Carl pulled out a pamphlet that displayed a picture of the gun he was holding as he answered in a flat tone, "No."

He continued as he placed the weapon on her chest while displaying a rather large-looking knife, "This is a Tech 9 semiautomatic pistol. Don't worry; it is unloaded. Now get undressed."

"You're kidding, right?" Heather pleaded, now convinced that this was no joke.

"If I forced you, would you undress?" Carl ordered even though posed as a question.

In response, Heather removed her blouse, tank top, and bra.

With her eyes moist and modest body language, she begged Carl, "No more."

Carl's unsympathetic response was nonverbal. He proceeded to load the gun and point it at Heather with one hand and then removed her pants and panties with the other.

After Carl succeeded in removing all of Heather's clothes, he told her, "You have to make love to me like you make love to your boyfriend."

Carl continued with his fantasy, which was all too real to Heather. "Did you ever have oral sex?"

Heather, shaking her head from side to side in an effort to beg as well as to inform, repeated, "No. No. No . . ."

Carl had his way with Heather. First he pushed her head toward his penis until her mouth was upon him. When he satisfied himself, he placed his mouth on her vagina and performed cunnilingus upon her.

She pretended to enjoy it as she hoped that Carl's assault might stop. Unfortunately this stratagem was unsuccessful.

Heather's mind momentarily stepped outside the madness of the moment to solve the riddle of why Carl would suddenly attack her so violently. She was unable to supply any possible reason. There obviously was no logical process to Carl's actions, nor was there any rational purpose that Heather's thoughts could imagine.

"You will have oral sex with me. You will love it," he assured himself and continued to terrorize Heather while clutching the gun in his right hand.

"Now we will have sex like you do with your boyfriend," Carl declared.

Carl then explained in more graphic terms that they would engage in intercourse. Heather informed Carl that she had endured a very bad childhood experience and that she really did not want him to enter her. Carl refused her plea but granted her request that he not ejaculate inside her.

Carl kept his word. He was a rapist with "honor." He withdrew and climaxed on Heather's stomach.

After he had calmed himself, he arose from the bed, wiped her belly with a towel, and sat on a chair while he rolled himself a joint. This was the first time since his onslaught that he was not pointing the gun at her. Carl returned to the bed and tried to rationalize his irrational and criminal actions toward Heather.

"This should not have happened. You are not responsible. When you told me that your boyfriend was Trinidadian, it set me off. The whole situation reminded me of my girlfriend. She left me after six years for a guy from Trinidad. She is pregnant with my child. I'm not thinking straight. You also resemble her. I guess I am trying to get back at the Trinidadian guy or my girlfriend. But trust me, I didn't mean to harm you."

Carl's justification by way of self-analysis was ineffectual in stemming the flow of Heather's tears. She had been violated by someone who she thought was trying to help her. As many victims of crimes, she blamed herself, thinking, "How could I be so dumb as to come to a man's house whom I hardly knew?"

Carl proceeded to tell Heather about his history with Sherrie, mentioning her by name. He chronicled his arrival from Jamaica and how he had met Sherrie. Carl described how he had advised Sherrie about what courses to take, what jobs to apply for, and what clothes to wear. He proudly stated that he had supported her during the time that they had lived together, a period where she had nothing. He had even paid for her college tuition.

"For all I've done for her, she rewarded me by betraying me for a guy from Trinidad. I'm going to kill her, her boyfriend, and then myself," Carl revealed.

Heather could not believe what was happening. She repeated in her mind what Carl had just divulged—that she reminded him of his girlfriend; they looked somewhat alike; they both had boyfriends from Trinidad.

When Carl, in an effort to validate his actions as well as his designs for Sherrie, proceeded to tell Heather how much he did for his girlfriend, how much he cared for her, and how she callously left him for a younger man her own age, Heather became physically ill. She barely was able to make it into the bathroom before vomiting.

After she emerged from the bathroom, Carl showed Heather the "Tech 9" semiautomatic pistol that he planned to use to kill Sherrie and then end his own life. She was terrified for Sherrie, a woman whom she had not even met. Heather wondered where she fit in this mad design. Fear overcame her again, not for some stranger, but for her own survival.

Carl continued to explain his intricate plan. He was going the very next day to the Manhattan law firm where Sherrie and her boyfriend worked.

"I will kill them both in the place where they met. I will ask the receptionist if there were any Trinidadian employees working there," Carl talked as though he were announcing tomorrow's train schedule.

In an effort to dissuade Carl, Heather reminded Carl that the next day was a Saturday and most law firms would be closed, and even if open, there was a good chance that Sherrie would not be in. Carl then told Heather about the contingencies inherent in his plan. If Sherrie was not at work, he would go to her house. Carl stated that he would force Sherrie's sister to tell him where she was. If her sister wouldn't help, he would seek Sherrie's brother and mother and so on. If anyone would refuse to cooperate, Carl would beat that person with his gun and then tie the individual up. As he went on, it became more and more clear to Heather that Carl was rambling like the madman that he most probably was.

Carl then informed Heather, "I will have to keep you here for the night and a good part of the day tomorrow when I will be busy carrying out my plan. It will be impossible for you to get out of my house. Every door and window will be locked. Even if you were able to open the window in the bedroom and jump to the ground, the fall and the rocks below would probably kill you. Will I have to tie you up? Do you promise that you won't try to escape?"

Heather responded and pleaded at the same time, not wishing to be tied up, "I won't try to leave. You can trust me. You said it's impossible to escape anyway. I just don't want you to hurt me."

Carl, in the magnanimous gesture of a megalomaniac, stated, "See, I'm putting the gun away in my briefcase. But don't get any ideas. This case has a combination lock. I keep my important things there such as my passport, social security number, and my plan for Sherrie. I'm also putting the only phone in this house in the case."

Carl started to get sleepy. True to his word, he did not tie Heather up, but he did cover her mouth with duct tape. Carl fell asleep on the bed lying face down. Heather was prone. They were both nude. Carl slept with his hand on Heather's back, not in any sexual fashion, but more in the way of a security measure to know when and if she left his side.

Heather did not sleep at all. She lied still throughout the long night, alternately crying silently and praying she would still be alive tomorrow.

Carl awoke sometime between seven and eight in the morning. Heather pretended to be asleep.

Carl, thinking he had awoken Heather, greeted her, "Aren't you going to give me a hug?"

Heather thinking that she was commanded, and not requested, complied.

Carl somehow deluded himself into believing that the hug that he had demanded was an invitation, placed himself on top of her, entered her, and satisfied himself with Heather. She was too frightened to resist, but clearly she was an unwilling participant.

Carl arose and removed the portable phone from the briefcase. He called Sherrie's job to ascertain whether she was working this Saturday. The office switchboard operator confirmed that she wouldn't be in. Carl then closed the briefcase, brought it along with him to the bathroom, and showered with the bathroom door open. Carl talked to Heather while showering.

When he had toweled himself dry, Carl asked Heather, "Do you want to call your boyfriend?"

Before Heather could respond, Carl answered his own question, "Maybe that's not such a good idea."

Heather thought to herself that Carl was a sadist as well as a rapist, teasing her that way. It was no wonder, she reckoned, as he already laid out his intention to murder another woman. Heather hoped that she wouldn't be the first to die in Carl's scheme.

Carl dressed and told Heather that he was going to pick up something for breakfast. "I will get you something too. I will be right back, so don't try to get away."

Heather assured Carl, "I won't try to leave."

Carl opened the briefcase, removed the gun, put it back in, placed the phone and a folder into the case, and closed it. He then left the apartment closing what sounded to be at least three locks.

Once Carl left, Heather showered in a futile effort to remove the filth and stench of Carl as well as the degradation of the evening and morning assaults. She scrubbed and scrubbed, but the soap and water could not make her feel clean.

She dressed and quickly explored possible avenues of escape. Heather tried the front door but was unable to open the locks as there were no knobs to turn. She tried the windows in the living room and in the bedroom, but she was unable to open them.

Just then from the bedroom window, Heather spied Carl parking his car. She instantly sat down on the bed in an effort to hide her intentions and to quiet her heart, which began to race again from the rush of adrenaline.

Carl entered the apartment with his briefcase in hand. He placed the briefcase down on the floor and immediately locked the front door from the inside with three different keys. He was carrying a bag with the McDonald's logo on it.

As he entered the bedroom, Heather tried as best as she could to ask nonchalantly, "You were true to your word. You were only gone twenty minutes. What did you buy?"

"I brought you some breakfast, an egg McMuffin and some coffee," Carl replied as he handed the bag to Heather.

"I see you've gotten dressed. You weren't planning to go anywhere, were you?" Carl smirked.

Heather gambled. "I was getting ready to go. You did tell me last night that you would let me go today."

Carl replied in a most serious way, "If you don't do anything stupid, I will release you later today. I will be back in a few hours as soon as I carry out my plan, just as I told you."

As if his spoken words had reminded Carl of an important appointment that must be kept, he walked toward the front door, unlocked it with the three keys, retrieved the briefcase, and departed after securing the multiple locks from the outside.

Heather peeked out the bedroom window to ensure that Carl was really leaving and not just testing her. Even after he had pulled his car out of the parking area, she still sat silently in disbelief as she was unsure that he was truly gone.

After about ten minutes, Heather began to examine ways of escaping without alerting Carl should he return. She settled on an interior wall that was attached to the condo next door. Heather banged on the wall repeatedly with her shoe, hoping that the occupant was at home and that the noise would bring someone to inquire about its source.

The clamor yielded results. After fifteen minutes, someone yelled a few times through the wall, "Stop banging!"

Heather was relieved, but she realized that she needed to be able to relay her plight through the wall so that it could be understood. She screamed her pleas to no avail. Heather realized that her message must be simplified.

She stated three times as loudly and as clearly as she could, "Come to the front door!"

Within a minute, Heather heard a woman's voice on the other side of the door. "What's going on in there?"

Heather cried in a frenzy, "I'm in trouble. I'm locked in here and being held captive. I was assaulted and raped. I need help before the man who did this to me returns!"

The nameless and faceless woman's voice softened with concern. "How can I help you? Should I call the police?"

Heather tried to steady her trembling voice by talking loud and clearly. "Please call my boyfriend first. Tell him I have been kidnapped and raped. Then call the police or have him call the police. But I don't know exactly where I am. Let them know.

After Heather had provided the woman with the telephone number of her boyfriend, the woman left to make the calls. Heather sat down drained. She waited, hoping to be rescued.

The police arrived in minutes. As the officers who responded were unable to break down the door, the Emergency Service Unit was called. Within minutes of their arrival, shortly after eleven thirty, the door was knocked off its hinges and pushed inside the apartment.

Heather cried hysterically. First the tears served as a catharsis from her ordeal. Then they turned to tears of relief and joy that her suffering, torment, and imprisonment were finally over.

She quickly remembered that another woman's terror may have already begun. Heather told the police what had transpired. She described Carl and the car he was driving. She informed them about the gun in the briefcase and what Carl planned to do with Sherrie. She knew only all too well that Carl meant what he said.

Heather had one request of the police: "Hurry! He will kill her."

Earlier that morning, Sherrie had accompanied her brother, Michael, to the hardware store to buy paint, some rollers and brushes, as well as a tray. Michael had planned to paint their mother's bedroom. He was a dutiful son, but was driven more by obligation to help his mom as he did live in her house.

After dropping off the supplies at his mother's house, Michael brought Sherrie to Brooklyn Hospital for her prenatal checkup. Sherrie was in her ninth month and the frequency of her visits had increased from monthly to weekly. The doctor informed Sherrie that she was doing fine and that the baby's growth inside her belly was progressing normally.

From the hospital, Michael dropped Sherrie off to do her grocery shopping at the Pathmark supermarket on Atlantic Avenue. From there, Michael was going to deliver some vitamin supplements for Sherrie to their sister CC's house. Sherrie now lived with her sister, CC, since Sherrie's separation from Carl.

The two sisters shared household duties. Since Sherrie was pregnant, CC insisted that she would do the house cleaning while Sherrie would do the shopping. CC did not want Sherrie to bend while cleaning or to do mopping and vacuuming. Besides, Michael would be able to help Sherrie out on many days by driving her to the supermarket.

CC was at home vacuuming the living room floor rug when she heard the doorbell ring. She knew it wasn't her mom or Michael as they both had keys. Sherrie would ring even though she too had a key if she had too many bags to carry. Yet it was too early for her to be finished with the grocery shopping. Then she remembered that Michael said he might come back after dropping

Sherrie off at the grocery store in order to help CC replace two overhead lights in the kitchen. She thought, "Michael must have forgotten his key again."

CC was forever telling Michael to place her key on his chain in case of an emergency. She was about to give Michael a good-natured lecture about consideration and his forgetfulness as she opened the door. CC was startled to see Carl standing in the hallway, holding a black briefcase in his left hand.

"Carl, what are you doing here?" CC asked.

Carl answered with his own question. "Where is your sister? I have some things of hers in the car and I want to give them to her personally."

CC protectively answered, "You can leave them with me. I don't know where she is and when she will return."

"Can I wait for her here?" Carl declared in a question while he walked across the threshold of the apartment.

"Carl, you know Sherrie doesn't want to see you, especially here," CC replied uneasily.

Carl gazed outside the living room window and saw something that made him spring into action. He closed the door and with his right hand pulled a rather large-looking gun from under his jacket and pointed it at CC.

"Carl, are you crazy? What are you doing?" CC mustered up the courage to ask before her mind went blank and her legs turned to jelly.

Carl's response was to move away from and to the left side of the door frame, while training the gun on CC. Carl pointed his left forefinger toward the sky while touching the tip of his nose in a silencing gesture.

Carl whispered, "Your brother will be walking down the hall toward your front door right about now. Open the door slowly and act real cool. Ask him calmly and normally where Sherrie is. Don't let on that I'm here if you don't want to get hurt."

CC opened the door, and sure enough, Michael was down the hallway about forty feet away. CC realized that when Carl looked out of her living room window, he must have seen Michael approaching. CC was scared not only for herself but also for Sherrie and now Michael. CC wanted to stop Michael from entering her apartment.

She thought quickly. "I just got through mopping the floor. It's all wet and you can't come in."

Michael replied while Carl delivered a threatening grimace right at CC. "I was going to help you a bit until I had to pick up Sherrie. But if I can't come in . . . " His voice trailed off into a little laugh that feigned regret for and actually meant relief at being unable to help CC with her chores.

"Where is Sherrie?" CC asked, not by a sincere desire to know, but now prompted and very frightened by Carl as he edged ever closer to the door frame with his gun pointed at CC's head.

"She's at Pathmark finishing her shopping," Michael replied while continuing toward the door.

"Run, Michael, run!" CC cried out, placing herself in great danger.

Carl shoved CC to the side and pointed the semiautomatic machine pistol at Michael, who was already sprinting back down the hallway toward the staircase and the exit. Carl pulled the trigger and held it for what seemed like barely a second. Four rounds had been discharged. Michael's gait faltered for an instant as one of the bullets grazed his right arm. Within two steps, Michael was again in full stride turning the corner to safety.

Carl did not pursue Michael. The information that Carl sought was obtained from Michael albeit unwittingly. Still, he had to deal with CC.

CC was shaking and crying, beseeching Carl over and over, "Don't kill me! Please, don't kill me!"

Carl thought a moment then reached for his black briefcase. He opened the combination locks and pulled out a roll of duct tape. He never uttered another word to CC. Carl motioned to her to sit down in the chair in the kitchen, which was right off of the hallway. He taped her to the chair and taped the chair to the kitchen table.

He then placed a piece of tape over her mouth carefully allowing her to have a clear air passageway by her nose.

As he left, he stated without a trace of rancor in his voice, "You will live. That is more than I can say for your sister."

Within minutes of Carl's departure, CC heard the doorbell ring. She exerted herself mightily but was unable to rise. She then pushed the chair and the table to which it was attached sideways as hard as she could in order to bang it against the kitchen wall. Even though she was bruising the side of her body and leg, she repeated this maneuver over and over again and was successful in creating a disturbance sufficient enough to alert whoever was outside the door that there was someone inside.

Within moments, the door was smashed in. The police, using a blade to cut the duct tape, untied CC thinking she was her sister, Sherrie. It had taken the police who had freed Heather longer than they wanted to travel to Sherrie's house. Although Heather had urged them to hurry, she did not know where to direct them. The police were able to trace the phone number registered to Carl in Far Rockaway. With the help of an emergency unit within the telephone company, they were able to ascertain the last few calls that were made from Carl's portable phone even though the phone was no longer in Carl's house. One of the calls was made to Sherrie's law firm. The firm provided the police with Sherrie's residence. This investigation was conducted in an efficient manner but did take some time.

The police were understandably concerned when they discovered that the woman that they had just cut loose was not Sherrie. She was still at risk and time remained their enemy. After CC related what had transpired in the apartment and that Carl was armed and had discharged his weapon, the squad of police officers contacted other units to meet them at Pathmark, a twenty-minute drive.

Michael, meanwhile, had sought to drive to his local precinct to report that Carl was holding CC in the apartment at gunpoint. He kept honking his horn as he was trailing four cars stuck behind a garbage truck that was making its Saturday pickup on the one-way street where he stood.

Michael was so emotionally frazzled when he finally arrived at the station house almost twenty-five minutes later that he almost neglected to remember that CC had asked him where Sherrie was before telling him to run. In his hysteria, the significance of the question was almost lost on him. No precious time was lost as the police that had responded to the apartment already had the pertinent information from CC and had left for Pathmark minutes ago.

When the first police car reached the front of Pathmark, the officers were approached by an agitated male standing in front of the entrance who informed them, "Someone stabbed a woman in there."

The officers exited their vehicle and ran into the store. They immediately observed a group of patrons outside an interior office and peering in. The officers made their way through the crowd and into the office. They saw two men, one the manager and the other the store security guard, wrestling Carl onto the ground. A few feet away was a noticeably pregnant woman who was lying on the ground bleeding from the face and neck area. One officer aided the men in subduing Carl. The other officer put on latex gloves and attended to Sherrie after calling EMS.

Carl had reached the Pathmark parking lot within fifteen minutes of leaving CC's apartment. He traveled above the speed limit and made every staggered light except one, which he had run. Carl surveyed the lot, which was full of cars. He opened the briefcase and thought that he might be detected if he brought the semiautomatic pistol into such a busy store. Instead, he selected as his weapon of choice a very sharp brown-handled knife with a six-inch serrated blade. Carl shut the briefcase, tucked the knife into his waistband by his hip, closed the car door, and walked purposefully toward the store.

When Carl had entered the supermarket, Sherrie was ready to check out her groceries on the third station away from the entrance. Carl pulled the knife from his pants and started moving toward Sherrie. Sherrie started to retreat toward the manager's office as soon as she saw Carl.

"Help me, help me! He's going to kill me!" Sherrie shouted when she observed the knife in Carl's hand.

Before the manager and the store detective with whom he was talking could react, Carl was upon Sherrie like the madman he was, attacking her with the knife. With a short chopping motion of his right arm, he cut her on the chin. The blow knocked Sherrie to the floor. Carl proceeded to stab her twice in the neck and a second time in the face before the store employees were able to pull him away from Sherrie, remove the knife, and subdue him. The blood covered her face and neck and flowed toward the ground, reddening Sherrie's maternity blouse.

Sherrie was taken by ambulance to Long Island College Hospital. She had surgery to close the wounds. The pain to her throat even after being stitched up was excruciating. She had trouble talking, swallowing, and even moving. She experienced premature contractions throughout the night due to the assault.

Carl was taken into custody. Before he was removed for the processing of his arrest, the police officers, who were now aware that Carl had a semi-automatic pistol, conducted a search of his vehicle upon Carl's consent. The gun was observed inside the briefcase, which was in an open and unlocked position on the front seat of the car. The silver duct tape and portable phone were also found in his car.

I presided over Carl's jury trial in Brooklyn for the attempted murder and felony assault of Sherrie, the attempted murder of Michael, and the kidnapping of CC. The entire allegation of Heather's rape in Queens was admitted into evidence as being highly probative and relevant of Carl's intent to kill and to injure Heather and to complete the narrative and to provide a proper contextual background as to the nature of Carl's relationship with Heather.

Carl's defense was that Heather and Sherrie were known to one another and that they had concocted the entire episode. Carl testified that his sex with Heather was consensual and that Sherrie was attempting to shake him down for money.

The defense attempted to discredit Michael by showing that he had prior convictions for leaving the scene of a vehicular accident and for criminal possession of cocaine at a time when he had an ongoing drug addiction problem. CC was similarly impeached by her admission that she had previously been in a drug treatment program for ninety days and that she was a recovering drug addict and alcoholic.

Heather and Sherrie were terrific witnesses and unshakeable. Carl was unable to explain away the events at the supermarket where unrelated witnesses, the store manager and detective, described the events of the stabbing in graphic detail. The police officers' testimony of their discovery of the semiautomatic pistol, silver duct tape, portable telephone, and black briefcase in Carl's car reinforced the truth of the testimony of the prosecution's witnesses. The jury convicted Carl of the charges, including attempted murder, kidnapping, and the possession of a weapon as a felony.

Heather had to relive her ordeal a third time. Four months later in a Queens courtroom, she testified against Carl in his rape trial. Once again, Carl was convicted.

Carl was sentenced to a term of imprisonment of thirty-four years for the attempted murder of Sherrie, the kidnapping of CC, and other charges in Brooklyn and fifteen years for the rape and kidnapping of Heather in Queens, both terms to run consecutively. In effect, Carl was sentenced an aggregate term of imprisonment of forty-nine years.

Carl was the paradigm of the classic batterer. He wanted to exert his power to control "his" woman. All the signs were present but initially went unrecognized by Sherrie. Selecting Sherrie's clothes and classes, insisting on picking her up and dropping her off at work, providing her with a cell phone so that he could call her at any time, as well as isolating her from her friends and relatives, indicated that Carl's intent was to control and to subjugate her. When Sherrie no longer permitted herself to be manipulated by Carl, he lost all his power over her. He reacted like a child whose toy had been taken away. Carl responded with anger and violence. He felt entitled to treat Sherrie the way he did. He was wrong, but persisted in attempting to exercise the only manner of control at his disposal—first stalking, then resorting to physical violence. Now he pays the price, for his response was criminal.

Sherrie was certainly traumatized, but from a different perspective she was quite fortunate. She survived and gave birth to a healthy baby boy. Sherrie married Lon. He treated and loved her boy as though the child were his own.

Hopefully Heather will recover from her psychic wounds and the violations to her body and soul. She was a hardworking woman looking for a job to better herself and to further her education. She was in the wrong place at the wrong time through no fault of her own.

Yet even in the moment when Heather was liberated and still extremely disturbed by the cruel assault perpetrated upon her, she worried about the safety of another woman whom she did not even know. Her story is about one woman putting aside her personal trauma and helping another survive.

Chapter Fourteen

Selfish Samuel

Samuel was charged with various crimes against Taisha, including burglary in the first degree and felony assault. Samuel's date book/diary had been inspected by the prosecution, and a duplicate had been turned over to Samuel's court-appointed counsel. At the subsequent proceeding, defense counsel asked of Samuel, sotto voce, about two entries in particular. The pertinent portions read: "Finally caught up with the bitch. Fucked her up. I might regret letting her live. . . . Almost got locked up. I do regret letting the bitch live. So now I will kill her." Samuel, in an effort to exculpate himself, informed his lawyer in a loud, matter-of-fact tone so all in the room could hear, "Not that bitch, another bitch!"

Taisha would be a mature woman now. In 1996, when the various events unfolded, she was a nineteen-year-old who was trying to hold her life together. She had been doing well academically in a Brooklyn high school and sailing through life. Like some very nice girls, she thought that she was in love. Some six months before, she had met an older boy, who seemed to her a man.

Samuel seemed so mature, a college boy. He seemed grounded as he also worked nearly full time as a file clerk for an insurance company in lower Manhattan. They dated a few months. Taisha enjoyed Samuel's company. They liked the same movies and enjoyed going to the corner candy store to share an ice cream soda like teenagers did in the 1950s. Samuel was rather plain looking and of average height and build. He was five foot eight inches and one hundred and fifty pounds. He was not particularly handsome but became so in Taisha's eyes when they would talk together.

One warm spring night in a moment of thoughtless passion and hormones gone wild, they consummated their love. Taisha became pregnant toward the end of her junior year. She was forced to drop out of school in the fall of what was supposed to be her last year in high school. Taisha planned to com-

165

plete high school and to go on to college. In her own mind she was merely postponing the inevitable. She would have her baby, stay home for a year or so, and with the help of Samuel and her parents, she would continue with her education and live happily ever after.

In early February of 1996, which should have been the beginning of Kaisha's final semester, she gave birth to a beautiful baby boy. Taisha and Samuel decided to name the baby Jashaun. Although there were a few weeks of very happy times, the joy of the new baby's arrival was short-lived. Perhaps it was the new responsibilities imposed on Samuel or the concomitant financial obligations, but whatever it was, Samuel's sweet attitude toward Taisha certainly changed. Then again maybe his true personality finally emerged. Yet, Taisha could not foresee the nasty and selfish side of Samuel.

Samuel had been accused of assaulting his former girlfriend in 1990. Those charges resulted in Samuel's plea to a violation, not a crime. In 1991, Samuel had also been indicted by a grand jury and charged with burglary and felony assault against the same ex-girlfriend's mother. After a jury trial, Samuel was acquitted of all felony charges but was convicted of misdemeanor assault and aggravated harassment. Samuel had made several threatening phone calls to his ex-girlfriend's house. A few days after the last phone call, he forced his way into the home of his former girlfriend and hit her mother a number of times in the face. He was extremely fortunate that she had not suffered a serious physical injury, which would have elevated the assault to a felony.

Taisha expected Samuel to help support the baby both emotionally and financially. They had talked many times of the love they shared for one another. When Taisha learned that she was pregnant, Samuel reiterated his devotion to Taisha by proclaiming, "Our baby will have everything that you want a baby to have. Our baby will want for nothing."

At the beginning, Samuel paid what he could toward the costs of rearing his son. Yet as Jashaun's first birthday neared, Samuel was becoming unraveled by the pressure of attending college, working, and giving much of his earnings to Taisha for their baby. Shortly after Jashaun's birthday, they argued regularly about Samuel's diminishing financial contribution for their son.

Taisha's requests were not unreasonable. Taisha's mother and father purchased the crib and stroller. They also paid for the food, diapers, and sundries needed for the baby's care. Taisha's parents provided a neat and clean place for them to live. Taisha merely asked Samuel to give her some money toward the weekly costs of raising their son.

In late January 1996, Taisha again engaged Samuel about his monetary obligations to their child. Despite their past differences over what each thought Samuel ought to pay, it was nonetheless quite unexpected when Samuel refused to contribute anything to the costs of raising Jashaun.

Taisha was shocked to hear Samuel's response to her request: "It is all your fault that we have a child! You should have used contraception. This is not a good time for me to have a baby! I am just starting out in my life. I can't afford to pay anything at all."

Taisha felt betrayed and hurt at the same time that she felt an uncontrollable rage well up inside of her. She fought back the tears that were soon to pour forth.

Taisha screamed, "If you won't support your son, then you will never see him!"

Samuel replied, "I will see my son whenever I want. If you try to stop me, you will be more than sorry. You will get hurt!"

Taisha's resolve was strong. Taisha went to Family Court and obtained an ex parte temporary order of protection based both on Samuel's threats and on an incident approximately one week later where he placed a knife to her throat. The order was in fact extended several times. The original protective order was served on Samuel.

Taisha never again would socialize with Samuel or ask anything of him. She did not request child support but rather brought a family offense petition. Taisha was through with Samuel. He was not yet finished with her.

On a cool day in late April, Taisha was returning home with Jashaun from the pediatrician. She wheeled the baby in his stroller down the block toward her parents' home. Taisha glanced down at Jashaun, noticing that the blanket covering him was partially blown off by the wind. She reminded herself that they would momentarily be warm inside. Sure enough, they were soon in front of her parents' house.

Taisha navigated the stroller containing her precious cargo slowly and with great care up the four steps leading to the front door of her parents' one-family private home. She opened up the Plexiglas exterior door and then placed her key inside the lock of the thick wooden inner door. After unlocking the inner door, she pushed it in and reached back for the stroller.

As she rolled the stroller into the house, she felt a hand heavy upon her mouth in an effort not to suffocate but to silence. Taisha was forcefully propelled into the house.

When Taisha turned around, she was unsure whether she was more scared or relieved to see that it was Samuel who was behind this attack. Before she had a chance to ponder her predicament, Samuel turned around to lock the front door.

He then ordered her in a loud, fierce voice while pointing, "Get your ass in that chair!"

When she sat down, Samuel was instantly upon her. He covered her mouth and nose with his hand. This time Samuel clearly meant to smother Taisha.

The utter panic of being unable to breathe made the episode seem as though it were minutes to Taisha, when in fact it only lasted seconds.

When Taisha struggled to free herself, Samuel repeatedly punched her in her face about a dozen times. He must have hit her on her left eye with at least three hard shots as it was immediately swollen nearly shut. Her eye was not yet scarlet or purple even though the skin surrounding the orbital was bleeding slightly.

Jashaun sat silently in his stroller by the front hallway inside the house while Taisha cried uncontrollably. Samuel pulled out a large hunting knife enclosed in a sheath from the back of his pants, seemingly from the waistband.

He quickly placed the knife to Taisha's throat and commanded her, "Shut the fuck up now!"

Abruptly, Samuel diverted his attention from Taisha and picked up the telephone in the living room. He placed the knife down alongside his leg as he sat down to dial the phone.

Taisha thought about running out of the house. Two things held her back. For one, Samuel was facing her while he was talking on the phone. Secondly, she could not bear the thought of leaving Jashaun behind.

When Samuel concluded his call, he picked up the knife and cut the phone wire near the wall jack.

He ordered Taisha while signaling with his knife, "Get up the stairs."

When they reached the top of the stairs, Samuel directed Taisha toward the bedroom down the end of the hall.

Samuel demanded more than inquired, "Where is the order of protection?"

"The order of protection is in the lower dresser drawer," Taisha replied.

She noticed that Samuel placed the knife down on the end of the bed. Samuel reached down, opened the drawer, moved some papers about, and removed the order.

He seemed to examine it and then placed it in his front left pants pocket.

Out of the blue, Samuel demanded, "Who is Ronnie?"

Fearfully Taisha answered, "He is a friend of mine."

Taisha knew that Samuel must have followed her or spoken to one of her friends. How else did he know of Ronnie? Ronnie was now a friend, but Taisha hoped that soon he would be her boyfriend.

Ronnie was not interested in having sex right away like the other boys she had met. They would talk and read together in her mother's house. On the few occasions when they went out together to a movie or to the diner for dessert, they would hold hands. Ronnie did not kiss Taisha good night until they had been out together on three dates. He was so sweet and seemed kind of shy. Ronnie actually asked Taisha for permission before kissing her. She of course said yes. He was awkward in his approach, which she found unusually refreshing. Taisha was reluctant to go too fast with Ronnie because in the back of her mind she remembered that Samuel too was respectful at the onset of their relationship.

Samuel asked Taisha to give him a description of Ronnie. She complied and also told Samuel where he lived when asked. Taisha was afraid to lie to Samuel because she believed that he already knew where Ronnie lived. She thought that Samuel was simply testing her.

Samuel picked up the knife and motioned with it while saying, "Go downstairs to the living room."

Taisha went down the steps while spying Samuel reentering her parents' bedroom. Taisha did not attempt an escape as she did not think that she could make it outside of the house before Samuel could get to her especially if she stopped to take the baby. Shortly, Samuel came down the stairs, knife in hand.

As Samuel proceeded to cut the telephone line in the living room, he informed Taisha by delivering a not so veiled threat, "I saw you buy a lottery ticket in the candy store the day before yesterday. I could have killed you then. I can kill you now. I can kill you anytime I want. I could wait until your mother comes home and kill both of you. I should kill you now so that your father will see you dead in his house, but none of this is in the plans that I have written in my book." Taisha now realized that Samuel had indeed been stalking her.

Taisha's head was hurting from the beating she had taken upon her arrival home. She felt like the Cyclops character from Greek mythology as she could see out of only one eye. Her left eye resembled that of a boxer on a losing end of a decision after a twelve-round brawl. It was now completely closed.

"You tell the cops that the mailman did this to you. Tell them that he broke into the house. I am telling you that I will see Jashaun whenever I want. If I tell you to bring him to see me, you will obey immediately!" Samuel bellowed.

Taisha was alarmed. Samuel was pacing back and forth aimlessly while waiving the knife almost as though he were deciding what to do with her. As quickly as he came, he departed. Samuel turned around with the sheath in his left hand and the knife in his right, opened the door, and walked out into the street.

Taisha observed Samuel pass through the front gate from the safety of the living room window. In her terror, she had forgotten that Samuel had cut the phone line in the living room. Upon seeing the severed wire, she ran up the stairs to call the police from her parents' room. Samuel had sliced that phone line too.

Taisha then ran back downstairs to the entrance of the house. She locked the Plexiglas door while standing behind it, waiting for a passerby to help her. She was petrified to go outside in case Samuel might return. While she did not wish to show Samuel how scared she was in his presence, upon his hasty departure, all her defenses came falling down as tears rolled down her cheeks.

After what was in fact about twenty minutes, but what seemed like hours to Taisha, a sturdy man in his mid-fifties walked by. Taisha somehow found the courage to unlock the door and venture out onto the front steps.

She implored the stranger, "Please call the police! I have been beaten and he may come back!"

When the stranger left, Taisha's fear returned. She quickly scampered back into the house and fumbled to lock both the inner and outer doors. Once inside, she waited and tried to steady her shattered nerves.

She repeated over and over again to herself in the manner of a supplication, "Help is on the way. The police will come."

Within minutes her prayers were answered. Two police cars with sirens blaring and light turrets blazing pulled up to the house. Taisha told the officers what had transpired and provided a physical description of Samuel. She also gave them the addresses where she thought that he may be. She called her mother at work from a neighbor's home.

The police implored her to seek medical attention for the injuries that she sustained to her head and to her left eye in particular. Reluctantly, she left Jashaun with her neighbor and allowed the police to summon an ambulance to transport her to Brookdale Hospital.

On the way to the hospital, Taisha realized that the police officers had given her good advice. Her left eye was aching as the swelling increased. Even with great effort she was unable to open her eye.

Upon her arrival, she was treated in the emergency room. A review of her vital signs revealed no abnormalities. Taisha was then taken to the radiology department for a CAT scan. The results were negative for any trauma to the head. Her injuries consisted of a swollen face and eye, the eyelid and surrounding tissue were black and blue, and the iris of her left eye was bloodshot. Although she was discharged from the hospital after several hours of observation, Taisha experienced great pain and was unable to see out of her eye for more than one week.

A few days later, a detective assigned to the investigation located Samuel on his college campus in Brooklyn. Samuel was carrying on as though life was normal and nothing had occurred. He had just finished attending a class and was on the way to his next one. The detective, a no-nonsense, sturdy Irishman named Quinn, arrested Samuel and placed him in handcuffs after verifying his identity. Detective Quinn seized Samuel's backpack and Walkman headset.

Later at the precinct as part of the inventory search, the items in the backpack were vouchered, namely, textbooks, notebooks, and a daily diary calendar. The books were first turned upside down, feathered, and visually inspected to ensure that they contained no weapons such as thin knives or razors or contraband. The inventorying of the items promotes three policies:

"the protection of the owner's property while it is in the custody of the police"; "insuring the police against false claims of lost, stolen or vandalized
property"; and "guarding the police and others from dangerous instruments
that would otherwise go undetected."[1]

Later when the assistant district attorney interviewed Taisha, she discovered that Samuel had told Taisha on at least one occasion that his plans for
her were in his book. The prosecutor applied to the court for a search warrant
to inspect the daily diary calendar for evidence of the crimes charged in the
indictment, including burglary, assault, and criminal possession of a weapon.

As the application was made only weeks prior to trial, the court directed
that notice be given to the defendant's attorney. A contested hearing was held
followed by oral argument. I ordered that a warrant be issued to allow the
prosecution to inspect the contents of the calendar diary.

Samuel was charged with various crimes against Taisha, including burglary in the first degree and felony assault. Samuel's date book/diary had
been inspected by the prosecution, and a duplicate had been turned over to
Samuel's court-appointed counsel.

At the subsequent proceeding, defense counsel asked of Samuel, sotto
voce, about two entries in particular. The pertinent portions read: "Finally
caught up with the bitch. Fucked her up. I might regret letting her live.
. . . Almost got locked up. I do regret letting the bitch live. So now I will
kill her." Samuel, in an effort to exculpate himself, informed his lawyer in
a loud, matter-of-fact tone so all in the room could hear, "Not that bitch,
another bitch!"

The diary chronicled Samuel's criminal acts in addition to confirming his
criminal intent.

The entry for April 20 read: "I did nothing of importance today, but did buy
a blade to handle my problems."

The entry for April 22, the date of the incident, indicated, "Finally caught
up with the bitch. Fucked her up. I might regret letting her live."

The entry for April 23, a few days prior to Samuel's arrest, revealed, "Almost got locked up. I do regret letting the bitch live. So now I will kill her."

At the pretrial hearings, the prosecutor sought the admission of uncharged
crimes or prior bad acts to demonstrate Samuel's intent, identity, and motive
as well as to describe the nature of Samuel and Taisha's relationship on its
case in chief or in the alternative, should Samuel testify, as impeachment material. Some acts were admitted while others were rejected when I balanced
the probative value against the prejudicial effect for each act individually as
well as for all of the alleged conduct cumulatively.

A summary of the prior bad acts and uncharged crimes sought to be introduced against Samuel consisted of the following: In early February 1996,
Taisha reported in a Family Court petition that Samuel placed a knife to her

throat after a heated argument about child support. On February 3, Samuel came to Taisha's door and repeatedly rang the bell and demanded to see Jashaun, all in violation of the protective order. A few days later, Samuel threatened Taisha on the telephone when she refused to allow him to visit with Jashaun without a Family Court order for visitation. In 1992, he was convicted of an assault against his former girlfriend's mother. In a series of taped messages between January and April 1996 to Taisha's parents' home telephone, Samuel repeatedly called Taisha a bitch and other choice words. In early March, Samuel attempted to remove Jashaun from his cousin's home by placing a knife to his own cousin's throat.

At the trial, Taisha was a very credible witness. The police officer's testimony of his observation of the severed telephone confirmed Taisha's version of the events. The hospital emergency room personnel and hospital records as well as the police officer's testimony corroborated the injuries sustained by Taisha.

The most serious crime with which Samuel was charged was burglary in the first degree, a class B violent felony, carrying a maximum sentence of twenty-five years in prison. Samuel, in an effort to negate one of the elements of burglary, namely, unlawfully entering or remaining in a dwelling, sought to show that Taisha had invited him into her home. Taisha was questioned extensively by defense counsel as to whether she had invited Samuel into the house but was afraid of her parents' actions or disapproval should she admit to this. She was queried as to some minor prior bad acts as a sixteen-year-old.

Taisha remained firm. She had not invited Samuel over, nor had she consented to his entry upon or his remaining in her parents' home.

The jury returned with its verdict within a few hours. Samuel was convicted of six crimes. I later sentenced him as a violent felony offender to, inter alia, an indeterminate sentence of incarceration of eleven to twenty-two years for burglary in the first degree and three and one-half to seven years for assault in the second degree, the terms of imprisonment to run concurrently. Samuel had been convicted of robbery as a felony in another state a few years before, but he was not sentenced as a second violent felony offender as the out-of-state conviction was not a violent felony under New York law. An order of protection was issued for a twenty-five-year period during which Samuel had to stay away from and could not write, phone, or contact Taisha. Samuel could not see his son whenever he wanted to. He would have to now convince the Family Court that it would be appropriate for Jashaun to visit him in state prison.

It is interesting to note that while Samuel thought he was entitled to see his son whenever he desired, he did not feel obligated to support Jashaun financially.

Chapter Fifteen

Dangerous "Love"

In the early morning while it was still dark outside, Robin was jolted awake even before her eyes opened. She felt two strong hands around her neck choking her but not completely stifling the air supply to her lungs. Suddenly, the hands released her neck, allowing the oxygen to proceed unimpeded through her throat. She sucked in the air as one who has been submerged many feet under water would when finally reaching the surface after much effort. When Robin was able to dissolve the remnants of sleep from her eyes, she saw someone looming over her menacingly with what appeared to be a carving knife. A man was uttering indiscernible words almost inaudibly. Then Robin heard him start to speak in a low, calm voice. She then realized who was choking her . . .

Ron and Robin had been college sweethearts in Massachusetts during Ron's sophomore and Robin's freshman year. Ron had come from a small town in northern Maine and Robin from a suburb just outside of Boston. They had separated for a year while Ron transferred to pursue an art major at a first-tier fine arts university in Brooklyn.

Ron had been fair to Robin. He had told her that since they were apart, he wanted to take this opportunity to date other women to make sure that their feelings for one another were genuine. Even though they called and e-mailed each other frequently, they realized that they were in fact in love and wanted to spend their lives together. Ron asked Robin to marry him. That summer they were wed in Massachusetts.

After their wedding and a short honeymoon, Robin moved into Ron's apartment near Prospect Park in Brooklyn. At first they lived quite happily together. Ron loved his courses and had already lined up a job teaching art in a private school for the following fall. Robin attended one of the City University campuses, concentrating on the sciences as she hoped to pursue a career as a pharmacist. They shared the shopping and cleaning chores. Both seemed to thrive in living the city life—movies, museums, off-off Broadway plays, and affordable ethnic restaurants—all subsidized by student discounts and parental aid.

Things were not quite perfect. By the beginning of June, it was clear that the sciences were not Robin's forte. She seemed to do better in the arts. Robin decided to switch majors to theater. Instead of taking a straight job during her first summer in New York, Robin worked for a not-for-profit theater workshop in lower Manhattan. This was a contentious issue between the newlyweds as Robin earned much less money than she would have in almost any other job. Ron also worked to make ends meet until the start of his teaching position in mid-September.

In the fall, Robin became pregnant. Ron wanted to have the baby, but Robin was worried about their financial situation. Although she never articulated this to Ron, Robin was also concerned about the effect a baby would have on her freedom to follow her newfound dream of becoming an actress. Ron was willing to undergo any hardship to have their baby. Robin convinced him, though barely, that she should complete college and they should establish their careers before starting a family. She had an abortion.

After graduation, Robin found part-time employment and continued to attend acting classes and theater group workshops to perfect her craft. This study was costly but viewed by Robin as necessary in order to become a polished actress. Robin's pursuit of an acting career became a deep source of conflict between Ron and herself. Ron had given up his dreams of becoming a working artist so that he could support Robin and start a family. Now he felt that she was following her dreams at the expense of his own. Ron also thought that her paltry salary and extra spending became an obstacle to them saving money to purchase their own home and to start a family.

Ron's fears were not unfounded. Over the next five years, Robin became pregnant twice more. The first time, they had a heated knock-down argument over whether Robin should have the baby. Ron presented compelling reasons for going ahead with the pregnancy. Ron did not believe in abortion even though it was legal in New York. He felt very guilty that he somehow acted in complicity with Robin by failing to insist that she not terminate her first pregnancy. He also believed that it was time to begin their family if they were to have a life together. Ron was also concerned, beyond the moral and religious issues, that if Robin were to have a second abortion, it may make it more difficult for her to become pregnant in the future.

Robin simply was not ready to raise a child. She thought that she was at a crucial juncture in the development of her own life's work and that a baby would just complicate her life and interfere with her own perceived progress.

Ron told her that this was a most selfish point of view and that she and he were not striving for the same goals.

Ron told her plainly, "You are jeopardizing our relationship."

Robin simply defied his wishes and aborted her pregnancy. This placed a great chasm in their relationship—one which they would never bridge.

After this abortion, Ron had great difficulty being close to Robin. He always had trouble verbalizing his feelings to her. For many months, their acts of sexual intimacy were few and far between.

Despite their infrequent liaisons, Robin became pregnant a little more than a year after her second abortion. She decided not to tell Ron. She once again terminated her pregnancy. This time her rationale was not only based on a desire to further her acting career, which was still barely nascent, but also on her indecisiveness as to whether she wanted to have Ron's baby and to spend the rest of her life with him. It was clear to her that their relationship was indeed shaky at best.

Within months of her last abortion, Robin had an affair with a fellow actor in one of her groups. Although she felt guilty about her dishonesty, she realized that perhaps her bond with Ron may have been irreparably damaged. Robin was still unsure of the final answer. She resolved in her own mind that the only way she could be certain of her feelings was to separate from Ron. After involved discussions over the next few evenings, it was agreed that they would live apart. In early September, Robin moved into her own apartment in the East Village section of Manhattan.

Ron's parents were distressed that their son was sad. Yet they were not unhappy that the two had separated. They never wholeheartedly sanctioned Ron's marriage to Robin. They fancied themselves as old New England Americans. They were able to trace their ancestor's arrival to America from England to the early 1700s. They fancied themselves as once removed from the *Mayflower*. They did not approve that Robin's parents were only second-generation Americans from Eastern Europe. Subliminally they acted in ways to subvert their son's marriage. On holidays when Ron would call to inform his parents that he would be visiting, they would always ask whether Robin would be coming with him. The question itself was strange enough, but when he answered in the affirmative, his parents would sound almost sad.

Ron's parents no longer hid their disdain for Robin or her family. The increased frequency of calls to Ron by his parents was noticeable. Most contained the theme that he should not take Robin back or that she was not and would never be good enough for him. Ron's parents either refused or were unable to recognize the palpable pain in his voice caused by his separation from Robin.

Ron did recognize his hurt and the void in his life created by Robin's absence. After some six weeks, he was resolved to contact her. Then she called him.

"How are you doing, Ronnie? I missed you."

"I missed you too. How have you been?"

Ron unsuccessfully tried to mask his emotions. He was elated to hear from Robin. Her calling spared him some pride and showed him that Robin truly cared. They talked for forty minutes and agreed to meet for coffee the next night.

The talk went well. Robin suggested that they should go out on a few dates to see how things progressed with them. During these outings, Robin was able to relate to Ron in a way that she never thought possible. When they lived together, he was distant and noncommunicative. Now he listened and appeared to be open-minded and receptive to the idea of fostering Robin's dream of becoming an actress. It was like she was talking to a new man. Over the next few weeks, Robin even felt secure enough to tell Ron of her short-lived extramarital affair with one of the actors in her group and of her secret third abortion. She believed that if they were to be reunited, then their relationship had to start and be based on a foundation of honesty and trust. Robin thought that if these issues could be resolved, then they could begin to compromise on the financial matters that seemed so divisive. Ron seemingly digested what she imparted and was still eager to resume their marriage.

A week went by after their last date before they spoke again. Ron called.

"Hi. Are you still willing to give our marriage a shot?"

"Of course. You know there's nothing I want more than for us to be together," Robin replied.

"There are certain things that I need to be done in order for us to have any chance at all," Ron implored.

"I'm listening." Robin waited with anticipation and hope.

"I want you back and I will support your quest to become an actress, but you must never return to the acting workshop where you now go."

"Why?" she asked.

Ron confessed, "I feel humiliated and embarrassed by your intimacy with another man whom you will continue to see. I also know men. I am sure other people in the group know about your affair with him and I don't think I can handle it."

There was silence on the phone as Robin thought about what was just said. She was optimistic and excited at the prospect of repairing their marriage. Robin realized that she did not want their relationship to end. She only wanted a commitment that Ron would work at making it a successful partnership.

Robin thought that if her past transgression really bothered Ron and he was honest enough to admit it, then she would leave her group. There were plenty of workshops out there, and she would simply have to find the right one, another one. In one way Robin was very happy that Ron was able to vocalize what he was feeling. She knew that Ron was making progress and he was asking something that she felt was quite reasonable.

"Sure, no problem. I want you to feel secure in our new relationship. I will pack my things and be there tomorrow afternoon. I love you."

"I love you too."

Ron immediately called his parents to relay the good news. It was mid-December and the Christmas holidays were fast approaching. Ron anticipated spending part of the holidays with his and Robin's parents.

The news was not received as joyously as it was imparted. Ron's parents clearly related their feelings on these most recent developments: "If you plan on coming here for Christmas, don't bring her. You are making a big mistake in taking her back. She has always been bad news. Don't you have any pride left? How did we raise you?"

Ron hung up the phone feeling numb. His parents still exerted great influence over him. Ron wondered for a second whether he was making the correct decision. He then listened to his heart and his heart won out over his mind. Ron then decided that he would have to make sure that Robin's past transgressions were all left behind.

Robin returned to their apartment the next afternoon. It was their apartment only it was smaller than she remembered it. Something was different. There was a wall up where the entrance to the second bedroom used to be.

"Why did you seal off the entrance to that bedroom?" Robin asked while pointing.

Ron explained, "I rented the second bedroom out to a graduate student. It makes things easier financially. I guess I never thought that you would ever come back. I put up the wall to give him and me some privacy. I opened another entryway on the backside of the room."

"How can we live together with a stranger? Isn't it a little bit crowded?" Robin inquired.

"He won't be back until after the New Year. He went home to visit with his family for the holidays. And don't worry about him. He is a month-to-month tenant. When he returns, I will tell him that he has to move. He will be out by February. I am holding one-month security. I know him. There will be no problem," Ron answered.

Things went well for the next four days. They cleaned up the house one day. The following days were spent eating take-out Chinese food, eating out, going to the movies, and watching movies at home on their VCR. They talked about their feelings and seemingly started to heal their wounded relationship.

On the fourth evening, Ron made a home-cooked meal: veal parmigiana with linguine and white clam sauce New England style. They both sipped a glass of merlot flirtatiously. Robin thought she may be actually falling in love all over again. They romanced one another and kissed like they did when they first began dating. Robin fell asleep in Ron's embrace dressed only in her panties without even bothering to wash the dishes or to place the unused food back in the refrigerator.

In the early morning while it was still dark outside, Robin was jolted awake even before her eyes opened. She felt two strong hands around her neck choking her but not completely stifling the air supply to her lungs. Suddenly, the hands released her neck, allowing the oxygen to proceed unimpeded through her throat. She sucked in the air as one who has been submerged many feet under water would when finally reaching the surface after much effort. When Robin was able to dissolve the remnants of sleep from her eyes, she saw someone looming over her menacingly with what appeared to be a carving knife. A man was uttering indiscernible words almost inaudibly. Then Robin heard him start to speak in a low, calm voice. She then realized who was choking her.

"You destroyed our marriage and I feel a tremendous sense of loss. You caused me terrible pain. I don't know what to do. Should I kill you or torture you? Should I first torture you and then kill you? Do you see what you've done to me?" he asked without requiring or expecting any answers.

Robin trembled as Ron placed the serrated edge of the knife up against her breasts just below the nipples. She was still breathing heavily in an effort to restore her breathing rhythm to normal.

She realized that this was not a bad dream when Ron said calmly and deliberately in a normal tone of voice, "This is a life-and-death situation."

Ron then changed positions. He had been straddling Robin by her upper thighs, but now he sat on her midsection slightly above her waist. He was looking at her head below as she lay flat on her back. Robin tried to wriggle herself free but stopped when Ron pressed the knife menacingly to the left side of her throat.

Ron lamented sedately, "We had a picture-perfect marriage. Look what you've done."

Robin sighed and bit her lip. The look on her face appealed to Ron more effectively than any words could convey. He almost decided to spare her from any more emotional pain and physical damage.

Ron, sensing her concern, attempted to ease her fear. "You will be okay, depending on how you act."

Ron got up and walked toward the kitchen. Robin partially sat up, forming a forty-degree angle with her upper body to the bed by leaning on her forearms. She arched her neck toward the kitchen in an effort to see what Ron was doing. He came back within a half minute carrying a can of soda, a green lemon juice bottle, and a shaker of salt. He was carrying something small that she was unable to identify as it was covered by his right hand.

Ron placed what he was carrying next to the knife, which was on the small end table adjacent to the bed. He then turned toward Robin, who remained propped up on the bed leaning on her elbows and forearms. He shoved her flat down on the bed and then sat on her.

Ron grabbed the knife and proceeded to cut her panties from her body. Robin was terrified. When Ron finished, he threw the panties toward the wall. Robin, feeling even more vulnerable as she was now naked, started to flail her arms at Ron in an effort to free herself. Ron then knelt on her arms after an initial attempt to restrain Robin by holding her wrists failed. He was now in a quadruped position with his back to her head and facing toward her feet, pinioning her arms with his legs and her legs with his arms.

Ron informed her deliberately, "If you don't stop moving, then I will have to tie you up."

Robin stopped struggling. Ron then placed the knife back on the end table while reaching for another object that was too slight for Robin to make out.

In his own mind, Ron was attempting to cleanse the impurities out of their marriage. Although he knew exactly what he was doing, Ron somehow thought that Robin was consenting to the purging of all of their problems. The abortions and the infidelity would be eradicated forever. Ron thought it was time for the ritual to begin.

Ron ran his hand across Robin's chest just underneath her ample bosom. Robin felt a little pain as his hand made contact with her body. She soon felt a wetness on her stomach and realized that it wasn't Ron's hand that caused this feeling. He had sliced her with a razor, cutting a three-inch red line under the middle of her breasts.

Once again Ron ran the razor across her upper stomach from left to right about two inches below the first slice. She was in emotional shock and denial and was unable to call out to make him stop.

After a few moments, reality penetrated Robin's psyche. She renewed her battle to free herself. Ron intensified the pressure on Robin's limbs and succeeded in thwarting her attempt to get off of the bed.

In a cold, distant voice, Ron opined, "It isn't so bad. Not yet at least."

He released her legs and reached for something on the end table. He poured some liquid on the bleeding wounds and then raised what Robin could see was the saltshaker and proceeded to shake salt on her body. As the salt was descending on the parallel cuts under her breast, she already felt a burning sensation from what she knew now was lemon juice.

Robin now felt extreme pain as Ron made a clear literary reference to her. "I pour salt on your cuts to disinfect the wounds that you had inflicted upon me."

Robin yelled out in anguish.

Ron's reply was in the form of another allegory. "You should be quiet. I am getting the hang of this blade. I will soon be able to handle it as an artist applies his paintbrush to the canvas."

Ron then repositioned himself to face Robin, placing his knees on her biceps. He then sat back and, rather gently considering the circumstances, pulled her head forward by the hair so that she could see the small slices on the front of her torso. After resting Robin's head back down on the bed, Ron made a cut on her upper left arm slightly below the shoulder. Robin yelped in pain. She tried to extricate herself, but Ron was able to keep her pinned down. Ron replaced the razor on the end table. He grabbed Robin's breasts with both hands and pinched her nipples, not in a sexual way, but in a manner meant to get the person's attention by inflicting a modicum of pain.

"You better behave. Your life and our relationship are in your hands," Ron warned.

He then reached for the razor. Ron then cut Robin on the upper portion of the outside of her left thigh. He then poured salt on the blood oozing out of her upper arm and thigh. The blood was flowing out of her leg more than from her other body parts that were cut. Robin noticed her thigh was more painful than the other wounds when the salt mingled with her blood. Her screams of pain, fear, and betrayal were much louder than before.

"It's not so bad. You're making too much noise," Ron exclaimed as he arose to turn on the radio as well as the television to a volume louder than one would normally set for enjoyment.

Upon his return, he grabbed her orange T-shirt, balled it up, and stuffed it into Robin's mouth. Ron then took her panty hose and tied them around her head and over her mouth so that Robin would be unable to easily remove the shirt that served to gag her.

Ron then stated, as though he were talking about the day's weather, "I should smack you to get your attention. Most women would be appreciative if their husbands never hit them."

Ron then sharply slapped both sides of Robin's face.

Robin almost ignored the hits she received. She was too preoccupied with thoughts of being trapped. She was unable to move her arms, which were pinned down by Ron's knees. The more Robin battled, the more labored her breathing became. After awhile, when she was barely able to take in air, she ceased her struggle to remove the gag from her mouth and to free herself from Ron's grasp.

Ron surveyed Robin's motionless body as if he were looking at a map in an effort to find the most direct route to where he was going. "Your forehead may be a good place to cut next, or maybe the nose or chin."

He then moved the razor vertically straight down from just under the bottom of the nose down the median of the extension of the septum to the top of the upper lip. Ron rattled on unintelligibly about the mixing of bodily fluids as he poured salt and then lemon juice on Robin's face.

Ron explained, "I am cauterizing the wounds of our relationship to help us to heal, but it is time to move on to the next level."

Ron walked toward the space of the apartment that he used as his art studio. He brought back a rope to the bed where Robin lay on her side with eyes stretched wide open. Ron pushed her chest to force her down flat on her back. He bound her wrists and ankles to her torso with the rope.

When he had finished tying Robin up, he picked up the phone and dialed a number. Robin gleaned from Ron's side of the conversation that he was talking to the superintendent of the building where they lived. Robin started to squeal as loud as anyone who was gagged could. Ron motioned her to be silent, but she persevered to no avail. The radio and television volume was so loud that she could not possibly be heard by the superintendent on the telephone. Even if she were heard, he would not know that she was in danger.

When Ron returned to the bed, he flipped Robin's legs up by the ankles toward her head. He informed her, "I will tell you exactly what I will do, so you can adjust."

Her heart was already pumping fast when Ron held up a pair of pliers, the handles covered with blue plastic. She noticed that the pliers could be converted into wire cutters. The tool had a dual use. Robin's nervous system went out of whack as she attempted to figure out which use Ron had in mind for her. Robin wriggled and shook uncontrollably.

Ron placed his left knee on her right thigh as he placed the wire cutter part of the tool on the second toe, right next to the big toe, applying a little pressure.

He directed, "Be still or I will cut it off."

He then proceeded to explain each part of the instrument and the function of the pliers as well as the wire cutter.

He said informatively, "I will use the pliers next."

Ron turned around to face Robin and then pinched her left nipple with the pliers. He then applied even more pressure with the pliers by squeezing the right nipple for a few seconds. Robin's pain was excruciating.

Ron then explained, "It wasn't so bad, was it? Are you ready?"

Robin's eyes opened ever wider if that were possible. She couldn't imagine what was to follow. She soon found out.

He placed the pliers on her clitoris and grasped it. It wasn't only the moderate pressure that caused her distress, but Ron was also pulling on the pliers as well as closing it. Robin felt as though Ron would remove her clitoris from her body. He would reduce the pressure and stop the pulling for seconds and then repeat the pressure sensation and rending several more times before removing the pliers from her body.

After a moment of relief, Robin panicked intensely when Ron placed the pliers inside her vagina while holding the end of the handles. Sadistically, Ron moved the pliers a number of times in and out of her while at the same time opening and closing it inside of her. When Robin tried to wriggle away from this torture, it ached even more.

"It shouldn't hurt that bad." The expert on pain opined, "Your cuts are only insignificant as you are superficial."

Ron then placed the tongs of the pliers on an ice cube and clamped on it. He then placed the ends of the pliers and the ice inside of her. Robin felt acute cold inside and out. She could not even obtain any cathartic easing of her anguish by yelling or crying out as she was still muzzled by the gag in her mouth.

He then elaborated, "I placed the pliers inside of you because someone else had been there. The ice cubes were used to numb you for what is to come next."

Without any further rationalization as before, he duplicated the pliers' maneuver, this time in her anus. He would place one tong then the other inside her rectum and pinch alternately the front of her pubic area and then her backside with the other tong. The moving and tweaking caused agonizing pain. Yet temporarily, Robin forgot the cuts and the fact that her vaginal area was still hurting. At that precise moment, she only felt the emotion of abject humiliation of being violated by someone whom she had loved.

The pliers were removed from her body. Robin saw Ron place the pliers upon the end table and then reach for another object that she was unable to readily recognize. Then Ron showed it to her. She shuddered. It was a high-powered stapler used to hold the thick wood of picture frames together. It was approximately seven inches in length and two and one-half inches in width. To dramatize its potency, Ron aimed it at the ceiling and shot it. The staples hit the ceiling with force but did not penetrate. Still they landed on the floor with a threatening thump.

As if Ron had not done enough physical and psychological damage, he went on, "I am going to staple the sides of your vagina to your thigh."

With that, he placed the stapler next to the skin protruding from her vagina and pushed it back onto her inner part of her right thigh. Robin although still tied up and gagged, struggled frantically to get away by moving her torso toward the end of the bed.

Ron grabbed her and warned, "If you don't stop moving, I will have to do other things."

Ron held the stapler still in midair, seemingly for seconds, while gazing directly at Robin's face, which was partially covered by the gag and hosiery holding it in place. Inexplicably, Ron was apparently moved by something that had not affected him before. Ron placed the stapler down and declared, "You win. I love you too much."

As suddenly as this nightmare began, it ended. At least the violence did. Ron undid the knotted panty hose around Robin's neck and removed the balled-up T-shirt from her mouth. Robin's wrists and ankles remained bound to her body when Ron inexplicably dialed 911.

Ron placed the phone to Robin's ear. When the police operator answered, Robin denied calling in an emergency.

Robin lied, "I meant to call information. I dialed you by mistake."

The savvy 911 operator asked, "Is someone there with you?"

When Robin answered, "Yes," the operator informed her that help was on the way.

Robin simply said, "Thank you."

Ron placed the phone back on the receiver and moved to a chair away from the bed.

"What do you intend to do?" Ron asked of Robin, who was still tied up.

"Leave," Robin stated simply.

Ron raised himself off of the chair and took two steps toward the bed. He then proceeded to untie the rope binding both of her wrists and ankles together. After she was unfettered, Robin stood up to retrieve her coat, which was draped over a chair. As she arose and put the coat on, Ron realized that she was naked except for the coat.

Ron ordered more than asked, "Stop; put on some clothes."

Robin thought about leaving, but she did not feel safe. Ron was only about two feet from her. They were now both standing by the kitchen refrigerator. Ron was situated between Robin and the exit. She decided that it would be more prudent to get dressed as she was still uncertain whether Ron could be set off again. Ron helped Robin pick up the clothes from the floor. She placed them on the sofa and then in an instant put on her ski pants' leggings, shirt, skirt, sweater, blazer, and finally an overcoat. When she placed the clothes directly on her wounds, she felt a new kind of sting. Yet she also sensed relief in that she was now closer to extricating herself from this real-life nightmare.

When she was finished, she asked, "Can I go?"

Ron answered by asking his own question. "Do you want your bag?"

Robin shook her head no and took two steps toward the front door. Ron put out his hands as if he was asking for a hug. Robin submitted to him and limply allowed Ron to hug her. Ron stood still on the side of the kitchen as Robin turned the lock, opened the front door, and went down the stairs as fast as her shaken body would go.

She almost ran past two police officers after she fumbled through her keys to unlock the exterior gate to the building.

The officers asked, "Did you call 911?"

Robin answered without detail, "No."

The officers proceeded to exact the needed information. "Did someone else call 911?"

"Yes," Robin responded.

At that point, the police officers both noticed the thin stream of blood that continued to trickle down Robin's lips and chin. One of the officers asked, "Who cut you?"

Robin resumed trembling as if the words triggered the reliving of her trauma. Still shaking, Robin removed her coat and showed the officers the cut on her arm. She then lifted up her shirt and displayed the wounds on her chest.

Again one of the officers asked, "Who did this to you?"

Robin this time answered clearly, if not calmly. "My husband. He is upstairs in our apartment."

As the police officers went upstairs, Robin crumpled onto the sidewalk. After a few minutes, she gathered herself and went to the pay telephone booth on the corner. She called her friend Edith. No one was home, so Robin left a message on the answering machine: "Help me!"

Edith was apparently screening her calls. She picked up and answered, "Robin, what's the matter? Are you okay?"

Robin, still quivering, began to tell Edith about her ordeal. After only a minute, her call was interrupted when the officers came down with Ron in handcuffs. The officers had arrested Ron after he identified himself. He had no complaints and no injuries. Ron appeared calm and collected. Ron and Robin were taken to the local precinct in separate patrol cars.

The EMS technicians treated Robin's wounds at the precinct, but not before one of the officers took Polaroid photos of each of her cuts. The EMS technicians suggested to her and the police that she go to the hospital for further medical care. The police transported Robin to the hospital. Some cuts were stitched up and others were taped close with a butterfly bandage. The wound to her psyche would not heal so easily.

Robin spent four to five hours at the hospital. A police officer interviewed her.

A hospital domestic violence counselor met with her as well. Edith also came to the hospital to see how Robin was doing. Even though Robin was patched up, she was still in appreciable pain. The cuts from her breasts were irritated and inflamed from the clothing touching her open wounds before she was treated. Her stomach hurt, and her vagina felt like it was burning. Whenever she moved, she felt a stab-like pain in both her vaginal and anal areas.

After Robin was discharged from the hospital, she returned to the precinct for a further interview by a team of detectives. When she had related the facts of the incident in full, the detectives asked her whether she would give them the keys to the apartment. She gave them the keys and permission to enter and to remove whatever they thought to be appropriate. The detectives retrieved and vouchered as evidence the razor, rope, saltshaker, lemon juice, T-shirt, panty hose, power stapler, and pliers. They took pictures of the apartment and the items seized in relation to where the bed was situated.

Robin stayed with Edith in her apartment in the lower east side of Manhattan. After a few weeks, she went home to spend some time with her parents in Massachusetts. When she returned to New York after three months, she rented an apartment in the upper west side. Robin was scared to spend the nights alone. First her brother stayed with her for two months. When he had to return to Massachusetts, she asked various girlfriends to remain with her for four to five nights at a stretch.

When Robin came back to New York, she filed for divorce. After Ron was served with the summons and complaint, his mother wrote Robin's parents a letter in an effort to resolve the indictment pending against Ron. A letter from Ron was included without containing an expressed apology. Robin's parents shared both letters with her.

After not speaking to Ron for nearly a year, Robin decided to call him.

She wanted to know the answer to a question, so she asked him, "Are you sorry at all at what you did to me?"

Ron replied, "I am sorry that all this happened, but the only way our marriage could have continued was for me to do what was necessary to cleanse our relationship. Anyway, you have an order of protection, so I can't talk to you." Ron then hung the phone up abruptly.

At the trial, Ron's attorney capably cross-examined Robin. Even though she was a National Merit semifinalist, Ron's trial attorney attempted to demonstrate that Ron was supportive of Robin when she changed her major from pharmacy to theater, implying, perhaps correctly, that her grades did not cut the mustard to be admitted to pharmacy school. Robin's shoplifting conviction while in high school was also brought out to further attack her credibility. The fact that Robin called Ron shortly before the trial was meant to test Robin's version of the incident. After all, Ron's attorney argued in summation, why would a woman who was so abused and who did not go along with the purging ritual as described in testimony at trial telephone the man who perpetrated these acts upon her?

The main focus of Ron's defense was one of consent. He testified that on the night when the crimes were alleged to have been committed, Robin and he talked about how he was devastated emotionally when she had undergone the abortions and how he wished they could start a family because he loved her. Ron told Robin that he had felt lost when he learned about her affair. Robin told him that the largest obstacle to their being reunited was Ron's failure to express his feelings. Their fundamental problem was a lack of intimacy on his part.

Ron testified that Robin agreed to go through the ritual of cutting and slicing wounds into her body and pouring salt and lemon juice onto them in an effort to rid her and their marriage from the past wrongs and blemishes that deeply stained their relationship. He also wanted to free himself from the emotional turmoil that she had imposed upon him. Ron basically substantiated the events of the evening and early morning as well as the order in which they had occurred. It was just as Robin had related. Ron used allegories to explain his acts that he alleged were performed with Robin's consent. Besides the obvious "salt on wounds," he explained that he tied Robin up because he was all tied up in her act of infidelity.

It was incredible to believe that Robin would permit, let alone invite, Ron to inflict her with such pain and torture. He also testified at trial along with one of his female friends that they believed that Robin had a motive to twist the events of the evening and early morning in issue. Ron's defense theory was that Robin wanted their apartment and she wanted him out even if that meant his incarceration.

Ron was convicted of, inter alia, attempted assault in the first degree, two counts of assault in the second degree, unlawful imprisonment, three counts of aggravated sexual abuse in the third degree, two counts of sexual abuse in the first degree, and seven counts of criminal possession of a weapon. At the sentencing, the parents of Ron and Robin were present. It was evident that each did not approve of the mate that their respective child had chosen. The failed marriage, the charges, and the convictions, as well as the imminent incarceration of Ron, did nothing to improve the situation. After considering Ron's previous unblemished history, but also the violations perpetrated upon Robin, I sentenced Ron to a term of imprisonment of six to eighteen years.

Ron seemed to be otherwise a hardworking, decent person. Yet I was astonished at how he could possibly think that Robin was consenting to the acts that he performed upon her. They were not only criminal but bizarre beyond anyone's value system. I hoped that in his case his incarceration would be rehabilitative in the sense that he would realize that he is not entitled to cure any conceived ills in his life by taking unilateral action that is harmful to another, especially an intimate partner.

Chapter Sixteen

Deadly Vignettes

Domestic violence cases are filled with motifs, subplots, and unusual stories. There are aspects of some cases that are not easily forgotten.

There was a young man who was convicted of misdemeanor assault and felony criminal contempt for acts perpetrated against his girlfriend. A review of his personal history revealed him to be a loved, very happy, and well-adjusted child until shortly after a traumatic event. When he was ten years old, he and his younger brother happened upon their grandfather's pistol. Their grandfather, a corrections officer, thought that his gun was well hidden. Apparently it was not. The two boys were inspecting the weapon when the gun accidentally went off, killing the younger boy. The older brother never recovered. He went from a cheerful boy to an introverted, troubled, and disturbed fellow who found his way into my court when he hit his girlfriend with a telephone. After serving six months in jail, I required him to undergo psychiatric counseling as part of a five-year probation period. This young man never appeared before me for any probation violation.

There was one defendant who would threaten his wife and who had hit his stepdaughter on one occasion. The really frightening facet of this case did not deal with humans. The defendant had broken the neck of his stepdaughter's cat and threw it against the wall as an intimidation tactic. There is a high correlation between animal abuse and domestic violence. This man had some kind of mental issue related to abuse of alcohol. After serving his jail time for assault and animal abuse, he was placed in a program for alcohol abusers. He left the program without permission and returned home in violation of the order of protection that I had issued. After a few weeks, his adult stepdaughter moved out, enabling him to return home without violating the protective order. While still under the court's supervision, the animal abuser died a few months later from complications related to his alcoholism.

Then there was the pharmacist who had graduated number two in his class. Prior to his being a defendant in the Domestic Violence Court, he had his license revoked due to other problems. After he had spent some time in jail for harassing and abusing his elderly mother, he was housed in an assisted care living facility in Brooklyn, as the restraining order prohibited him from living with his mother. On one of his probation monitoring updates in court, the ex-pharmacist had to be instructed that he could not, as he had been doing, gather the unused medication of the other residents of the facility. He explained that he had been collecting the dosages that remained at the end of each day, ostensibly to prevent the other housemates from inadvertently taking someone else's medicine. The court reminded him that his business was no longer pharmacy and that someone working in the residence would address his concerns regarding the prophylactic removal of unused medicines to ensure the safety of the other residents.

There were the handful of perpetrators that I label the "Caustic Killers." These defendants, both men and women, used caustic substances to disfigure or to blind their former lovers and spouses. There were a few who poured lighter fluid or another accelerant on the objects of their scorn and then attempted to put them on fire.

How could I ever forget the torturous beating from neck to toe and the cigarette burns that a husband from a Middle Eastern country inflicted on his wife? The defendant was able to negotiate a sentence of five years in prison as the husband's family agreed to allow the wife and children to live rent free in an apartment that they owned. This was not a quid pro quo for the promised sentence, but it certainly made it more palatable for the prosecution to offer a plea and for me to abide by it. No one was truly happy about the length of the husband's sentence.

The defendant continued to write to his wife in violation of the protective order. The new indictment was handled by Judge Matthew D'Emic, a colleague and good friend who also headed a domestic violence part and now also presides over the state's first mental health court. After a jury trial, the husband was convicted of three counts of criminal contempt as a second felony offender and sentenced to three consecutive terms of two to four years in jail, in all an additional six to twelve years in prison. Prior to the later convictions, his wife moved out of her in-laws' building, and with the help of Elisa, a dedicated career prosecutor, the wife's application to remain in the country as a victim of domestic violence was granted by the Justice Department (formerly the Immigration and Naturalization Service, now the Department of Homeland Security).

There were a few celebrity defendants, including one heavy metal guitarist and a rapper, both of some fame. The guitarist had a case involving a rather unusual situation. He and his fiancée had renewed their love for one another during a substance abuse rehabilitation program. A few months later, he had discovered that his former fiancée had married another, months prior to their public reaffirmation of their love for one another. His reaction was strange. Instead of being angry at his former fiancée, he telephoned her husband and challenged him to a fight. When the newlywed did not show up at the announced hour for the fisticuff duel, the guitarist paid a visit to the bridegroom and knocked down the front door of his house. Luckily no one was hurt.

The rapper had entered a guilty plea to felony contempt for violating an order of protection. The court suggested that the defendant do a "rap" condemning domestic violence as part of his sentence, which included probation. The defendant and his attorney thought this to be reasonable. When they returned to court for sentencing, they reported that the producer did not believe that a "rap song" about domestic violence was going to sell to the purchasing public. This was a sad but true commentary on our society.

There was one defendant, a Vietnam veteran, who lived with his elderly aunt who had Alzheimer's disease. Mysteriously, he was entrusted with the care of his aunt. His aunt would moan throughout the night and constantly slam the doors to her bedroom and the bathroom. After months of being awakened by his aunt's screaming and groaning, he came upon what he believed to be the perfect solution. He tied her and her bedroom door down each night. This clearly was elder abuse and inhumane treatment. Each morning she was covered with her own urine and feces. The nephew was prosecuted, and the aunt was moved to a nursing home. Once she was removed to a nursing home, the nephew no longer posed a danger to anyone. Only then did I fully understand the adage "not fit to live with another." This defendant had to live alone.

This chapter is aptly named "Deadly Vignettes." It is easily discernible that the first letter of each word of the chapter's title when placed together forms DV, the acronym for domestic violence. The chapter consists of various stories of domestic violence described in abbreviated fashion. Each story was picked as part of the chapter to show that each case has various twists and turns on the same theme—power and control that becomes violent and criminal.

JAKE FELT JUSTIFIED

Julia and Jake had been together for nine years. Although Julia had told Jake on more than one occasion that she was unhappy in their marriage, Jake never suspected that Julia was having an affair and Julia did not think of leaving

Jake. After all, they had two children together, Jake Jr. and Michael, eight years old and five years old, respectively.

Yet some months before, Julia met Louis, a very handsome and attentive man, in front of her apartment house. Louis flirted with her, bought her breakfast, and then took her to lunch in his Volvo. Over time, they started to spend more and more time together walking and talking in the park and their relationship became intimate.

One day Jake came home early from work. He observed his two sons playing together on the living room floor. He walked into the bedroom only to discover his wife, Julia, naked and in bed with another man, who was also nude. Jake went at this unknown man with the intention to kill him with his bare hands any way he could, but Julia tussled with him while the unknown man, later to be known to him as Louis, rushed to put his pants on, gathered his shirt and shoes, and escaped through the window. Jake was extremely angry but not enough to be violent toward Julia—not yet at least.

Jake ordered Julia to get dressed, take their children, and get out of their apartment forever. He screamed, "You stepped all over my manhood! I do not want to see you here ever again, but I will continue to see my boys!" Jake also took Julia's cell phone, beeper, and credit cards away from her.

During the ensuing weeks, Jake would pick up Jake Jr. and Michael and take them to school and oftentimes pick them up. Jake would deliver the boys back to Julia. Julia and the children were staying at Julia's mother's apartment. Then one day, Jake Jr. told Jake that Julia had told the boys to call Louis "Daddy." Almost one week later on the following weekend, Jake went to visit Julia. He asked Julia's mom to watch the boys for a few hours. He asked Julia to return home with him. She agreed.

Julia entered their apartment first. Jake locked the door. He took out the .38 caliber handgun that he had owned for ten years and shot Julia six times, killing her. No one was going to tell his boys to call another man "Daddy" or "Father."

At his murder trial, it was clear that Jake felt justified in doing what he did. His lawyer skillfully argued to the jury that although the sex act occurred weeks before, the precipitating act that caused Jake extreme emotional disturbance was Julia's telling the boys to call Louis "Daddy" a week prior to the shooting. There was a reasonable view of the evidence to support Jake's contention, so I was obligated to charge the jury that if they found that Jake acted under extreme emotional disturbance, then Jake would be guilty of only manslaughter in the first degree, even though he intended to kill Julia and in fact caused her death. The jury agreed with the defense, and Jake was convicted of manslaughter. I sentenced Jake to eighteen and one-half years in jail.

HANGIN' HANK

Hank had been a drug abuser for years. His wife, Jennifer, had remained with him through two stays at a residential drug treatment program. She wanted to believe that he would be able to return to the family to help in raising and in supporting their two daughters. When he had been clean, Hank was a skilled union carpenter who was a good provider for his family. When he was high, Hank was physically and verbally abusive.

Jennifer had finally given up her hope in reuniting the family with Hank. After his discharge from his latest drug treatment program, Hank continued to be abusive toward Jennifer. His abuse was physical as well as verbal. It was bad enough that she had to experience such maltreatment, but Jennifer could not bear having her girls observe their father mistreating her so.

Jennifer went to the criminal court to file charges of aggravated harassment and misdemeanor assault and to secure a full stay-away order of protection. The restraining order mandated that Hank "stay away from Jennifer's home, place of business, or any other place where she may be." Additionally, it provided that Hank was not to contact her in any manner such as by letter or telephone. The court's order allowed Hank to petition the family court for visitation or custody of their two children.

Hank was not coping well with his situation. Not only did he miss being with Jennifer and his children, he felt totally powerless to do anything about it even though the protective order provided him with legal recourse. He thought of a bizarre plan that would get everyone's attention. His kids would take notice and Jennifer would be remorseful for forcing him to do what he had designed.

The next day at about six thirty in the morning, Hank proceeded to Jennifer's apartment building with a very strong rope and a chair. He rang a number of the apartments from outside the front entrance of the building. One of the tenants rang back and Hank entered the building.

The building was one of those prewar apartment houses with typically high ceilings. Hank stationed himself right outside of Jennifer's apartment. He placed the chair about two feet away from the apartment door. He then fashioned a noose out of the rope's end and threw it over a pipe that ran parallel to the floor and was about two feet below the ceiling.

Hank then stood on the chair and adjusted the rope so that it would be taut when the noose was placed around his neck. He then removed the noose from his head and tied the end of the rope tightly around the door handle of the unit nearest to Jennifer's apartment. He again went onto the chair and grasped the noose with both hands and lifted his feet up off the chair to test whether the rope would support his weight. It did. He stepped off of the chair to admire his work.

Hank thought his scheme was perfectly planned. He would hang himself outside of Jennifer's door. When she would exit her apartment to take the children to school, she would find his hanging, lifeless body and realize what a terrible mistake she had made. He was only mildly concerned that his two girls might also see their father hanging as a result of his suicide.

It was almost seven o'clock when Hank was prepared to put his plan into action. He strode upon the chair, placed the noose tightly upon his neck, and kicked the chair away. He was hanging freely and knew that soon he would be dead.

Almost immediately, Jennifer came out of the apartment holding a bag of garbage to be thrown out.

Upon seeing Hank dangling from and slightly swaying on the rope, Jennifer dropped the garbage and cried out instinctively, "Oh, my God! Call the police!"

Jennifer retraced her steps back into her apartment. She slammed the door in an effort to ensure that her children would be spared the horror of seeing their father hanging dead.

Only a few seconds had elapsed since Hank had kicked the chair away from under him. He had seen and heard his wife scream. Hank irrationally thought that she was again depriving him of what he had wanted, the ability to startle her with his own hanging. He thought that she was calling the police and would now spoil his surprise.

Incensed with anger at Jennifer in thwarting his design, Hank's body was pumped up with adrenaline. With a superhuman effort from his strong and wiry body, he pulled himself up on the rope with his hands and somehow extricated his head from the noose. Although his neck was scarred with the fresh rope burn upon it, Hank ignored the pain and jumped down the four feet to the floor. He immediately began to pound both fists on Jennifer's apartment door.

"Don't call the cops to ruin my plan! How dare you, you fucking cunt?" Hank screamed.

When the police arrived minutes later, Hank was still shouting and banging on the door. Even while being handcuffed, he was yelling, "She cheated me! She ruined my plan!"

This case was one of violence by Hank against himself with the intent to inflict permanent emotional harm upon his family. Hank was indicted for the highest level of crime that he could be charged, a nonviolent E felony for violating the order of protection—the least serious felony. It carries a maximum indeterminate period of incarceration of one and one-third to four years in jail.

There is a strong correlation in domestic violence cases between suicide and the murder of one's intimate partner. It was clear to both the prosecutor and the court that if there was a next time, Jennifer and/or the kids might not be as fortunate. They might be victims of a future homicide.

The easy solution would have been to place Hank in jail for the maximum period of incarceration, one and one-third to four years, in addition to issuing a full order of protection for the permitted statutory maximum of seven years. Yet when Hank would be released from jail, he would still be possessed by his demons and may very well still cause harm to his family.

Hank initially was sentenced to six months in jail and then five years' probation, including a residential drug treatment program and psychological counseling followed by a domestic violence accountability program to cover the original charges and the violation of the order of protection. His violation of the order of protection was horrific with potentially awful psychological ramifications for his wife and children. Still it was only punishable by a maximum sentence of one and one-third to four years' incarceration. I wanted to monitor Hank's progress directly and to keep the specter of a greater period of incarceration over his head in the hopes that he would not traumatize his family again. I placed him in jail for six months and wanted to monitor him for five years on probation. As part of his probation, I mandated an alcohol treatment program.

Unfortunately Hank violated the rules of the drug treatment program after a few months and was resentenced for violation of his probation to the statutory maximum of one and one-third to four years in jail. He neglected to avail himself of the services offered. Hank failed to get the mental help that he sorely needed. Although he has been punished and isolated from society for years, his issues remain, and upon his release from prison, his family may have to confront his demons once again.

VIC THE VET

Vic had lived in upstate New York for many years. He worked in an alcohol rehabilitation center for former servicemen through the Veteran's Administration. At one time, Vic had a drinking problem himself.

During the Vietnam conflict, Vic had served as a medic in combat zones. He had seen many casualties of war. Vic had tried to provide comfort and aid to those who were wounded. Sometimes he succeeded. When he did, Vic felt good and somewhat fulfilled. Too many times he was unable to keep the seriously wounded alive until the doctors could treat them. These experiences and his routine observations of lifeless boys in body bags spun Vic into a deep depression and drinking sprees. He became a binge drinker. The time between binges became shorter and shorter as Vic witnessed more and more death and felt more and more pain.

After his honorable discharge from the army in 1968, Vic lived in Brooklyn. He was still a heavy drinker, but his intake had subsided somewhat after leaving Vietnam. Vic met a young woman named Meg. She was a kindergarten teacher. They developed a relationship and dated each other exclusively for a year and a half.

A few years after his relationship with Meg had ended, Vic moved out of Brooklyn to live in upstate New York. Vic's drinking waxed and waned and waxed again until he finally sought help. Through Alcoholics Anonymous and a veteran's support group, Vic stopped drinking, one day at a time. He eventually explored the underlying reasons for his drinking, but never sustained his therapy long enough to reach below the surface of his issues. Vic started to work at the Veteran's Administration shortly after dealing with his alcohol addiction.

Meg meanwhile moved on with her life. She quickly met someone after Vic. She married her new boyfriend within months. Meg became pregnant within a week of her wedding. She had a baby girl that was born two months premature. A few years after the baby was born, Meg left teaching to enter the business world. She became a sales executive for a manufacturing firm.

Nearly twenty-eight years elapsed since Meg and Vic had ended their relationship. Vic was reading one of the previous Sunday newspapers from New York City. He noticed a wedding announcement of a young lady who was listed as Meg's daughter. Vic noted the age of the young lady, subtracted the years since he had been with Meg, and thought that the bride-to-be was his daughter. Vic's calculation had actually been off by two years.

Vic was furious at Meg. Although he had not thought of Meg for more than two decades, he now became convinced that she had deprived him of the joy of being a father. Not only was he stripped of the experience, but he was denied the knowledge that he even had a daughter. Vic took notice of Meg's residence and work addresses. He was not going to be refused the pleasure of fatherhood any longer. Vic's campaign began immediately. He looked up Meg's telephone number and called her.

Without introduction or greeting or any indication that nearly thirty years had passed, Vic blurted out, "Why didn't you tell me we had a daughter?"

"Who is this? This sounds like Vic. Is that you, Vic?" Meg asked in real surprise.

"You guessed right, Meg. I read that our daughter will be married in a few weeks. Why wasn't I told? How could you keep her from me for all these years?" he demanded.

"What do you mean our daughter? Your daughter? She is not your daughter. I guarantee it," Meg answered.

"I don't believe you. I don't know why you are lying to me, but I will get answers. This is not over. It's only the beginning," Vic exclaimed before hanging up.

Over the next few months, Vic engaged in his newfound obsession. He barraged Meg with phone calls and letters at her office and home. Vic would not accept the fact that Meg's daughter was not his, even when Meg repeatedly told him so. On one occasion, Meg put her daughter on the phone to tell Vic that she was not his child. As Meg was unable to dissuade Vic of this notion, she was left with no other choice than to file charges of aggravated harassment and to seek a protective order against him.

Vic entered a plea of guilty to the misdemeanor of aggravated harassment and was sentenced to a conditional discharge, which included the issuance of a one-year order of protection. The order restrained Vic from calling or writing Meg or her daughter and ordered Vic to stay away from their homes and places of business.

All was quiet for the next several months. Then the writing and the calls resumed. Still, Meg was unwilling to pursue further charges. The prosecutor, an understanding woman who had dealt with Meg from the time she filed the original complaint until Vic's plea and sentence, had explained that if Vic should violate the conditions of the order of protection, he would then be facing felony charges of criminal contempt.

Meg had told Vic that if he did not stop calling her, she would have to bring felony charges against him. Apparently undeterred, Vic kept calling and writing. Meg did finally follow up on filing felony contempt charges, but only after Vic actually came into the city to Meg's place of business and caused a scene.

Vic was facing several felony and misdemeanor contempt charges as well as a series of aggravated harassment offenses. The court appointed an attorney for Vic. The attorney demonstrated great care and diligence in filing a motion to dismiss the charges in the interest of justice. The primary compelling reason cited was the post-traumatic stress disorder suffered by Vic as a soldier. He had seen so many of his comrades die in Vietnam.

After the court was assured that Vic no longer believed that he was the father of Meg's daughter, the felony charges were dismissed. Vic entered a plea of guilty to the misdemeanor charges of criminal contempt and aggravated harassment. He was sentenced to three years' probation, including psychological counseling at the Veteran's Administration in upstate New York. A final full order of protection was issued with Meg and her daughter as protected parties. The order of protection directed Vic to stay away from Meg and her daughter. Additionally it prohibited Vic from traveling into New York City for any reason over the next three years without prior court approval. Vic was informed that any violation of the court's order would result in his being sentenced to two years in jail.

Many years have gone by since Vic's plea. There have been no further phone calls to Meg or her daughter. There has been no violation of the order of protection.

ROSA'S RUSE

Rosa and her husband, Raul, were walking purposefully. Both of their T-shirts had blotches of sweat on them because of the ninety-plus-degree temperature and high humidity. Rosa's attention became fixed, and she excitedly pointed out the man across the street to Raul.

"There is the pendejo who shamed me!" she screamed, with anguish etched upon her face.

The two of them ran across the street. As they reached the sidewalk, they both pulled out knives that had razor-sharp blades. Raul with the skill of a surgeon was cutting and slicing the flesh on the man's face, neck, checks, and arms. Rosa was flailing her arm with the knife like a shoemaker using an awl to create holes in the side of the leather for the laces. She kept piercing the man's arms and legs with the point of the blade.

When the man was lying defenseless and still, Raul kicked him in the stomach, spit on him, and cursed him, "Tu madre es una puta." This translated meant, "Your mother is a whore."

One of the merchants with a store on the street observed the onslaught by Raul and Rosa and called 911. By the time the police arrived, the couple had completed the carnage. The man lay on the street with blood streaming out of the slices and gushing out of the holes in his body.

The injured man, whom the police learned to be Pedro, was brought to the nearest hospital. Pedro had lost a lot of blood. After he was given a transfusion and sutured up with more than three hundred stitches on his neck, face, and arms, the police were given permission by the doctors to interview him.

The police were surprised to learn that Pedro was able to identify one of his assailants, Rosa. Pedro had just concluded having an affair with Rosa. He knew that she was married but did not know her husband. Pedro surmised that the man cutting him along with Rosa was her husband.

Pedro related that he too was married. He was worried that his wife and children, whom he loved, would learn about his affair. Pedro was willing to jeopardize his marriage by fooling around outside it, but he was not willing to throw it away for Rosa's needs. Rosa was becoming too serious in their relationship, jealous of Pedro's wife, and obsessed with the idea of the two of them becoming a permanent couple. A life together with Rosa was not Pedro's notion of his future. The day prior to the assault upon him, Pedro had told Rosa that they must end their relationship. He had made up what he thought to be a good story.

"I cannot see you any longer. It is not safe for either of us. My wife is mistrustful of me. She suspects that I am having an affair. She told me, 'I will cut you up if you ever cheat on me and you will never see your children again,'" Pedro declared.

Rosa was not fooled. With tears in her eyes and anger in her heart, Rosa told Pedro, "This is bullshit. You are breaking up with me. You are giving me a line of crap. If you think a wife scorned is one to be reckoned with, watch this woman's fury. You'll be sorry. You'll see!"

Pedro did not see or hear or from Rosa for the rest of that day. Yet on the next afternoon, a strange man and Rosa surprised him on the street. Pedro did not realize that he was under attack until he had been cut and stabbed a number of times. Pedro described the assault to the police as being lightning quick and performed with precision that was violently vengeful. Pedro therefore guessed that the strange man must have been Rosa's husband.

Rosa and Raul were both arrested. They both gave consistent statements to the police. Rosa had been raped by Pedro and had so informed Raul. Raul asked Rosa to walk the streets in the neighborhood with him in hopes of seeing and identifying her attacker. Rosa had suddenly seen Pedro on the street and identified him to Raul as her assailant. They both lost control of their emotions and attacked Pedro with the knives that they had been carrying.

Raul and Rosa were each assigned separate attorneys. Raul's lawyer, a private attorney from a county panel who had agreed to represent indigent defendants for a reduced hourly rate, was skeptical of the story that Raul had related. She was convinced that Raul believed the story to be true, but she simply was not buying it.

Raul's attorney subpoenaed the records to the phone in Rosa and Raul's house as well as the records to Pedro's telephone. The investigation revealed what the attorney had believed was in fact the truth. There were numerous calls back and forth between Pedro and Rosa. They had indeed been having an affair.

Rosa had one small child and was pregnant. It was unclear who the father of the unborn baby was. As the facts unfolded and the entire true version was disclosed to the prosecutor, the crime committed by Raul was viewed in a different light.

Raul was not justified in his criminal action. Yet he thought he was assaulting and seeking revenge on a man who had violated his wife in a base and vile manner. Although his acts were of a criminal nature, Raul was almost a victim himself, perhaps twice a victim. He was lied to by his wife. Rosa used Raul to inflict punishment on Pedro, her lover. Raul did not know about Rosa's infidelity. Raul believed that he was vindicating a wrong done to his wife. Rosa lied again in telling Raul why she wanted to harm Pedro.

Both Rosa and Raul were offered a plea bargain of six months in jail in addition to five years on probation. Rosa's jail sentence was to be served on sixteen weekends so that she could take care of her baby, the unborn child within her, and herself. The sentences were to be staggered. Raul would begin his six months in jail first. When his incarceration was completed, Rosa would begin to start serving her sentence on the weekends. This arrangement was approved by me in order to provide the maximum coverage for Rosa and Raul's young child.

Irony struck Raul again. While he was serving his six-month sentence, the Immigration and Naturalization Service discovered that Raul had overstayed his entry visa into the United States. He was deported after serving his sentence of incarceration. If Rosa were also an illegal alien, her status may have gone undetected as she was only imprisoned on weekends.

Raul certainly was not blameless. His actions were criminal. His deportation was proper. Yet one can feel some sort of compassion for him. Rosa set him up after being unfaithful. Now he is without the only family he has loved and known while banned from the country where his loved ones reside. I am not certain that Solomon would have approved of the justice that I dispensed to Raul when juxtaposed against Rosa's punishment.

VOODOO VILLAIN

Jean was from Haiti. He stood accused of kidnapping his former girlfriend, who was the mother of his child, of burglarizing her apartment, and of violating an order of protection. Jean was able to post a bail bond of two hundred thousand dollars. He was mandated to attend a domestic violence accountability program and was placed on an eight o'clock curfew each night as additional conditions of bail.

While Jean was out on bail during the pendency of his case, he was involved in gun trafficking. During a two-month period, Jean was regularly selling guns to two individuals who were really undercover police officers. The undercover officers purchased a number of weapons from Jean. They could have arrested him weeks ago, but they were working Jean in order to identify those who provided Jean with weapons. The goal of the undercover operation was to remove as many guns from the streets as possible and to go higher and higher into the gun trafficking enterprise in an attempt to bring down the main supplier.

The officers did not know that Jean had a pending case for an assault on the mother of his child. One day, Jean approached the two and asked them for help should he need it.

"I have this girl who is giving me some problems. I have my magic man working on some voodoo powder potion to chill her for good. If he can't do what I want, can I count on you boys helping me out? I will need you to make her disappear. Okay?"

Very surprised, one of the undercover detectives answered, "If you give us a good deal on our next shipment, we can do anything."

Jean replied, "You don't need to do anything now. I think my magic man can handle this, but just in case I may need you."

The officers spoke to their superiors. It was decided that even though they wanted to discover who Jean's suppliers were in order to arrest and to prosecute them, it would be too risky to continue the investigation while Jean was plotting to kill an innocent woman. The authorities had a moral and legal obligation to protect Jean's former girlfriend from potential harm.

The weapons investigation was aborted. Jean was quickly arrested for the illegal sale of firearms and for conspiracy to commit murder. Bail was denied on the new charges, and Jean was remanded to the Department of Corrections.

After a jury trial, Jean was convicted of, inter alia, kidnapping in the first degree, burglary in the first degree, criminal possession of a weapon in the second degree, several counts of criminal sale of a firearm in the third degree, and criminal contempt. He was acquitted of the charge of conspiracy to commit murder. The jury was not convinced that Jean was intent on killing his ex-girlfriend with voodoo powder, perhaps because his plan was so outlandish. The two undercover officers did take this threat seriously. They believed that Jean was deadly serious. Jean was sentenced by me to consecutive terms of imprisonment of twenty years to life on the top kidnapping charge and five to fifteen years on the weapons possession charges, in all, twenty-five years to life.

THE AX MURDERER

Months prior to the opening of the Domestic Violence Court in 1996, a case most disturbing came before me for disposition. A man in his twenties was accused of burying a hatchet in his girlfriend's head. His girlfriend was of similar age.

This murder as alleged was gruesome in nature. The defendant was competent to stand trial. He did not have anything approaching an insanity defense. There was no apparent motive for the murder.

What was even more troubling was the plea bargain offered. The prosecutor, an experienced woman in the homicide bureau, had offered the young man a plea to manslaughter in the first degree with a promised sentence of six to twelve years in jail.[1] This was a rather generous offer for this crime. There had to be some kind of problem with the prosecutor's case. The defendant was going to accept the offer to the manslaughter disposition if I were to give my approval.

I had some reservations. For one, I was concerned why the offer for such a heinous crime was such a lenient one. I was also troubled that the defendant was Caucasian and his murdered girlfriend was African American. In Brooklyn, as well as in other inner-city areas, a great proportion of the defendants are minorities. Judges are, in fact, sensitive to the perception that minorities receive more severe sentences than Caucasians.

The former Kings County district attorney, Charles J. Hynes, had been the fire commissioner of New York City. More importantly, years ago he had been appointed by the then governor, the late Mario Cuomo, to be the special prosecutor in the racially charged and potentially divisive "Howard Beach" case where two African American men were beaten by a group of young white men with bats. One of the victims had been tragically killed by oncoming traffic when he tried to flee from his attackers.

District Attorney Hynes's office also handled the murder of Yankel Rosenbaum, an Australian Hasidic Jew studying in New York who was killed by a mob of black youths shortly after the death of Darren Cato. Darren was a young African American boy who was accidentally killed when hit by a car driven by a Hasidic driver. Both incidents threatened to tear apart not only the racially diverse Crown Heights section of Brooklyn but the entire city too.[2]

Brooklyn has a disparate racial, ethnic, and religious population of about two and one-half million people. There are more than fifty languages spoken in Brooklyn. I wanted to be assured that neither the race of the defendant nor of the decedent was a factor in the plea bargain.

The reasoning for offering the plea was a sound one. Apparently a corpse exhibits some similar characteristics when it is entering rigor mortis as when rigor mortis is ending. The medical examiner listed the time of death based on the ending of rigor mortis thinking that the corpse was beginning the process. The prosecutor explained that the time of death listed in the autopsy report was at a time when the defendant had an alibi for the crime. This understandable error could very well have caused a jury to find there to be a reasonable doubt, resulting in a possible acquittal.

The rationale for offering such a plea to the defendant was reminiscent of another case before me when I was the domestic violence judge. The defendant there was offered and had accepted a seven and one-half to fifteen-year sentence for assault in the first degree. As part of the proposed plea bargain, the defendant would not be subsequently prosecuted for the murder of his wife, should she die, as the law allowed. The defendant had beaten his wife severely. She had been in a coma for about one year. It was more likely than not that the victim would die in the near future. There was a problem of proof regarding the cause of death as the victim's husband had made no statement and there were no witnesses to the incident. The court approved the husband's plea to the attempted murder as well as the assistant district attorney's promise not to prosecute the defendant in the future for the murder of his wife if she should die.

I agreed to take the defendant/ax murderer's plea to manslaughter in the first degree and to impose the negotiated sentence. My first ax murder case was unfortunately not my last, but it will remain etched in my memory forever.

MARIO THE MANIPULATOR

Mario's case was in and out of the courthouse for more than three and one-half years. Numerous adjournments had been granted each time Mario had changed attorneys. His attorneys—there had been three or four—had moved to have Mario examined by two psychiatrists on two occasions to determine his fitness to stand trial. One time, it was believed that he faked a fall in order to feign amnesia. Mario's shenanigans prompted the court-appointed psychiatrists to brand him a malingerer.

The process of having a defendant examined is meant to ascertain whether an accused understands the nature of the charges against him and is able to participate or aid his attorney in presenting a defense. If a defendant is found to be unfit to stand trial, then one is temporarily confined in a psychiatric hospital until the time when he or she becomes fit for trial. If it is determined that there is no likelihood that the defendant will become competent in the reasonable future, then he or she should be civilly committed.[3]

Each time the court orders a defendant to be examined by two psychiatrists, the case must be adjourned for at least thirty days for the psychiatrists to complete their exams and to file their reports. Either side or the court can request such an examination. Either side can contest the finding of fitness or incompetence to proceed to trial. A hearing is held with the examining psychiatrists, relatives, and any other retained psychiatric experts testifying. This process is necessary but understandably time consuming.

Most of the time, a finding of incompetence is uncontested. The accused is held in a psychiatric hospital while a plan of treatment is devised that will promote the defendant's fitness to proceed. The temporary stay can easily exceed six months and often is more than one year. The defendant is entitled to a review by the court of his fitness to proceed to trial every six months.

On occasion, there are a few individuals who somehow have an unusual ability to abuse the process. They are expert malingerers. They are very successful in affecting a mental condition to avoid going to trial. The skilled few are able to fool the examining expert psychiatrists upon whom the court relies in great part in arriving at its conclusion. Thus, sometimes defense counsel, the prosecutor, and the judge are also duped by the expert malingerer.

Mario had been in an upstate psychiatric hospital on one occasion after being found unfit. He had been confined in a psychiatric hospital for more than eight months while his case was pending. His other ploys at pretending to be incompetent were luckily caught by the examining psychiatrists.

Mario was charged with the murder of his fiancée, Paula. On a cool spring night nearly four years before the final disposition of Mario's case, Mario and Paula had spent a night on the town. Mario had rented a stretch Lincoln limousine for the night. The betrothed couple first went for drinks at the River Café to enjoy the magnificent view of the Manhattan skyline from the foot of the Brooklyn Bridge. Then they went to dinner at a prime seafood place in Manhattan. Mario had bought tickets to a hot Broadway show. After the show they returned to Brooklyn for dessert at a popular diner directly across from the federal courthouse on the other side of Cadman Plaza Park. Mario had done it up in a big way.

After the pie à la mode that they had both enjoyed in the diner, Mario and Paula returned to the limo. The chauffeur remained in the driver's seat after Mario requested that the smoked-glass partition be raised to separate the couple from the front of the vehicle. For the next several hours, the car remained parked on Cadman Plaza West. The couple was enveloped in complete privacy. The driver was unable to see or hear what, if anything, was happening in the rear of the limo.

At about four-thirty in the morning, Mario started to bang on the smoked-glass partition. The driver was startled awake from his slumber and lowered the divider.

Mario was sobbing while screaming at the same time, "Call a doctor! Call 911! She's not breathing. I think she's dead!"

When questioned by the authorities, Mario maintained that he had fallen asleep in the back of the limo a few minutes after he and Paula had finished a short period of necking. He had no idea how Paula had died.

The autopsy and other forensic evidence revealed that Paula had suffocated by manual strangulation. Mario was the prime suspect as it was believed that no one else had entered the rear of the limousine after the partition had been raised. There was no other direct proof that Mario was the murderer. Until he was awakened by Mario's screaming and banging, the driver saw or heard nothing unusual from the rear of the car.

The homicide detectives and the detective investigators did their work. Conversations with Paula's family revealed that they believed that Mario had beaten her up frequently. The police were informed that only months ago Mario had purchased a life insurance policy on Paula. There was speculation among Paula's relatives that Mario had plotted to kill her to collect on the insurance policy. A couple of Paula's friends were told by her that she was considering ending her engagement. As Mario had the opportunity and motive, he was indicted for Paula's murder.

After more than three and one-half years of delays caused by repeated requests for adjournments by Mario to hire new counsel, for the newly retained attorney to familiarize him- or herself with the case, and for a number of examinations of Mario by court-appointed psychiatrists to determine his fitness to stand trial, the case was finally set down for jury selection.

On the adjourned date prior to the judge ordering a panel, Mario entered a plea of guilty to the top count of the indictment, reckless and depraved indifference murder. Mario was promised the minimum sentence allowed, fifteen years to life.

Ten days later, the courtroom was packed with friends and relatives of Paula at Mario's sentencing proceeding. The judge, who took the plea bargain while pronouncing the promised sentence of fifteen years to life, announced that he would recommend to the parole board that Mario serve a minimum of twenty-five years in jail.

This announcement clearly was met with approval from Paula's family and friends. Yet, this began a new round of motion practice. Mario's attorney successfully argued that the heralded recommendation to the parole board at the time of sentencing was, in effect, a sentence of twenty-five years to life in jail, the maximum allowable under the law, and more time than what Mario was promised. Mario asked not only for a re-sentence before another judge but requested that his plea of guilty be vacated as well. The court granted that part of Mario's motion to be re-sentenced before another judge but denied the application to vacate his guilty plea.

Mario's case was sent to my part for sentencing. Mario's attorney once again made an application to vacate his guilty plea, claiming that he would be irreparably harmed when he appeared before the parole board because of the original judge's declaration even if he were re-sentenced before a different judge.

The prosecution did not oppose the motion and in fact joined in Mario's request. The prosecutor argued that it was the court's right and responsibility to impose a tougher sentence for such a serious crime. He argued that Mario, throughout his life, showed little regard for the opposite gender. He declared that this was a crime of depravity by a man with a history of domestic violence abuse. Any person who regularly beat up his girlfriend and then plotted to kill her to cash in on her life insurance policy was deserving of the maximum sentence that the law would allow. The prosecutor stated on the record that he wanted the opportunity to try Mario, so that if he were convicted, the court would be able to impose a maximum sentence of twenty-five years to life.

Paula's family was ambivalent. On the one hand, they wanted Mario punished as severely as possible for the murder of their loved one. Yet, they all were united in their desire to have Mario's admission stand on the record. The only way Mario could be punished for more than the original promised sentence of fifteen years to life in jail would be if the court were to allow him to withdraw his guilty plea. Then should he be convicted, the court would be able to sentence Mario to up to twenty-five years to life.

The family was somewhat relieved by the cathartic effect of Mario's admission to murdering Paula. They also knew that at a trial, not only would Mario declare his innocence, but a conviction was never a certainty, especially where there was no witness to the criminal act.

I believed that I had to act firmly and decisively. "Any longer sentence will not return Paula to her family. If I were to grant your application to have your plea back, to allow you to go to trial and to delay these proceedings further, it would be tantamount to permitting you to manipulate the system once again. You [Mario] do not control these proceedings; you do not control the court. I will hold you to your plea of guilty to murder in the second degree. I am now prepared to go forward with the sentencing."[4]

Paula's family members made statements echoing their mixed emotions about holding Mario to his plea versus allowing him to go to trial with the possibility of a higher sentence by permitting him to withdraw his plea.

Mario made his statement: "I only pleaded guilty to give Paula's family closure."

I sentenced Mario to a period of incarceration of fifteen years to life. No one left the courtroom happy, including me.

A VALENTINE'S DAY MOTHER AND CHILD REUNION

I had experienced an emotional and touching moment during trial testimony many years ago. A sixty-five-year-old woman was accused of having hit her ninety-three-year-old mother over the head with a coffee mug, causing the mother physical injuries and much pain. The daughter had refused a plea offer of probation and psychiatric treatment.

The daughter had a difficult time of it. Life had not been terribly kind to her, but she believed that she had it worse than the reality of her situation. The daughter had divorced thirty years before and had never been quite the same since then. She had lived with her mother since her divorce. She was indeed fortunate at the age of sixty-five to have her mother not only alive but alert and fairly vibrant mentally, emotionally, and physically. She was also lucky to have a roof over her head as she never made a lot of money when she was able to find work, which was infrequently. Her mother owned the house where they both lived.

The mother and daughter, both senior citizens, generally got along with one another. They also had their moments when each would get on the other's nerves. This was not a one-way street. Mother would annoy daughter and vice versa.

On the day of the physical altercation, the disagreement was of no moment. The daughter in frustration hit her mother over the head with a fairly weighty coffee mug. The nonagenarian fell to the ground unconscious. She had sustained a concussion and a laceration to the head from the blow as well as black and blue marks to her hands and knees from the fall.

Despite the entreaties from her elderly mother and other members of her family and rejecting her attorney's advice, the daughter refused the prosecutor's offer of probation, including psychiatric counseling if she were to enter a plea of guilty to assault in the second degree, a felony. She was determined to take her case to trial.

For the months leading up to the trial, the daughter remained in jail as she was unable to make one thousand dollars' bail. She had nowhere to live as her other relatives were unwilling to take her in. Her mother was willing, but the court had issued a full order of protection mandating that she stay away from her mother and from her mother's house. It was ascertained at trial that her mother did visit her at Riker's Island, often spending almost two hours each way traveling there by public transportation. Many times she waited for an hour for her daughter to be produced for the visit.

On Valentine's Day, the mother was called to testify at her daughter's trial. This was something the mother was reluctant to do. Her daughter needed some psychological help, and the mother was worried that, after she was gone, no one would intercede on her daughter's behalf. Since her daughter refused help voluntarily or as part of a plea of guilty, the mother was determined to help her daughter in the only way she knew and in the only avenue left to her. She would testify at trial so if her daughter were to be found guilty, I could mandate a referral to a mental health professional.

After the mother had concluded her trial testimony, she expressed her love and concern for her daughter who was incarcerated during the trial. The mother requested me to allow her to give her daughter a kiss. I gave her permission. Thank goodness my court officers had faith in my judgment. Never before had I permitted an incarcerated defendant to have physical contact with a complainant.

The two women, both senior citizens, kissed and hugged with sincere love and emotion.

"How are you doing, sweetheart?" the mother asked the daughter.

"I am doing fine, Ma. How are you feeling?" the daughter replied.

The mother, with love and a lifetime of devotion to her child, implored, "Okay, but I want you to get some help so you can come home."

There was not one dry eye in the courtroom. The daughter discontinued counseling a few months after her mother passed away. With the consent of the prosecutor and probation, she was not in violation of her probation, as she was no longer a danger to anyone. After a few years on probation without incident, it seemed that the daughter was doing well. Her probation was terminated early. It was a final gift to a mother who had always loved her daughter.

SLAUGHTERHOUSE SLAYING

Mary claimed that Lionel, her boyfriend, had physically abused her in the past. They had lived together for almost three years. They argued often but almost always made up within an hour or two. He was exciting to Mary and so challenging. She was very jealous and many times thought that he was going out with other women. There were also long periods that she truly loved him and when he made her happy. Mary was generally glad that Lionel was her boyfriend and lover.

Lionel worked at a slaughterhouse in Brooklyn—not a butcher shop, but a place where live animals were killed. Almost daily, Mary would meet Lionel at the slaughterhouse when his shift was over. Mary wanted to make sure that Lionel would be coming home to her and not disappearing into the late hours of the night or early morning. She would have to walk through an anteroom and then through a second huge area where the livestock stood, and then into another large space where the animals—goats, chickens, calves, and sheep—were slaughtered.

Lionel went to work at the slaughterhouse early one weekday morning in the middle of the summer. As Lionel emerged from the subway at 6:45 a.m., a time when most people were just waking up to begin their day, it was already hot and humid. He walked five long blocks from the station to the shop. He passed two blocks of commercial and industrial buildings followed by three blocks of concrete rubble that could have easily been bombed-out Dresden after the Second World War. As Lionel neared the entrance of the slaughter shop, he noticed the hundreds of flies, seemingly standing still in space, with their wings fluttering. The flies, surrounding the scores of huge meat hooks hanging by the loading docks, anxiously awaited the carcasses that would soon be brought out.

, When Lionel entered his work area, he put on his white body apron that would shortly be splattered red with the blood of the animals that he would kill. Lionel did not often think about the violent aspects of his job, but when he did, it was the bearing of the animals that confounded him. The animals in the area adjacent to the killing stage had to sense the carnage nearby. Yet they never resisted to entering the place where they would soon be slaughtered. They never uttered a squeal out of anguish or fear. Lionel thought that this was odd.

Around three in the afternoon, about an hour before the end of his shift, Lionel beeped Mary and left a message for her to meet him at his workplace. Mary came into the slaughterhouse at about 3:45 p.m. as was her custom. She came into Lionel's work area.

Lionel said, "I am going to meet my friend Rick later, and I can't hook up with you until at least seven thirty."

This started a tremendous argument because Mary assumed that Lionel was going to meet another woman. This was not an uncommon occurrence between the two of them even at Lionel's job. The animals didn't seem to mind the arguments and neither did Lionel's boss.

"I'm going to leave and never come back," Mary finally retorted.

"Just go then." Lionel concluded the spat and turned his attention to a goat that he had just killed.

Mary couldn't bear the fact that Lionel didn't seem to care that she was leaving him now and maybe forever. His detachment only served to enrage her more.

"Oh, you don't care; you don't care!" Mary screamed as she seized one of the butchering knives nearby.

Mary started walking toward him as he was leaning forward and downward to continue to cut up the goat that he was handling. Lionel was unaware of what was transpiring before him. He stood up and the knife that Mary was holding entered his chest. Instinctively, he stepped back. Mary, still clutching the knife, threw it to the ground when she saw Lionel holding his chest, futilely trying to stem the gushing of the blood from his breast area.

Mary started banging on the wall for someone to help her. Lionel's foreman came in, and Lionel, who was still standing, implored his foreman to call an ambulance. The foreman, who was so used to killing animals and seeing their blood, was astonished to see a man cut up and human blood staining the floor of the slaughterhouse. He was momentarily frozen until the enormity of the situation penetrated his consciousness causing him to run out and call 911.

Lionel then fell down on the ground where his own blood blended in with the animal's blood that branded the floor. Mary knelt down beside him in an effort to stop the bleeding and to comfort Lionel.

The police arrived seconds before the EMS unit. The officers were directed by the foreman to where Lionel was lying. In response to their question as to the identity of the perpetrator, the foreman told them that Lionel's girlfriend "must have stabbed him." The EMS technicians treated Lionel as they were whisking him off to the hospital. Mary was arrested and brought to the precinct.

Mary made a number of statements claiming that the stabbing was an accident, but they were inconsistent in one very important respect. At the crime scene Mary told the first officer to respond to the radio run of a stabbing in progress, "I got into an argument with my boyfriend, and he asked me for the knife. I threw it at him and it hit him in the chest." She repeated this version of the incident approximately one hour later at the precinct.

About one and one-half hours after her second statement, Mary was again advised of her Miranda rights at the precinct. She reported in pertinent part, "I came at him with the knife like I was going to stab him. He stood up and I poked the knife at him, but I didn't realize that I stabbed him. I only wanted to scare him. The next thing I see, Lionel is grabbing his chest and I saw a lot of blood." This version was given again soon thereafter before an assistant district attorney and memorialized in videotape.

Each time that Mary provided a statement to law enforcement officials of what had occurred, she gave an inconsistent version of the events that led up to the stabbing. Every time Mary was questioned, she expressed an interest in and concern for Lionel's condition. In each of her three statements at the station house, Mary reported that Lionel had been physically abusive toward her in the past, using his hands most of the time. One time he had hit her with a stick, busting up her left eyebrow. Another time, Mary had Lionel arrested for punching her in the mouth. It was clear that on the day of the incident, Lionel had not hit Mary, nor had he threatened her in any way.

It was undisputed that the knife penetrated the left side of Lionel's breastbone and ruptured his aorta. He fell to the ground bleeding just like the animals that he had butchered. In less than three minutes after being placed in the ambulance, he was dead.

Mary had given two different theories of an accident. It would be most difficult to convince a jury that the trial variant, whatever it might be, was the truth. She had very little choice but to let her lawyer work out the best possible disposition.

Mary, who was soon to turn thirty, was an attractive woman whom most men would call pretty. She had experienced a most difficult and hard life.

Mary's mother had disowned both she and her sister after her father had died from AIDS-related causes. Her grandmother raised her, but she was purported to have been abusive to Mary and her sister. Mary ran away from her grandmother when she was only fourteen and had been on her own since then. Although the incidents of past abuse allegedly inflicted by Lionel against her and evidence of battering and its effects would not be admissible at trial as Mary was not entitled to a defense of justification, the prosecutor was receptive to Mary's history with Lionel and was sympathetic to her background.

After the prosecutor consulted with Lionel's family, I allowed Mary, with the People's consent, to enter a plea of guilty to manslaughter in the first degree. In essence, Mary admitted to killing Lionel while having the intent to inflict serious physical injury upon him.

At her sentence, Mary was contrite and faced Lionel's family, apologizing to them for her actions and for their loss of their loved one. Her face and words exhibited the ring of truth and earnestness. It was sincere but not enough to undo the pain and the damage that had been done. I sentenced Mary to twelve years' incarceration as agreed upon in the plea bargain.

SLY SHERYL AND THE UNUSUAL BIRTHDAY PRESENT

The headline read: "Brooklyn Sanitation Worker Shot Dead while Serving Girlfriend with Protective Order." Eighty-five percent of my cases in the Brooklyn Domestic Violence Court dealt with male defendants who were accused of some type of criminal abuse against their female intimate partners. More than 10 percent concerned elder abuse and same-sex intimate violence. In less than 5 percent, women were accused of perpetrating violence against men with whom they had an intimate relationship.[5] Many times the women claim to have been abused. They allege that their conduct was not criminal but justified as done in self-defense or violent resistance or female resistance. Yet sometimes it is clear that the acts were simply criminal, to exert their power in an attempt to control.

Sheryl and Daryl had met in 1993, dated, and then lived together from 1995 to 2001. They had a son born in 1997. Shortly after the birth of their son, Sheryl became possessive of Daryl and extremely jealous even though she had no reason to be. The two began to argue a lot, and Daryl's love for Sheryl gradually disappeared from the strain of Sheryl's unfounded accusations. He moved out in June of 2001.

Daryl was a New York City sanitation worker and had been employed there for nine years. He had a steady income and was a good provider who supported his two children well and gave Sheryl money for herself without being ordered to do so by any court. He never missed a scheduled visit with the children and was eager to spend as much time with them as Sheryl would allow.

Daryl thought their separation would indicate to Sheryl that he had made a clear break in their relationship. Daryl had a very active social life after leaving Sheryl. This seemed to drive Sheryl over the edge. If she could not have him, no one else would either.

Sheryl called him many times each day on his cell phone while he was working on the street. Daryl had to tell her what he thought she had known but apparently did not: "We are through. I will be a good father to our kids, but you and I are no longer an item. You should not be calling me unless it concerns our children."

Despite this direct approach, Sheryl persisted in harassing Daryl. She continued to call him numerous times each day. She would go to Daryl's apartment uninvited and ring his doorbell continuously until he would be forced to answer. When on one occasion Daryl refused to answer, she created such a racket that he feared the landlord might ask him to leave. On two occasions she went to his sanitation terminal at the beginning of his shift and created such a scene, cursing at him and screaming, that he was afraid that he might eventually lose his job if she persisted.

Daryl went to Family Court and obtained a temporary order of protection. Two days later, he asked his sister, Carol, to go with him to serve Sheryl with the stay-away order and the notification of the upcoming court date. Carol really did not want to get involved because Sheryl was still the mother of her nephew, but it was Daryl's birthday and she knew that Daryl had no other way to deal with this very bad situation.

They drove to Sheryl's apartment and saw her coming out of the front entrance of the building. Daryl's sister exited the car and attempted to give Sheryl the court order. Sheryl asked Carol what it was. Carol told her. Sheryl said she would accept it if she first would be able to speak to Daryl for five minutes alone. Carol went back to the car to tell Daryl of Sheryl's request. Daryl acquiesced.

Sheryl walked over to Daryl's car, sat down in the front passenger seat, and closed the door. Carol stood on the sidewalk about twenty feet away from the car. After about three minutes, she heard two shots. Carol then saw Sheryl exit the car and run down the street. Carol ran over to the car and saw Daryl motionless with two wounds, one to the chest and one to the side of the head. Daryl was pronounced dead at the scene when the ambulance arrived.

Sheryl was apprehended and indicted for murder. She entered a plea of guilty before another judge. The promised sentence was twenty years to life. Later that judge allowed her to withdraw her guilty plea and she went to trial.

Sheryl was convicted and sentenced to twenty-five years to life in jail. Her conviction was reversed by the appellate court, based on the trial court's failure to charge the jury on the law of justification or self-defense. Self-defense or justification defense allows a person to use deadly physical force to defend herself if she reasonably believes that the other person is using or about to use deadly physical force upon her. The conduct is then deemed justified under the law and not criminal.

Upon remand from the appellate court, the case was sent to my part for retrial. The jury was impaneled and the evidence unfolded as explained except for Sheryl's testimony. Sheryl claimed that upon entering the car, she and Daryl struggled when Daryl grabbed for a .22 caliber pistol in the console of his car. The gun went off twice during the tussle, hitting Daryl both times. After summations, I charged the jury on the law, giving a justification or self-defense instruction.

The jury was hung, that is, split on whether Sheryl was guilty of murder. Sheryl was lucky that this was a jury trial. If it had been a bench trial, I would have found her guilty of murder. Why would Daryl shoot her when he did not even intend to talk to her? His presence at her building was only necessitated by his need to drive his sister, Carol, to serve Sheryl with a full stay-away order of protection. The verdict made no sense at all. As the petitioner in Family Court, Daryl was a party to the proceeding. As a party, he was not allowed to serve the order of protection.

The defense attorney and prosecutor requested permission to speak to the jury to ascertain how the vote was split. I allowed them to do so as both wanted to know whether a third trial could be averted. I wanted to avoid another trial because the parents and family of Daryl had gone through so much—a guilty plea, withdrawal of that plea, a trial and conviction, a reversal of that trial, and then a second trial that resulted in a hung jury. In my mind, the emotional ordeal that Daryl's parents had endured and would continue to endure was more than anyone should have to experience. Sheryl gave different versions of the events. When she originally entered a plea of guilty, she admitted to intentionally killing Daryl; in her motion to withdraw her plea, she contended that it was an accident; at trial, she testified that she was justified.[6]

The jury informed the attorneys that they were deadlocked ten to two for conviction of murder. The two jurors who voted for an acquittal thought that Sheryl may have acted in self-defense. The district attorney's office offered Sheryl a plea to manslaughter in the first degree and a sentence of fifteen years' imprisonment. Sheryl, armed with the knowledge that the jury almost convicted her of murder, agreed to accept the plea. I approved the plea agreement. It was the best outcome considering that Daryl's parents would be spared further emotional turmoil and they would hear Sheryl admit to intentionally shooting their son.

THE DEVIL MADE ME DO IT

It was questionable where the murder took place, but Joyce, barely thirty-six years old, lay dead in her bathtub. Roger had strangled her. He tried to blame his actions on his addiction to drugs.

I believed that the research literature on drug addiction or alcoholism as the cause of violence is clear—the abuse of drugs or alcohol may exacerbate domestic violence, but it is not the cause of it. Many criminals attempt to hide behind their addiction for their violent acts, but there are many addicts who are not violent and who do not engage in acts of domestic violence.

Although Roger was only forty years old, he was already a career criminal. He had five misdemeanor and two violent felony convictions. The two felony convictions were for an assault in 1991 and for a robbery in 1996. Roger had been sentenced to one year and five years in jail for the assault and robbery convictions, respectively. He had a number of bench warrants on his record for not returning for scheduled court appearances. Roger also violated the conditions of his parole on the robbery conviction.

Roger claimed that he and Joyce had been lovers for a few months. Joyce informed him that she was pregnant. Although Roger maintained that her unborn child was not his, he nonetheless moved into her apartment ostensibly because of Joyce's pregnancy.

Within weeks of his moving in, Joyce purportedly told Roger that she was not pregnant. Roger became incensed and enraged that Joyce had lied to him and tricked him into living with her.

Roger was a self-proclaimed drug addict. His drug of choice was cocaine. That very night he had a bitter verbal dispute with Joyce over her feigned pregnancy and her manipulation of him. Then Roger claimed to have resorted to his old friend, his regular escape from reality, crack cocaine. It was only then that he strangled Joyce to death.

The next morning, Roger began shouting out of the window of his apartment, "Help! I need a doctor. We're hurt. Help!"

A man who was sweeping the sidewalk in front of his private home across the street from Joyce's apartment heard Roger's pleas for medical assistance. The man was coincidentally an employee of the coroner's office, the Office of the Chief Medical Examiner of the City of New York. He knew exactly what to do. He called 911 and asked for the Emergency Medical Service (EMS) and the police to respond to Joyce's apartment building. Upon EMS's arrival, the man directed the technicians to the floor from where Roger had yelled.

When entering Joyce's apartment, the EMS technicians thought that Roger needed medical attention as he exhibited lacerations to the neck and scratches to the left wrist and chest right below the left nipple. It was later discovered that these wounds were self-inflicted.

Roger first motioned them away from himself and then directed the technicians to the bathroom, where Joyce lay motionless in the bathtub. "Not me, in the bathroom. The one who needs help is in the bathroom!"

After it was determined that Joyce was dead, one of the technicians asked Roger, "How did this happen?"

Roger responded, "You'll find out how she died when you cut her open. I only wish I could have died with her."

A few minutes later, Roger admitted to the technicians that he and Joyce had a fight the day before and that he had placed her in the bathtub.

The Office of the Chief Medical Examiner's office conducted an autopsy of Joyce's body. An external exam revealed marks on her neck. An internal examination uncovered a rupture or fracture of the cricoid cartilage of the neck. Both of these observations were consistent with the medical examiner's conclusion that Joyce's death was caused by manual strangulation and blunt force trauma to the head.

Roger at first claimed that he did not remember what had occurred in Joyce's apartment that fateful evening. He was taken to Kings County Hospital for observation after his arrest. He acted violently while at the hospital.

Roger was declared fit to proceed to trial after an examination by two court-appointed psychiatrists. Eventually he gave up trying to blame his conduct on drug addiction and placed the blame of Joyce's death and murder squarely where it belonged: upon his own shoulders. Roger entered a plea of guilty to the crime of murder in the second degree and was sentenced to a term of imprisonment of eighteen and one-half years to life. At his sentence, I was relieved for Joyce's family that he expressed remorse for her death and acknowledged that he was responsible for her murder.

Chapter Seventeen

What Can We Do to Protect Abused Women and to Aid Them to Help Themselves?

The executive and legislative branches of government, both state and federal, have done much in the last twenty-five years to provide the police and the courts with many of the tools necessary to combat the scourge of domestic violence.[1] The criminal justice system continues to pour more resources into the prosecution of domestic violence crimes through mandatory arrest policies and primary aggressor anti-stalking and anti-strangulation statutes; through the elevation of violations of protective orders to the status of felonies where an aggravating factor is present or when the accused had violated such a court order in the recent past; through the mandatory meting out of harsher sentences without parole for perpetrators of violent crime; through the enforcement by prosecutors of their "no drop" policy of prosecuting domestic violence crimes even without the help of the complainant;[2] through the enactment of rape shield laws and criminalization of human trafficking; through our government's federalization of certain domestic violence crimes and a prohibition against weapon possession for those persons convicted of felonies and domestic violence misdemeanors and those subject to an order of protection;[3] and the creation of specialized courts such as domestic violence and integrated domestic violence courts.[4] What more can we do? How can we help?

Technological developments have helped in our response to and can continue to aid in combating domestic violence. Computers in patrol cars that contain information or copies of protective orders can be used to eliminate the need of a victim as a complaining witness. This was first utilized in Quincy, Massachusetts, and is now available in other locales, including New York. There a police officer observes a woman crying and sitting in a car with a man at a known spot where lovers park. The officer asks the woman if everything is all right. She answers yes. The officer returns to his vehicle and runs the license plate, and the car is registered to Mr. Jones. The same individual is listed as an enjoined party in a protective order with Mrs. Jones listed as the protected party. The officer returns to the car and asks whether the man is Mr. Jones and whether the woman is Mrs. Jones. If both answers are in the affirmative, an arrest is made and the prosecution may proceed without a victim. Cameras with film or digital cameras have recently been provided to every patrol car in New York City. This should be done in every community throughout the country so that evidence can be gathered at the earliest possible stage in order to help ameliorate and to counteract the degree of victims' recantation and lack of cooperation and in order to help prove a case even without the victim/complainant. Domestic violence 911 calls should be monitored and mapped. This would provide the police with hot sheet information.

In Largo, Florida, the criminal justice community had developed a system, albeit on a small scale, of utilizing the Internet to play the 911 domestic violence call at the defendant's initial arraignment along with a display of photos of the victim taken by the arresting officer at the crime scene, as well as the initial police report. It is anticipated that criminal court pleas at the first appearance will rise from 16 percent to 64 percent. With the arrival and improvement of a digital phone system, such a system may one day become a reality. The success of this project is important to the administration of justice for three reasons. First, in misdemeanor courts the dismissal rate in domestic violence cases is typically between 50 and 70 percent. Any action that would reduce dismissal rates other than on the merits of a case ought to be explored by the criminal justice system. Secondly, if more cases can be disposed of at an early stage in the proceeding, then the courts will be free to turn their attention and resources to trying those remaining cases. Thirdly, the discovery of the contents of the 911 tape by defense counsel at an early stage will aid in the evaluation and preparation of the case. The use of the Internet/Intranet for the display of photos of the victim at the crime scene as well as the early disclosure and the release of the 911 tape and the initial police write-up should be a priority welcomed by the prosecution and the defense bar. Psychologists, sociologists, actuaries, and criminologists should work on perfecting risk and lethality assessment instruments that help in the statistical prediction of homicides among defendants accused and/or convicted of domestic violence–related crimes. Courts should use and expand the use of these risk assessment and lethality assessment tools available today to make better determinations regarding the setting of conditions of bail and sentencing.

I envision a technological system where a judge can access a victim's emergency room records at the initial criminal court arraignment so that better and more informed bail determinations can be made. All states ought to enact legislation mirroring the federal bail statute[5] where the presiding judge may consider the safety of the complainant in setting appropriate bail conditions.[6] Sadly, the safety of a victim of a crime is not a factor that a judge can take into account in all jurisdictions in domestic violence cases. Electronic monitoring through probation departments as a condition of bail should be available to state judges as it is in the federal system. Laws should be passed similar to "Clare's Law" in Great Britain and a police initiative in New Zealand called the Family Violence Information Disclosure Scheme whereby persons are allowed to inquire from the police whether their partner has a domestic violence conviction.[7]

Police precincts are often the first stops for victims of domestic violence. Copies of orders of protection should be available to victims and officers on the beat. The copies of the protective orders or computer-generated facsimiles ought to be available at the local station house. This would enhance the image and public perception of community policing of domestic violence cases. This is a great and easy way for the police departments to engage in positive public relations. The local precinct is and should be positively portrayed as a bastion of safety and protection.

With the development by many states of a domestic violence registry, the placement of orders of protection in the station house may be achieved nationally through computer technology. The official entering of all orders of protection, both civil and criminal, in the respective state and national violence registry in every instance would enable women to be protected from their abusers whenever and wherever they may travel or live.[8] Permanent orders of protection, even civil orders, may be the most effective intervention for the protection of victims from their abusers.[9] Orders of protection when working in combination with a monitoring court, such as the Brooklyn Felony Domestic Violence Court, may ultimately prove to be the best way to deal with the scourge of domestic violence. Sadly, only 20 percent of the approximately two million women in the United States who are physically abused, stalked, or raped by partners each year obtain protective orders.[10] As women become more confident in the criminal justice system's response and method of handling complaints of domestic violence, this statistic may hopefully change. Each state must give full faith and credit to an order of protection as long as the defendant or respondent had notice and an opportunity to be heard.

While we have started to protect the victim in the criminal realm, we must do more in terms of the civil arena and social services both prior to and after any criminal conduct. How then can we afford to neglect the needs of victims in areas other than criminal justice?

We need community prevention efforts to reduce incidence of domestic violence in the first place. Our ministers, priests, and rabbis should not encourage battered wives to remain in the home for the sake of keeping the family together. Our clergy should understand that by doing so they assume the responsibility of the next beating or worse. Our neighbors should be vigilant to report or to intercede when observing abuse. We should stop and ask women on the street who display visible bruising if there is any way to help them. There should be more school-based programs and educational programs in youth centers to alert youngsters of teen dating violence. High schools should develop a curriculum of instruction concerning teen dating violence and what is not acceptable behavior. College orientation should require every student to attend a program on sexual assault, including a clear message that no means no and yes must be stated and not simply implied by failing to say no.

For those suspected of child abuse, there should be programs entailing home visitation by nurses, social workers, paraprofessionals, and members of the community to prevent violence as well. Probation and parole officers should ensure that those who have been convicted of domestic violence crimes abide by the conditions of the orders of protection.

We need more and better shelters for abused women, shelters that do not require the victim to choose between staying with an abusive spouse and giving up her fourteen-year-old son to foster care because the shelter prohibits teenage boys to reside there. Shelters are an integral and very often necessary vehicle that a woman must have available in effectuating a safety plan. A safety plan and thus a shelter are indispensable when a woman is to leave an abusive partner.

Women should not need to make impossible and improper choices as they once had to do routinely. Sarah Buel, a former victim of domestic violence and former prosecutor of domestic violence cases in Norfolk County, Massachusetts, and now a nationally treasured expert in the field, relates a story of how one of her friends and her young son would be repeatedly battered by her husband. The wife would invariably separate from her spouse. Ms. Buel would take her friend's child in as a foster child. Ms. Buel never would understand why her friend always took her husband back as Ms. Buel's focus was on the son. Then days after her friend and son were brutally murdered by her husband, Ms. Buel learned how the unthinkable became possible. She discovered that that state's equivalent of the bureau of child welfare or agency for children's services required at that time, and in fact put in writing to the mother, that her son would only be placed back with the mother if the family unit were intact—that is, she had to stay with the father.[11] Now that was more than thirty years ago. Recently, however, women in many parts of the country were asked to choose and to balance whether to complain about being a victim of domestic violence and risk being charged as a neglectful parent in a family court proceeding.[12] This scenario pits the possible loss of custody of a mother's child against her remaining with an abusive spouse. We, the criminal justice system, the child protective system, and society at large, should never again place women in the position of making a "Sophie's choice" in these kinds of matters.

We can try to ensure that women and children live without fear in their homes. We can try to think outside the box. In Israel, a small program called Bet Noam has taken an innovative approach to combating domestic violence.[13] This program should be explored here in America. The men who are accused of committing domestic violence are removed from their homes. The women and children would then be able to continue their lives without interruption. There would be no displacement of residence for the mothers and children, no change of employment for the women, and no transfer of schools for the children. Bet Noam, meaning Nice House, is a residence for male accused batterers with a capacity to house thirteen men plus a sleep-in counselor. The men go to work each day. Upon their return to the residence, each man on a rotating basis has chores to do such as shopping, cooking, and cleaning. Each night after dinner, the men have a group counseling session. Each man also undergoes individual intensive counseling once a week. The men live in the residence for a four-month period from Sundays through Thursdays. On the weekends, Friday and Saturday in Israel, they must stay at another place but not at the residence of their wife and children. After completion of their four-month period, the accused must leave the residence. Each man is mandated to continue therapy once a week for one year. A new man is then rotated into the residence. There are far more applicants than there are available spaces. Each man hopes that the judge presiding over his criminal case will take into consideration the accused's participation in the adjudication or sentence, although the judge is not required to do so. One of the salutary benefits to women is that this four-month period has given the wives an opportunity to commence divorce proceedings without emotional or physical resistance. The women have been provided with a cooling-off period in which they are permitted to contemplate the direction in which to take their lives in a calm manner away from physical intimidation or subtle coercion. One difficulty that the organizers have met in starting and expanding this program is the political and societal perception that Bet Noam is a program that is beneficial to batterers, not to those who are abused. This too may be an obstacle in developing such a residential program in the United States. Yet, with proper education this may be possible.

What more can we do? The police and the FBI do not ask the president of the bank that has been robbed five times why the bank still keeps money in their vault. Why are we so hard on women who do not leave their abusers as soon as we would like? It is important not to ask why, but it is equally important to provide the tools to enable these women to leave when they chose to leave an abuser. Remember these women may be smarter than we are, as a woman is 75 percent at greater risk of being murdered when she is ending the abusive relationship, preparing to leave, or actually leaving her abuser.

First, we must support a victim with compassion, caring in an understanding manner. We should listen to her concerns and not be dismissive. We should be a friend. We should find out who this woman is rather than who we think she is. We should not blame the victim, as many times she is already incorrectly blaming herself. The victim should be made to realize that no one deserves to be threatened or beaten. Victims are often unaware that there is help available. We should provide information where a victim can get help and how to access relevant hotlines and direct her to an advocate for battered women. Advocates will be able to explain to the victim her rights under the federal and state domestic violence laws. An advocate can supply information on how to locate and access the local police precinct, emergency shelters, the family and criminal courts as well as the local prosecutor's office; can explain how to obtain civil or criminal orders of protection and oftentimes walk the victim through the process; and can help develop a safety plan or develop strategies that will reduce the risk of further violence.

There are many resources that victims or their families or friends can access to obtain assistance. To name a few here may be helpful:

1. National Domestic Violence Hotline: www.thehotline.org;
2. National Network to End Domestic Violence: www.nnedv.org;
3. National Coalition Against Domestic Violence: www.ncadv.org;
4. Safe Horizon: www.safehorizon.org;
5. Women's Law, A Project of the National Network to End Domestic Violence: www.womenslaw.org.

There are family justice centers where victims can get all this information and legal assistance in areas such as housing and employment. These are approximately eighty family justice centers in existence or in formation throughout the country, including in Brooklyn, Manhattan, and the Bronx in New York; Minneapolis, Minnesota; Salt Lake City, Utah; Tacoma, Washington; South Bend, Indiana; Knoxville, Tennessee; and San Diego, California.[14] Access to resources and services are necessary so that victims and their children can go forward with their lives. This involves not only ensuring their physical safety, but it must also include working on numerous other problems—who will pay the rent or who will watch the children when she goes to school, to work, or to get retrained. Job and housing assistance provide the economic means necessary for a victim to leave an abusive relationship. We need more of these to help women to transition into permanent housing. In New York City, shelter population for the homeless has increased substantially due to domestic violence.[15] We need to cut out the red tape in long-term housing placement and adequate child care.

We have made much progress since the 1960s when the police, the courts, the medical profession, and society as a whole did not consider domestic violence a crime but merely a private matter.[16] Although we can and will do much better, this country in dealing with domestic violence is light-years ahead of much of the world. It is unbelievable that in this day and age the high court of a developed, cultured, and civilized Western European democracy in the relatively recent past has declared that it is not a crime to discipline or hit one's wife so long as it is not done too often or too harshly. It is equally unfathomable that rape assailants can go without punishment in certain countries if marriage is proposed to the victim.

In 1997, I testified before the Commission on Domestic Violence Fatalities convened by then governor George Pataki.[17] I had a rather large wish list at that time suggesting ways to improve the handling of domestic violence cases. Many of those suggestions have been implemented. Yet despite our recent and rapid progress in dealing with domestic violence, we have a long, continuous, and persistent journey ahead. Domestic violence is often deadly violence. Where the relationship between the murderer and the victim are known, 49 percent of women murdered in New York City are killed by their husbands or boyfriends.[18] We must not allow domestic violence to fade into the flavor or fad of the day, month, or year.

Chapter Eighteen

What Should We Do
with the Perpetrators?

Perpetrators who are convicted of violent acts against their intimate partners should be punished or incarcerated as the law allows. Courts such as the Brooklyn Domestic Violence Court should engage in intensive judicial supervision of probationers and those who are awaiting disposition of the accusations against them. Those who violate orders of protection or who commit acts that are criminal but are not of a violent nature may receive some jail and probation. Convicted defendants, whether probationers who served less than six months in jail or parolees who have served years (remember almost all of them will be released from prison at some time), should be placed in long-term cognitive behavioral therapy programs, not anger management programs, as part of their probation or parole.

When domestic abuse reached the point of being physical, coercive, sexual, or other criminal conduct, it would come to my court. What I have come to learn from working as a judge, attending domestic violence training, and talking to victim advocates and feminists is that domestic violence is an attitudinal issue that pervades our society.

The "X" and "Y" generations[1] are titillated by stories of guns, violence, and especially sexual and physical domination of women by men. Should we have expected less when culture and society has been historically and predominantly misogynistic?

A prominent feminist told me long ago that domestic violence is not only a crime but conduct by men based on a sense of entitlement.[2] She informed me that this feeling of entitlement could only be eradicated by an attitudinal change in society. It was evident to me that this shift would be creeping and snail-like. After this conversation, I realized that even the Beatles, who sang and wrote such beautiful music that endures, produced a song that included male entitlement and threats of domestic violence ("Run for Your Life").[3]

Still there is hope and we are still experimenting with solutions. As mentioned in chapter 2, the statistics seem to indicate that the incidence of intimate partner abuse has been significantly reduced since 1994.

Professionals in the field believe that much of domestic abuse is learned behavior. If violence and abusive behavior are learned, then perhaps they can be unlearned.

How can an attitude of entitlement and thus domestic violence be unlearned? Anger management is not the answer. Anger management is not for perpetrators of domestic abuse. It is for people who have anger toward most anyone—strangers, police, road rage, and so on. The literature seems to indicate that even batterer intervention programs have no long-term effect in reducing the incidence of abuse,[4] although I did find it useful as a monitoring tool to reduce any possibility of abuse while the case was pending.[5]

Can we afford to await the many years, perhaps hundreds of years, to have society's attitude change to one of equality and away from entitlement? I would answer this question with an emphatic "no!" Our police, courts, and other institutions must triage this problem, while attitudes change universally. Strong judges should protect the constitutional and procedural rights of defendants, while holding batterers accountable and protecting the safety of the complainants while the criminal or family court case is pending and, when legally possible, even after the case is concluded, through the monitoring of probationers and parolees.

Individuals, however, do change. It is clear that the laws in our country have been enacted and have fostered change. The women's and victims' rights movements have been the engine driving legislation. The violence against women laws may have influenced a modification in attitudes and resulted in a greater awareness of the issues and a concomitant reduction in the incidence of domestic abuse since 1994. Is it also because of the development of domestic violence courts, dedicated domestic violence prosecution bureaus, and better trained police and improved education for advocates and other professionals who deal with battering and its effects? Is it because of a greater access to civil services for those victims who secure civil or criminal protective orders? Is it due to the work of cognitive therapy programs that employ strategies to deal not only with the perpetrator but also with the victim?[6]

An often overlooked, but what I believe to be an important, attitude changer are male groups against intimate partner violence such as "A Call to Men," which are run by strong men such as Ted Bunch, Tony Porter, and Ulester Douglas.[7]

I often had asked defendants, "How would you feel if someone had abused your daughter, mother, or sister?" I then would point out that the complainant was someone else's daughter, mother, or sister. I am unsure whether this had a long-term effect on the defendant, but it did cause many defendants to pause and think about what I had just said.

I am not sure whether it is any of these individually or all of them working together in combination. What I do know is that when I started this work in 1996, I knew that there was a great deal that I did not know. I realized that it was important to keep an open mind to new strategies and possible solutions, especially in dealing with perpetrators and reducing the violence. Even when I had served almost a dozen years presiding over domestic violence felonies, I still tried to be receptive to innovative ways to help ameliorate the problem of intimate-partner abuse. We must continue to recognize that domestic violence is a most complex issue. No one who works in this field in any respect should think they have seen and know everything.

What to do with the perpetrators is an evolving answer. We are still working on this one.

Chapter Nineteen

Reflections

There is no disguising the fact that the first generation of judges to preside over problem-solving courts was taking a real risk. Brooklyn judge John Leventhal's experience with problem-solving courts began back in the spring of 1996 in a conversation with administrative judge Michael Pesce. Pesce presented Leventhal with a fascinating opportunity, the chance to preside over a judicial experiment, the first of its kind in the state: a specialized domestic-violence court. Pesce was looking for a judge who was willing to explore new ways of handling cases, someone who was as good at forging partnerships as he was at parsing the law, and who did not shy away from gut-wrenching decisions. The court would handle crimes that stood out not only for their violence, but also for the fact that the accused and the victims were intimately involved. The thinking behind the specialized court was simple: domestic violence cases demand a unique set of skills and knowledge from judges, attorneys, and social workers. Aggregating these cases in a single courtroom would make it easier to protect victims and to make more informed decisions about court orders.

Leventhal was intrigued. The idea of a domestic violence court reminded him of why he went into the law in the first place. "A lot of judges and lawyers want to help people and the society at large," he reflected, "but it's rare to get a case that actually means something to humanity. At the domestic violence court, I feel like I'm doing meaningful work every day."[1]

This is how it all started. The quote about how rewarding and important the work that I was doing is as true today as it was the day that I had said it, even though now my work as an appellate judge is much different.

In early June of 1996, I had hoped that Judge Pesce had selected me to preside over the then pilot project domestic violence court because he thought I had the talents needed to handle the special challenges presented. The cases you have read are often complex emotionally due to the once or continuing intimate relationship between the complainant and the accused. Unlike crimes committed by strangers, victims of domestic violence are often reluctant witnesses. They may still love the accused. They may have children together. The accused may be the breadwinner of the family and perhaps the one who provides the family with health insurance and other benefits. Besides the financial and emotional ties, fear from real or unsaid threats may contribute to the reluctance. Consequently the complainants try to drop the charges, refuse to cooperate with the prosecution, and sometimes testify for the defendant at trial.

Secretly, I thought that Judge Pesce had chosen me because other jurists had declined to head the first specialized domestic violence court in the state and the first dedicated domestic violence felony court in the nation. After all, I had only been a judge for a year and one-half. At the time, the perception among the judiciary was that nothing good would come of such an assignment. Only four months earlier, a domestic violence homicide had caused the newspapers to blame a judge for the death of a woman who had been murdered by her boyfriend. The mayor of the city and the governor called for the impeachment of this judge. This public uproar resulted in the convening of the commission on judicial misconduct and led to the eventual removal of the judge.[2] One can imagine that judges were not knocking on Judge Pesce's door to volunteer to be a judge presiding over domestic violence felonies.

Nonetheless, I had agreed to take the assignment. Up until that time, I had only four experiences with domestic violence. All were deadly or nearly so. As an attorney engaged in the private practice of law, I had represented a woman who had shot her boyfriend on the curtilage of her home.[3] As a judge, I presided over a bench trial where the defendant was convicted of killing his father- and mother-in-law with hunting knives and taking his wife and son hostage and approved a plea of guilty to manslaughter by an "ax murderer."[4]

The most personal brush with a domestic violence homicide occurred the year before I became a judge. I was dropping shirts off at the local dry cleaners in Brooklyn with my two young sons. A pretty young woman in her mid-thirties was laughing at the antics of my then two-year-old son, Adam, and four-year-old son, Danny. As we left the dry cleaners, a man entered. I walked to the end of the street with my two boys and heard loud pops sounding like lightbulbs being stomped on. When I walked the boys to their nursery school around the corner and up the stairs, I realized that my youngest son had left his lunch box in the dry cleaners. I returned to the store within three to four minutes to what was then a secured crime scene. The young woman lay motionless on the floor of the store, shot dead by the man who had entered as we left. Later I read that the man was the young woman's jilted boyfriend. Like many domestic violence homicides, the man committed suicide the next day.[5]

These four incidents left quite an impression on me and made me realize the awesome responsibility that I had undertaken when I accepted the assignment to preside over the Brooklyn felony domestic violence court.

I made one request of Judge Pesce. On a Wednesday in early June of 1996, I asked to begin the assignment in September so I could read up on issues and the law peculiar to domestic violence. Although he agreed, there was such a clamor for a domestic violence court that the pilot project opened up the following Tuesday.

During that summer, I visited Quincy, Massachusetts, to observe a misdemeanor court where a dedicated domestic violence prosecutor's bureau prosecuted violations of probation before one judge. In Massachusetts, misdemeanors are punishable by up to two and one-half years in jail, unlike New York and many other states where the maximum penalty is one year. I observed the judge handle violations of probation in domestic violence cases. I was impressed that one judge handled all the violations of domestic violence offenders but was startled by the rather large violation calendar. I was determined to reduce violations of probation in my court by returning probationers back to court every two to three months of the first year even when no violation had occurred. This strategy worked and the statistics supported this effort.[6]

Right away I learned about the Violence Against Women Act, battering and its effects and how it is part of a justification defense, the use of experts by the defense and prosecution in these cases, how to form a partnership or what some call a coordinated community response to address issues that might arise, and how to make the court run more efficiently yet always fairly. These and other issues were addressed.

Yet after two years of what I was told would be a one-year assignment, I felt emotionally burnt out. Day after day, seeing and hearing about assaults both physical and sometimes sexual; battering with fists, teeth, and even metal baseball bats; torture; burning of flesh; basically inhuman treatment of persons who may have once been loved by the abuser took its toll on me. I asked Judge Pesce to be relieved of my assignment as I felt that it was affecting my emotional well-being. He consented to my request and asked me to wait one month until he could find a replacement.

The next week the chief judge of the state of New York, the Honorable Judith S. Kaye, paid a visit to my chambers. She asked me how the court was running and how I was doing. I relayed my concerns about continuing in my assignment. Judge Kaye reminded me of the importance of the work that I was doing and what we all had achieved and appealed to my vanity by telling me that the court started as a pilot project and was now a model court cited by the Justice Department and the northeastern states as one to be emulated. Nonetheless, I told Judge Kaye of the effect these cases had on me.

I could never relax. "Vacations, weekends, you can't get away. You watch the news: Is it Brooklyn, is it my case, did I let him out?"[7] Whenever there was a domestic dispute or homicide in Brooklyn, I would call to see whether it was one of my defendants. I would not feel comfortable taking vacation for more than a week or two as I wanted to monitor my defendants; accountability and victim safety were paramount to the court's success and as important to the mission as protecting a defendant's constitutional and procedural rights. I was always worrying that something awful may happen. Even after eight years of presiding, my "fear of tragedy hadn't waned: What haunted me was the specter, the prospect that, God forbid, there would be a fatality or a terrible beating. . . . I would think I were to blame.[8] I told Judge Kaye that my inclination was to decline to continue in the part, but I would think about my decision overnight."

That night I thought about it mightily. I acknowledged that what Judge Kaye had told me was right. We were doing such good and rewarding work. I would just have to try to become used to seeing intimate violence without it destroying me emotionally. One cannot help being affected by seeing such intimate partner abuse and its effects daily and routinely. Yet one can try to limit its impact on one's inner self. I told her I would continue. I realized that the work was both difficult and sometimes very depressing. But at the end of the day, it was also uplifting.

There was another defining moment in my experience. In the aftermath of the terror attack of September 11, 2001, the criminal justice system was being torn asunder by a cascade of retirements and the diversion of funds being poured into security. Governor Pataki declared a state of emergency and suspended a defendant's statutory right to a speedy trial. No murder trials were being conducted as the forensic pathologists from the Office of the Chief Medical Examiner were all down at the World Trade Center site trying to identify the remains of the victims and heroes killed in the terrorism attack. The Probation Department and other agencies were being hit by massive retirements. I feared that the partnership that we had developed and worked so hard to keep intact was in danger of being decimated. The then Commissioner of Corrections and Probation informed me that the Department of Probation would no longer be able to provide intensively supervised probation to any defendants who received up to six months in jail and up to five years of supervision. The ISP or intensive supervised probation was an important tool utilized by the court to monitor domestic violent offenders to ensure that no future harm would occur to a targeted victim.

After several phone calls had produced no resolution to what I perceived to be a big problem, I felt forced to write the commissioner a letter. I pointed out to him that I would sentence a defendant to ISP. He would then decline to supervise the defendant intensively. I would then order the Department of Probation to do so. He would then refuse. I would then hold the Department of Probation in contempt of court. I pointed out that the appellate court would then decide who was correct. The commissioner, knowing that ISP was an important component of the success of the court in monitoring probationers, acceded to my "request" and the defendants on probation continued to be supervised by the ISP unit. I always had a great relationship with the commissioner, and it continued after our one-time disagreement. He was trying to do the best for his department with the limited resources available, and I had to do what I thought was best for the court. In fact, when I testified before the Dunne Commission,[9] I underscored the great relationship that I had with the Department of Corrections and Probation and the commissioner in particular.

As I have said many times:

> The rewards in presiding over a dedicated domestic violence part have been many. . . . When I accepted the assignment to preside over the state's first domestic violence court, little did I know that I would be able to turn (with a lot of help) a pilot project into a national model. This chain of events was probably the most significant factor that influenced the decision of two governors to designate me to serve on one of our state's intermediate appellate courts. In retrospect, I realize that my life goal of helping people, which brought me to law school's door in the first place, was fulfilled by my work in the Brooklyn Domestic Violence Court.[10]

In retrospect, I feel fortunate to have had the opportunity to preside over the nation's first felony domestic violence court and the first domestic violence court of any kind in New York. When the Brooklyn Domestic Violence Court was about to commence operations in 1996, judges were apprehensive about taking such an assignment when weighing the risks versus the rewards. Now, judges are eager to do such significant work. In some small way, I hope that I contributed to the success of what was then a pilot project and what now has become a national model to emulate.[11] I am gratified that because of what was accomplished, many domestic violence courts and integrated domestic violence courts have been established. In short, I have received much more than I have given by having the opportunity to do this important work.

Power and Control Wheel. Source: Domestic Abuse Intervention Project, 202 East Superior Street, Duluth, MN 55802, 218-722-2781, www.theduluthmodel.org.

Notes

INTRODUCTION

1. Jennifer Gonnerman, "The Judge of Abuse: Domestic Violence, A New Court Fights an Old Problem," *Village Voice*, January 28, 1997.
2. The Police, "Every Breath You Take," *Synchronicity*, A&M Records, 1983.

CHAPTER ONE

1. James Ptacek, *Battered Women in the Courtroom: The Power of Judicial Responses* (Boston: Northeastern University Press, 1999).
2. David Adams, *Why Do They Kill? Men Who Murder Their Intimate Partners* (Nashville: Vanderbilt University Press, 2007). A myth about abusive men is that they are mostly uneducated or unemployed.
3. Senate Judiciary Committee, *Violence against Women, A Majority Staff Report, United States Senate* (Washington, DC: 102nd Congress, October 1992), 3.
4. Uniform Crime Reports, Federal Bureau of Investigation, 1991.
5. Senate Judiciary Committee, *Violence Against Women: A Week in the Life of America* (Washington, DC: 102nd Congress, October 1992).
6. "Defending Our Lives: Study Guide," prepared for *Defending Our Lives*, directed by Margaret Lazarus (1973; Cambridge Documentary Films).
7. Ibid.
8. Ibid.
9. Ibid.
10. Ibid.
11. Senate Judiciary Committee, *Violence against Women: Victims of the System, United States Senate* (Washington, DC: 102nd Congress, 1991).
12. "Defending Our Lives: Study Guide."

13. Ibid.

14. Ibid.

15. Susan A. Wilt, Susan M. Illman, Maia Brody Field, *Female Homicide Victims in New York City, 1990–1994* (New York: New York City Department of Health, Injury Prevention Program, 1997).

16. Lillian Wan, "Note: Parents Killing Parents: Creating a Presumption of Unfitness," *Albany Law Review* 63 (1999): 344.

17. Janice Drye, "The Silent Victims of Domestic Violence: Children Forgotten by the Judicial System," *Gonzaga Law Review* 34 (1999): 230.

18. David Wolfe and Barbra Korsch, "Witnessing Domestic Violence during Childhood and Adolescence: Implications for Pediatric Practice," *Pediatrics* 94 (1994): 594–99. For young children, in particular, episodes of abuse tend to elicit feelings of self-blame and fear.

19. Barry Zuckerman et al., "Silent Victims Revisited: The Special Case of Domestic Violence," *Pediatrics* 96, no. 3 (1995): 511–13. Children who witness domestic violence may suffer post-traumatic stress disorder, especially if the violence is severe or chronic, frequent, and perpetrated in close proximity to the children.

20. Audrey Stone and Rebecca Fialk, "Criminalizing the Exposure to Children of Family Violence: Breaking the Cycle of Abuse," *Harvard Women's Law Journal* 20 (1997): 205–27.

21. Ibid., 208.

22. Wolfe and Korsch, "Witnessing Domestic Violence," 594–99. See note 44.

23. Nancy Erickson, "The Role of the Law Guardian in a Custody Case Involving Domestic Violence," *Fordham Urban Law Journal* 27 (2000): 829.

24. Amy Haddix, "Comment: Unseen Victims: Acknowledging the Effects of Domestic Violence on Children through Statutory Termination of Parental Rights," *California Law Review* 84 (1996): 763.

25. S. R. Dube et al., "Childhood Abuse, Neglect, and Household Dysfunction and the Risk of Illicit Drug Use: The Adverse Childhood Experiences Study," *Pediatrics* 111 (2003): 564–72.

26. Domestic violence is seen by varying groups, depending on the vantage point and the context, as either a behavioral, psychological, societal, feminist, sociological, or criminal issue. In truth, it is all these. In a particular instance, the domestic violence may involve one or more of these factors.

27. Barbara Hart, National Coalition against Domestic Violence, 1988.

28. Carole Wolfe Harlow, *Victims of Violent Crime* (Washington, DC: U.S. Department of Justice, Bureau of Justice Statistics, 1991).

29. Shannon M. Catalano, *Intimate Partner Violence, 1993–2010* (Washington, DC: U.S. Department of Justice, Office of Justice Programs, November 2012), NCJ 239203, www.bjs.gov/content/pub/pdf/ipv9310.pdf.

30. Ibid.

31. Cheryl Hannah, "No Right to Choose: Mandated Victim Participation in Domestic Violence Prosecutions," *Harvard Law Review* 109 (1996): 1849; but see Linda

Mills, "Killing Her Softly: Intimate Abuse and the Violence of State Intervention," *Harvard Law Review* 113 (1999): 550.

32. *Civil Rights, U.S. Code Annotated 42* (1994), § 13981.

CHAPTER TWO

1. See Matter of Duckman, 92 N.Y.2d 141 (1998). Two dissenting judges held that the judge's removal from office was unwarranted. Judge Titone wrote: "The implication of the present disciplinary proceeding is that judges whose rulings displease the political powers that be may be subjected to a modern-day witch hunt." See also Clyde Haberman, "The Case for Duckman as a Scapegoat," *New York Times*, July 14, 1998.

2. The victim advocates and the resource coordinator and subsequently a children's counselor performed triage for wrap-around services and were a precursor to the Family Justice Center later established by the District Attorney's Office.

3. See Judith Kaye and Susan Knipps, "Judicial Responses to Domestic Violence: The Case for a Problem Solving Court," *Western State Law Review* 27 (2000); see also John Leventhal, Daniel Angiolillo, and Matthew D'Emic, "The Trials, Tribulations, and Rewards of Being the First Felony Domestic Violence Court," *American Bar Association Judges Journal* 53, no. 2 (2014).

4. It is also the first court part in New York dedicated exclusively to processing crimes of domestic violence.

5. Matthew Goldstein, "Monitoring Suspects Key to New Part: Domestic Violence Court Applauded For First Five Months of Operation," *New York Law Journal*, March 3, 1997.

6. The court takes steps to lessen the ability of the defendant to place pressure on the complainant to drop the charges. Besides informing the defendant that the name of the case is not his wife or girlfriend against him, but the People of the State of New York against the defendant, and that the order of protection is the court's mandate not that of his intimate partner, other steps are taken. For example, when the complaining witness comes to the courtroom and states that she wants to be heard to ostensibly drop the charges, the defendant is informed that this development will not affect the prosecution of the case. Complainants are not heard in open court. The victim advocate assigned to the case is notified that her client is in the courtroom. The advocate then speaks to the complainant privately in the advocate's office near the courtroom. If there is something that the advocate feels is relevant and appropriate for the court to know, the advocate will relate that in open court.

7. This became less important with the creation of the Integrated Domestic Violence (IDV) Court, where cases involving misdemeanor crimes as well as Family Court matters such as visitation, custody, and child support are before one judge. The IDV judge has the ability to go into the Family Court and Criminal Court computer databases as well as the Domestic Violence Registry and the Sex Offender Registry.

CHAPTER THREE

1. Battered women syndrome, oftentimes called battered person syndrome, and now commonly referred to as battering and its effects, had not been recognized by New York appellate courts as a legally cognizable theory related to self-defense or justification until 1995 (see *People v. Hyrckewicz*, 221 A.D.2d 990 [4th Dept. 1995]).

2. *People v. Pons*, 68 N.Y.2d 264, 267 (1986): "Calling justification a 'defense' is a misnomer. Justification does not negate a particular element of the crime nor does it operate to excuse criminal activity." If the use of force is justified, the force is legal and proper (ibid.; *People v. McManus*, 67 N.Y.2d 541, 545 [1986]). It is the prosecution's burden to show beyond a reasonable doubt that the use of force was not justified (ibid.; *People v. Higgins*, 188 AD2d 839, 840 [3d Dept. 1992]; *People v. Seeley*, 179 Misc.2d 42, 46 [Sup. Ct Kings Co. 1998]).

3. See *People v. Seeley II*, 186 Misc. 2d 715 (Sup. Ct Kings Co. 2000), for a discussion of when the use of expert testimony relating to battered woman syndrome is admissible by the prosecution to explain the unusual behavior of the complainant and when an expert can testify for a defendant and the scope of the expert's testimony.

4. In *People v. Ianniello*, 21 N.Y.2d 418, 424 (1968), the New York Court of Appeals "noted that given the investigatory as opposed to the accusatory purpose of a Grand Jury presentation, a witness has no right to be represented by counsel as an advocate before the Grand Jury. Yet, the Court identified three legal rights of a witness which may be critically affected before the Grand Jury, and as to which the witness should be entitled to consult with counsel: the decision whether to assert the privilege against self-incrimination; the decision whether to answer a question that has no apparent bearing on the subject of the investigation; and the decision whether to invoke a testimonial privilege, such as the attorney-client privilege" (*People v. Smays*, 156 Misc.2d 621, 625–26 [Sup. Ct NY Co. 1993]).

CHAPTER FIVE

1. Jeffrey Sipes, "Hitting Home," *Brooklyn Bridge*, April 1997.
2. Ibid.

CHAPTER SIX

1. Murray Weiss, Larry Celona, Angela Allen, and Kate Perrotta, "Enraged Ex Guns Down Love Duo On Street: Cops," *New York Post*, December 16, 2000.
2. Sarah Kershaw, "Suspect in Midtown Killings Shoots Himself in the Head," *New York Times*, December 17, 2000.
3. Sarah Gardiner and Patrice O'Shaughnessy, "Manhunt's Over Slay Suspect Shoots Himself," *Newsday*, December 17, 2003.
4. Ibid.

5. Sarah Goodyear, "Rehab Madness: Do Programs for Men Who Batter Women Work? No One Really Knows," *Village Voice*, February 13, 2001.

6. Ibid.

7. Dareh Gregorian, "Double Killer Shoots Self in Front of Cops," *New York Post*, December 17, 2000.

8. See, for example, Melissa Labriola, Michael Rempel, and Robert C. Davis, *Testing the Effectiveness of Batterer Programs and Judicial Monitoring* (National Institute of Justice, Center of Court Innovation, November 2005), www.cour tinnovation.org/sites/default/files/battererprogrameffectiveness.pdf; Washington State Institute for Public Policy, *What Works to Reduce Recidivism by Domestic Violence Offenders?* (January 2013), www.wsipp.wa.fov/Report File/1119/Wsipp What-Works-to-Reduce-Recidivism-by-Domestic-Violence-Offenders Full Report.pdf; Iowa Department of Corrections, "Return on Investment: Evidence-Based Options to Improve Outcomes" (May 2012), www.doc.state.ia.us/Uploaded Document/446.

9. Gardiner and O'Shaughnessy, "Manhunt's Over Slay Suspect Shoots Himself."

10. Gregorian, "Double Killer Shoots Self in Front of Cops."

11. Gardiner and O'Shaughnessy, "Manhunt's Over Slay Suspect Shoots Himself."

12. Martin Mbugua, Don Singleton, and Maki Becker, "Slay Suspect Shoots Self Taunts Cop Hours After Midtown Love-Triangle Killings," *Daily News*, December 17, 2000.

13. Gregorian, "Double Killer Shoots Self in Front of Cops."

14. Emily Gest, "Midtown Killer Dies From Own Bullet," *Daily News* (New York), December 19, 2000.

15. Goodyear, "Rehab Madness."

CHAPTER SEVEN

1. See *People v. Seeley II*, 186 Misc. 2d 715 (Sup. Ct Kings Co. 2000), for a discussion of when the use of expert testimony relating to BWS is admissible by the prosecution to explain the unusual behavior of the complainant.

2. Joan M. Schroeder, "Using Battered Woman Syndrome Evidence in the Prosecution of a Batterer," *Iowa Law Review* 76 (1991): 553.

3. *People v. Ortega*, 15 N.Y.3d 610 (2010) and *People v. James*, 19 A.D.3d 616 (2005).

4. Lenore Walker, *The Battered Woman* (New York: Harper Colophon Books, 1979). See also Lenore Walker, R. K. Thyfault, and Angela Browne, "Beyond the Juror's Ken: Battered Women," *Vermont Law Review* 7 (1982).

5. Edward W. Gondolf and Ellen R. Fisher, "Battered Women as Survivors: An Alternative to Treating Learned Helplessness," *Contemporary Sociology* 18 (1989): 11–25.

6. Ibid.

7. Evan Stark, "Re-presenting Battered Women: Coercive Control and the Defense of Liberty," in *Violence against Women: Complex Realities and New Issues in*

a Changing World (Québec: Les Presses de l'Université du Québec, 2012). See also Evan Stark, *Coercive Control: The Entrapment of Women in Personal Life* (New York: Oxford University Press, 2007).

8. Ibid.

9. Ibid.

10. Ibid.

11. Joan B. Kelly and Michael P. Johnson, "Domestic Violence: Differentiation among Types of Intimate Partner Violence: Research Update and Implications for Interventions," *Family Court Review* 46 (July 2008): 476.

12. Lundy Bancroft, *Why Does He Do That?: Inside the Minds of Angry and Controlling Men* (New York: Berkley Publishing Group, 2002). Bancroft describes ten styles of abusive men among the more than two thousand that he has encountered in his fifteen years as a counselor, evaluator, and investigator: the demand man, Mr. Right, the water torturer, the drill sergeant, Mr. Sensitive, the player, Rambo, the victim, the terrorist, and the mentally ill or addicted abuser.

13. Mary M. Cavanaigh and Richard J. Gelles, "The Utility of Male Domestic Violence Offender Typologies: New Directions for Research, Police and Practice," *Journal of Interpersonal Violence* 20 (February 2005): 155, 162.

CHAPTER EIGHT

1. Devlin Barrett, "Street Walking Nightmare," *New York Post*, November 17, 1999.

2. "New York's New Abolitionists," *New York's New Abolitionists*, www.newyorksnewabolitionists.com (accessed November 20, 2015).

3. Ibid.

4. "Trafficking Victims Protection and Justice Act," 2015 N.Y. Laws ch.368, eff. January 19, 2016.

CHAPTER NINE

1. Katherine Finkelstein, "Gay Man Charged in a Killing Can Use 'Battered Wife' Defense," *New York Times*, April 25, 1999, www.nytimes.com/1999/04/25/nyregion/gay-man-charged-in-a-killing-can-use-a-battered-wife-defense.html.

2. J. D. Glass, "2 Studies That Prove Domestic Violence Is an LGBT Issue," *Advocate*, November 4, 2014, www.advocate.com/crime/2014/09/04/2-studies-prove-domestic-violence-lgbt-issue.

3. "Domestic Violence in the LGBT Community: LGBT Fact Sheet," Center for American Progress, June 14, 2011, www.americanprogress.org/issues/lgbt/news/2011/06/14/9850/domestic-violence-in-the-lgbt-community.

4. Ibid.

CHAPTER TEN

1. "Administration on Aging," U.S. Department of Health Administration for Community Living, www.aoa.gov/AoA_programs/elder_rights/EA_prevention/whatisEA.aspx.
2. Ibid.

CHAPTER ELEVEN

1. Should a defendant violate a temporary order of protection, which is usually a condition of bail, the court may then change the conditions, including raising the bail amount (*CPL* §§530.12, 530.13); *Cf. Release or Detention of a Defendant Pending Trial, U.S. Code* 18 (2008), §3142 (safety of victim may be considered by federal magistrate at initial arraignment in setting appropriate conditions of bail); see also John Leventhal, "States' Bail Statute Must Be Amended," *New York Law Journal*, January 1, 2004.
2. In some cases, an inmate may be sentenced in New York to a term of incarceration of up to two years in a city prison if he were to be convicted of two misdemeanors and he were to receive two consecutive one-year terms (P.L.§70.30[2][b]).

CHAPTER TWELVE

1. Joan Kelly and Michael Johnson, "Domestic Violence: Differentiation among Types of Intimate Partner Violence: Research Update and Implications for Interventions," *Family Court Review* 46 (2008): 476.
2. Evan Stark, "Re-presenting Battered Women: Coercive Control and the Defense of Liberty," in *Violence against Women: Complex Realities and New Issues in a Changing World* (Québec: Les Presses de l'Université du Québec, 2012).
3. "Abuse Defined," *National Domestic Violence Hotline*, www.thehotline.org/is-this-abuse/abuse-defined/; see figure 19.1, "Power and Control Wheel," Domestic Abuse Intervention Project by the Duluth Model, www.theduluthmodel.org/pdf/powerandcontrol.pdf. (The Power and Control Wheel was developed in Duluth by battered women who were attending education groups sponsored by the local women's shelter. The wheel is used in our Creating a Process of Change for Men Who Batter curriculum, and in groups of women who are battered, to name and inspire dialogue about tactics of abuse. While we recognize that there are women who use violence against men, and that there are men and women in same-sex relationships who use violence, this wheel is meant specifically to illustrate men's abusive behaviors toward women.)
4. Kelly and Johnson, "Domestic Violence," 476.
5. Ibid.

6. Ibid.
7. Ibid.

CHAPTER FOURTEEN

1. *Colorado v. Bertine*, 479 U.S. 367, 372 (1987); *Illinois v. Lafayette*, 462 U.S. 640, 646 (1983); *People v. Gonzalez*, 62 N.Y.2d 386, 389 (1984).

CHAPTER SIXTEEN

1. At the time of the defendant's conviction, manslaughter in the first degree was punishable by an indeterminate sentence as opposed to the current state of the law in New York. Now, should a defendant be convicted of the same crime, he would receive a determinate sentence.

2. The defendant, Limrick Nelson, was acquitted of murder in state court. The U.S. Attorney for the Eastern District of New York in Brooklyn tried Mr. Nelson for violation of Mr. Rosenbaum's civil rights. The first trial resulted in a conviction but was reversed based on challenges as to the composition of the jury. The second trial resulted in a jury verdict finding Mr. Nelson in violation of Mr. Rosenbaum's civil rights. The jury, however, found that Mr. Nelson was not responsible for Mr. Rosenbaum's murder.

3. *Jackson v. Indiana*, 406 U.S. 715 (1972). Release or civil commitment could be sought and obtained prior to the expiration of the maximum authorized commitment period when there is a substantial probability that a defendant would be unlikely in the foreseeable future to improve sufficiently to regain competency to stand trial; see also *People v. Schaffer*, 86 N.Y.2d 460, 465 (1995).

4. Maureen Fan, "Slay-trial Judge Sparks Fury," *Daily News*, March 12, 1997; see also Angela Allen, "Limo Killer Cuts 15-Year Plea Deal," *New York Post*, March 12, 1997; see also Brad Hamilton, "Judge Upholds Original Plea as Murderer Gets 15 to Life," *Brooklyn Daily Eagle*, March 12, 1997.

5. Joan B. Kelly and Michael P. Johnson, "Domestic Violence: Differentiation among Types of Intimate Partner Violence: Research Update and Implications for Interventions," *Family Court Review* 46 (July 2008): 476.

6. Nancie Katz, "Killer Changes Her Story Again Says Beau Shot by Accident," *Daily News*, December 3, 2002, www.nydailynews.com/archives/boroughs/killer-story-beau-shot-accident-article-1.49873.

CHAPTER SEVENTEEN

1. It can be argued that the Violence Against Women Act legislation championed by then senator Joseph Biden and various states' legislation criminalizing certain con-

duct against women in the 1990s are the most important enactments since the various states' passage of the Married Women Acts in the nineteenth century, which gave women the right to contract, to own property, and to inherit independently of their husbands, and the passage of the Nineteenth Amendment giving women the right vote. See, e.g., *Slansky v. Slansky*, 293 N.E.2d 302, 304 (Ohio Ct. App. 1973) ("As the Nineteenth Century precursor of today's women's liberation movement, this Act was part of a national campaign to sweep away the common law web of limitations and disabilities which had entangled a married woman's rights to own and dispose of property, to make binding contracts, and to sue and be sued in an individual capacity"). The effect of the Married Women's Property Acts was to abrogate the husband's common law dominance over the marital estate and to place the wife on a level of equality with him as regards the exercise of ownership over the whole estate. The tenancy was and still is predicated upon the legal unity of the husband and wife, but the Acts converted it into a unity of equals and not of unequals as at common law. No longer could the husband convey, lease, mortgage, or otherwise encumber the property without her consent. The Acts confirmed her right to the use and enjoyment of the whole estate and all the privileges that ownership of property confers, including the right to convey the property in its entirety, jointly with her husband, during the marriage relation. *Sawada v. Endo*, 561 P.2d 1291, 1295 (Haw. 1977) (citations omitted).

2. Cheryl Hannah, "No Right to Choose: Mandated Victim Participation in Domestic Violence Prosecutions," *Harvard Law Review* 109 (1996): 1849; but see Linda Mills, "Killing Her Softly: Intimate Abuse and the Violence of State Intervention," *Harvard Law Review* 113 (1999): 550.

3. See *Unlawful Acts, U.S. Code 18* (2005), § 922 (g) (1), (8) and (9); see also *People v. Adams*, 193 Misc.2d 78 (Sup. Ct Kings Co. 2002).

4. Susan Keilitz, Rosalie Guerrero, Ann M. John, and Dawn Marie Rubio, *Specialization of Domestic Violence Case Management in the Courts: A National Survey* (Williamsburg, VA: National Center for State Courts, 2000).

5. *Release or Detention of a Defendant Pending Trial, U.S. Code* 18 (2008), §3142; See also John M. Leventhal, "Perspective: State's Bail Statute Must Be Amended," *New York Law Journal* (2004).

6. The Office of Court Administration has proposed legislation that would allow a judge to consider that factor.

7. These Domestic Violence Disclosure Schemes permit members of the public, where they have a concern that their partner may pose a risk to them or where they are concerned that the partner of a family member or a friend may pose a risk to that individual, a right to request of the police whether a partner has a history of abusive offences or whether there is other information to indicate that there may be a risk from the partner. http://content.met.police.uk/Article/Domestic-Violence-Disclosure-Scheme---Clares-Law/140002279281/ 1400022792812

8. See, e.g., *Computer System to Carry Orders of Protection and Warrants of Arrest, New York Executive Law* (2013), §221-a.

9. Victoria L. Holt, Mary A. Kernic, Marsha E Wolf, and Frederick P. Rivara, "Do Protection Orders Affect the Likelihood of Future Partner Violence and Injury?" *American Journal of Preventive Medicine* (January 2003): 16. (Researchers at the

Harborview Injury Prevention and Research Center found that women who obtained and maintained civil protection orders were safer than those without them in the five-month period after they were initially threatened or abused. The study established that intimate partner abusers in the protection order group were significantly less likely to have threatened the women or to have inflicted psychological or physical abuse on them. Four months later, the protection order effect had grown even stronger.)

10. Ibid.

11. "Defending Our Lives: Study Guide," prepared for *Defending Our Lives*, directed by Margaret Lazarus (1973; Cambridge Documentary Films).

12. *Nicolson v. Williams*, 203 F.Supp.2d 153 (E.D.N.Y. 2002). District Court finds that New York City's Agency for Children's Services policy of bringing "failure to protect" neglect petitions against victims of domestic violence to be unconstitutional, affirmed in part *sub nom. Nicolson v. Scoppetta*, 344 F.3d 154 (2d Cir.2003). Court of Appeals affirms District Court's findings of fact and continues injunction in effect but defers questions regarding constitutionality of policy pending answers by New York's Court of Appeals to certified questions concerning interpretation of state law, i.e., whether allowing a child to witness domestic violence constitutes a danger or risk to the child's life or health and whether the child's witnessing domestic violence, without additional particularized evidence, justifies removal of the child from the home. The New York Court of Appeals in *Nicolson v. Scoppetta*, 3 N.Y.3d 357 (2004) has found in answering one of the federal appeals court certified questions that a parent victim of domestic violence is not responsible for neglect merely because the child has been exposed to the violence inflicted upon the abused parent. In essence, a policy of removal of a child from the caretaker abused parent merely because child witnessed violence is an unlawful one.

13. John Leventhal, "Observations of a New Country in an Old World and a New Way of Dealing with an Old World Problem," *The Jurist*, Summer 2004.

14. See familyjusticecenter.com to locate a center.

15. Mireya Navarro, "Domestic Violence Drives Up New York Shelter Population as Housing Options are Scarce," *The New York Times*, November 10, 2014. The Police Department attributes 70 percent of the increase in public housing crime in the last three years to domestic violence.

16. But see, *Town of Castle Rock, Colorado v Gonzales*, 545 U.S. 748 (2005) [Colorado law does not give petitioner-mother a right to police enforcement of a restraining order. The police had discretion in this apparently mandatory statute. The creation of a personal entitlement to something as vague and novel as enforcement of restraining orders could not simply go without saying. The right to enforce a restraining order did not have ascertainable monetary value. The mother had no property interest in police enforcement of the order and thus no procedural due process claim.] The Inter-American Commission on Human Rights in *Jessica Lenahan (Gonzalez) v. United States of America* issued a landmark decision finding the United States responsible for human rights violations against Jessica and her three deceased children. See also, *DeShaney v. Winnebago County DSS*, 489 US 189 (1989) [State had no constitutional duty to protect child from his father after receiving reports of possible abuse. The purpose of the due process clause of 14th Amendment is "to protect

people from the State, not to ensure that the state protected them from each other." The 14th Amendment does not transform every tort committed by a state actor into a constitutional violation.]

17. Despite recommendations, local-level domestic violence fatality incident review boards were relatively rare in New York State ten years after the Pataki Commission on Domestic Violence Fatalities. See Deborah J. Chard-Wierschem and Mellissa I. Mackey, "Domestic Violence Serious Incident/Fatality Reviews in New York State," in *Domestic Violence: Research in Review* (New York: Office of Strategic Planning, Bureau of Justice Research and Innovation, New York State Division of Criminal Justice Services, October 2006). Now there is a statewide commission and a local committee in New York City and other counties in the state.

18. Susan A. Wilt, Susan M. Illman, Maia Brody Field, *Female Homicide Victims in New York City, 1990–1994* (New York: New York City Department of Health, Injury Prevention Program, 1997).

CHAPTER EIGHTEEN

1. Generation X, commonly abbreviated to Gen X, is the generation born after the Western post–World War II baby boom. Millennials (also known as the Millennial Generation or Generation Y) are the demographic cohort following Generation X.

2. John Leventhal, "Spousal Rights or Spousal Crimes: Where and When Are the Lines to Be Drawn?" *Utah Law Review* (2006): 351.

3. The Beatles, "Run for Your Life," written by John Lennon and Paul McCartney, *Rubber Soul*, Parlophone Records (1965): www.comprar-cd.mus.br.

4. Melissa Labriola, Michael Rempel, and Robert C. Davis, *Testing the Effectiveness of Batterer Programs and Judicial Monitoring* (National Institute of Justice, Center of Court Innovation, November 2005), www.courtinnovation.org/sites/default/files/battererprogrameffectiveness.pdf.

5. *People v. Bongiovanni*, 183 Misc.2d 104 (Supreme Court, Kings Co. 2000). The court held that placing a defendant in a batterers' intervention program is not punitive and no greater an imposition on liberty than issuing a pre-trial order of protection prohibiting the defendant from returning to the marital residence: "Until there is a determination of guilt or innocence the court is responsible not only to seek justice by safeguarding the rights of the defendant; it must also insure that the complainant is secure and that societal peace is preserved during the pendency of the action. Directing a defendant to attend alternative to violence courses helps insure this. Rather than implying guilt, attendance at the program, in tandem with its educational benefits, reminds the defendant, as does the order of protection, that although at liberty, he is still bound by the dictates of the court, which can rescind his liberty on his failure to abide by those dictates. In requiring attendance at such programs, the court feels it is less likely that a temporary order of protection will be violated. Such a condition thus assists the court in its responsibility to secure the peace and protect the family." Cited with approval in *Halikipoulos v. Dillon*, 139 F.Supp.2d 312 (E.D.N.Y., 2001) (upholding a shoplift program as a condition of bail).

6. See, e.g., Emerge, a certified program in Massachusetts. The people coming to this program "are asked to recognize how they have chosen such behavior as a pattern in their relationships and families and how those choices have harmed others." ("Emerge seeks to educate individual abusers, prevent young people from learning to accept violence in their relationships, improve institutional responses to domestic violence, and increase public awareness about the causes and solutions to partner violence. With the development of parenting education groups for fathers, Emerge has expanded its mission to include a goal of helping men to become more responsible parents. Emerge teaches that domestic violence is a learned behavior, not a disease or a sickness. Emerge supports grassroots, institutional and cultural efforts to stop partner violence, sexual assault and child abuse. Emerge recognizes that other oppressive life circumstances such as racism, poverty and homophobia create a climate that contributes to partner violence," www.emergedv.com).

7. For U.S Men's Anti-Violence Organizations, see Men Can Stop Rape, www.mencanstoprape.org.

CHAPTER NINETEEN

1. Greg Berman and John Feinblatt. *Good Courts* (New York: New Press, 2005), 98.

2. See chapter 2, "Build It and They Will Come."

3. See chapter 3, "Lucky Laurie."

4. See chapter 4, "Yuri the Hunter," and chapter 16, "Deadly Vignettes" ("The Ax Murderer").

5. Robert McFadden, "Brief Romance, Growing Fears, Then Two Deaths," *New York Times,* April 9, 1994, www.nytimes.com/1994/04/09/nyregion/brief-romance-growing-fears-then-2-deaths.html.

6. See chapter 2, "Build It and They Will Come."

7. Amy Waldman, "Striking Back: The City's New Assault on Domestic Violence," *New York Times*, June 28, 1998, 1.

8. Berman and Feinblatt, *Good Courts*, 103.

9. Task Force on the Future of Probation in New York State: John R. Dunne, Chair (2007).

10. John Leventhal, Daniel Angiolillo, and Matthew D'Emic, "The Trials, Tribulations, and Rewards of Being the First Felony Domestic Violence Court," *American Bar Association Judges Journal* 53, no. 2 (2014).

11. Jonathan Lippman, "Ensuring Victim Safety and Abuser Accountability: Reforms and Revisions in New York Courts' response to Domestic Violence," *Albany Law Review* 46, no. 3 (2012–2013): 1428. ("The creation of the DV courts was made possible by the modeling of specialized DV courts by the Center of Court Innovation, the court system's research and development arm, and by the leadership of the Honorable John M. Leventhal of the Brooklyn Felony Domestic Violence Court.")

Bibliography

"Abuse Defined." National Domestic Violence Hotline. www.thehotline.org/is-this
-abuse/abuse-defined/.

Adams, David. *Why Do They Kill? Men Who Murder Their Intimate Partners.* Nashville: Vanderbilt University Press, 2007.

"Administration on Aging." U.S. Department of Health Administration for Community Living. www.aoa.gov/AoA_programs/elder_rights/EA_prevention/whatisEA
.aspx.

Allen, Angela. "Limo Killer Cuts 15-Year Plea Deal." *New York Post*, March 12, 1997.

Bancroft, Lundy. *Why Does He Do That?: Inside the Minds of Angry and Controlling
Men.* New York: Berkley Publishing Group, 2002.

Barrett, Devlin. "Street Walking Nightmare." *New York Post*, November 17, 1999, 38.

Berman, Greg, and John Feinblatt. *Good Courts.* New York: New Press, 2005.

Catalano, Shannon M. *Intimate Partner Violence, 1993-2010.* Washington, DC: U.S.
Department of Justice, Office of Justice Programs, November 2012. NCJ 239203.
www.bjs.gov/content/pub/pdf/ipv9310.pdf.

Cavanaugh, Mary M., and Richard J. Gelles. "The Utility of Male Domestic Violence
Offender Typologies: New Directions for Research, Police and Practice." *Journal
of Interpersonal Violence* 20 (February 2005): 155, 162.

Chard-Wierschem, Deborah J., and Mellissa I. Mackey. "Domestic Violence Serious
Incident/Fatality Reviews in New York State." *Domestic Violence: Research in
Review.* Office of Strategic Planning, Bureau of Justice Research and Innovation,
New York State Division of Criminal Justice Services, October 2006.

"Defending Our Lives: Study Guide." Prepared for *Defending Our Lives*, directed by
Margaret Lazarus (1973; Cambridge Documentary Films).

"Domestic Violence in the LGBT Community: LGBT Fact Sheet." Center for
American Progress. June 14, 2011. www.americanprogress.org/issues/lgbt/
news/2011/06/14/9850/domestic-violence-in-the-lgbt-community.

Drye, Janice. "The Silent Victims of Domestic Violence: Children Forgotten by the
Judicial System." *Gonzaga Law Review* 34 (1999): 230.

Dube, S. R., V. J. Felitti, M. Dong, D. P. Chapman, W. H. Giles, and R. F. Anda. "Childhood Abuse, Neglect, and Household Dysfunction and the Risk of Illicit Drug Use: The Adverse Childhood Experiences Study." *Pediatrics* 111 (2003): 564–72.

Erickson, Nancy. "The Role of the Law Guardian in a Custody Case Involving Domestic Violence." *Fordham Urban Law Journal* 27 (2000): 829.

Fan, Maureen. "Slay-trial Judge Sparks Fury." *Daily News*, March 12, 1997.

Finkelstein, Katherine. "Gay Man Charged in a Killing Can Use 'Battered Wife' Defense." *New York Times,* April 25, 1999. www.nytimes.com/1999/04/25/nyregion/gay-man-charged-in-a-killing-can-use-a-battered-wife-defense.html.

Gardiner, Sarah, and Patrice O'Shaughnessy. "Manhunt's Over Slay Suspect Shoots Himself." *Newsday*, December 17, 2003.

Gest, Emily. "Midtown Killer Dies from Own Bullet." *Daily News*, December 19, 2000.

Glass, J. D. "2 Studies That Prove Domestic Violence Is an LGBT Issue." *Advocate*, November 4, 2014.

Goldstein, Matthew. "Monitoring Suspects Key to New Part: Domestic Violence Court Applauded For First Five Months of Operation." *New York Law Journal*, March 3, 1997.

Gondolf, Edward W., and Ellen R. Fisher. "Battered Women as Survivors: An Alternative to Treating Learned Helplessness." *Contemporary Sociology* 18 (1989): 11–25.

Gonnerman, Jennifer. "The Judge of Abuse: Domestic Violence, A New Court Fights an Old Problem." *Village Voice*, January 28, 1997.

Goodyear, Sarah. "Rehab Madness: Do Programs for Men Who Batter Women Work? No One Really Knows." *Village Voice* (New York), February 13, 2001.

Gregorian, Dareh. "Double Killer Shoots Self in Front of Cops." *New York Post*, December 17, 2000.

Haberman, Clyde. "The Case for Duckman as a Scapegoat." *New York Times*, July 14, 1998.

Haddix, Amy. "Comment: Unseen Victims: Acknowledging the Effects of Domestic Violence on Children Through Statutory Termination of Parental Rights." *California Law Review* 84 (1996): 763.

Hamilton, Brad. "Judge Upholds Original Plea as Murderer Gets 15 to Life." *Brooklyn Daily Eagle*, March 12, 1997.

Hannah, Cheryl. "No Right to Choose: Mandated Victim Participation in Domestic Violence Prosecutions." *Harvard Law Review* 109 (1996): 1849.

Hart, Barbara. National Coalition against Domestic Violence. 1988.

Harlow, Carole Wolfe. *Victims of Violent Crime*. Washington, DC: U.S. Department of Justice, Bureau of Justice Statistics, 1991.

Holt, Victoria L., Mary A. Kernic, Marsha E. Wolf, and Frederick P. Rivara. "Do Protection Orders Affect the Likelihood of Future Partner Violence and Injury?" *American Journal of Preventive Medicine* (January 2003).

Iowa Department of Corrections. "Return on Investment: Evidence-Based Options to Improve Outcomes" (May 2012).

Katz, Nancie. "Killer Changes Her Story Again Says Beau Shot by Accident." *Daily News*, December 3, 2002. www.nydailynews.com/archives/boroughs/killer-story-beau-shot-accident-article-1.49873.

Kaye, Judith, and Susan Knipps. "Judicial Responses to Domestic Violence: The Case for a Problem Solving Court." *Western State Law Review* 27 (2000).

Keilitz, Susan, Rosalie Guerrero, Ann M. John, and Dawn Marie Rubio. *Specialization of Domestic Violence Case Management in the Courts: A National Survey.* Williamsburg, VA: National Center for State Courts, 2000.

Kelly, Joan B., and Michael P. Johnson. "Domestic Violence: Differentiation Among Types of Intimate Partner Violence: Research Update and Implications for Interventions." *Family Court Review* 46 (July 2008): 476.

Kershaw, Sarah. "Suspect in Midtown Killings Shoots Himself in the Head." *New York Times*, December 17, 2000.

Labriola, Melissa, Michael Rempel, and Robert C. Davis. *Testing the Effectiveness of Batterer Programs and Judicial Monitoring.* National Institute of Justice, Center of Court Innovation, November 2005. www.courtinnovation.org/sites/default/files/battererprogrameffectiveness.pdf.

Leventhal, John M. "Perspective: State's Bail Statute Must Be Amended." *New York Law Journal* (2004).

———. "Observations of a New Country in an Old World and a New Way of Dealing with an Old World Problem." *Jurist*, Summer 2004.

———. "Spousal Rights or Spousal Crimes: Where and When Are the Lines to Be Drawn?" *Utah Law Review* (2006): 351.

Leventhal, John, Daniel Angiolillo, and Matthew D'Emic. "The Trials, Tribulations, and Rewards of Being the First Felony Domestic Violence Court." *American Bar Association Judges Journal* 53, no. 2 (2014).

Lippman, Jonathan. "Ensuring Victim Safety and Abuser Accountability: Reforms and Revisions in New York Courts' Response to Domestic Violence." *Albany Law Review* 46, no. 3 (2012–2013): 1428.

Mbugua, Martin, Don Singleton, and Maki Becker. "Slay Suspect Shoots Self Taunts Cop Hours after Midtown Love-Triangle Killings." *Daily News*, December 17, 2000.

McFadden, Robert. "Brief Romance, Growing Fears, Then Two Deaths." *New York Times*, April 9, 1994. www.nytimes.com/1994/04/09/nyregion/brief-romance-growing-fears-then-2-deaths.html.

"Men Can Stop Rape." Men Can Stop Rape. www.mencanstoprape.org.

Mills, Linda. "Killing Her Softly: Intimate Abuse and the Violence of State Intervention." *Harvard Law Review* 113 (1999).

Navarro, Mireya. "Domestic Violence Drives Up New York Shelter Population as Housing Options Are Scarce." *New York Times*, November 10, 2014.

"New York's New Abolitionists." New York's New Abolitionists. www.newyorksnewabolitionists.com (accessed November 20, 2015).

"Power and Control Wheel." Domestic Abuse Intervention Project by the Duluth Model. www.theduluthmodel.org/pdf/powerandcontrol.pdf.

Ptacek, James. *Battered Women in the Courtroom: The Power of Judicial Responses.* Boston: Northeastern University Press, 1999.

Schroeder, Joan M. "Using Battered Woman Syndrome Evidence in the Prosecution of a Batterer." *Iowa Law Review* 76 (1991): 553.

Senate Judiciary Committee. *Violence against Women, A Majority Staff Report.* Washington, DC: United States Senate, 102nd Congress, October 1992.

———. *Violence against Women: A Week in the Life of America.* Washington, DC: United States Senate, 102nd Congress, October 1992.

———. *Violence against Women: Victims of the System.* Washington, DC: United States Senate, 102nd Congress, 1991.

Sipes, Jeffrey. "Hitting Home." *Brooklyn Bridge*, April 1997.

Stark, Evan. "Re-presenting Battered Women: Coercive Control and the Defense of Liberty." In *Violence against Women: Complex Realities and New Issues in a Changing World.* Québec: Les Presses de l'Université du Québec, 2012.

———. *Coercive Control: How Men Entrap Women in Personal Life.* New York: Oxford University Press, 2007.

Stone, Audrey, and Rebecca Fialk. "Criminalizing the Exposure to Children of Family Violence: Breaking the Cycle of Abuse." *Harvard Women's Law Journal* 20 (1997): 205–27.

The Beatles. "Run for Your Life." *Rubber Soul.* Parlophone Records, 1965.

The Police. "Every Breath You Take." *Synchronicity.* A&M Records, 1983.

Waldman, Amy. "Striking Back: The City's New Assault on Domestic Violence." *New York Times*, June 28, 1998.

Walker, Lenore. *The Battered Woman.* New York: Harper Colophon Books, 1979.

Walker, Lenore, R. K. Thyfault, and Angela Browne, "Beyond the Juror's Ken: Battered Women." *Vermont Law Review* 7 (1982).

Wan, Lillian. "Note: Parents Killing Parents: Creating a Presumption of Unfitness." *Albany Law Review* 63 (1999): 344.

Washington State Institute for Public Policy. *What Works to Reduce Recidivism by Domestic Violence Offenders?* Olympia: Washington State Institute for Public Policy, January 2013.

Weiss, Murray, Larry Celona, Angela Allen, and Kate Perrotta. "Enraged Ex Guns Down Love Duo On Street: Cops." *New York Post*, December 16, 2000.

Wilt, Susan A., Susan M. Illman, and Maia Brody Field. *Female Homicide Victims in New York City, 1990–1994.* New York: New York City Department of Health, Injury Prevention Program.

Wolfe, David, and Barbra Korsch. "Witnessing Domestic Violence during Childhood and Adolescence: Implications for Pediatric Practice." *Pediatrics* 94 (1994): 594–99.

Zuckerman, Barry, Marlyin Augustyn, Betsy Groves, and Steven Parker. "Silent Victims Revisited: The Special Case of Domestic Violence." *Pediatrics* 96, no. 3 (1995): 511–13.

About the Author

Hon. John Michael Leventhal has served as an the Associate Justice of the New York State Supreme Court, Appellate Division, Second Department from 2008 to the present. Justice Leventhal was first elected to the Supreme Court, Second Judicial District in November 1994 and reelected in 2008, during which time he presided over the nation's first felony Domestic Violence Court. Prior to his election to the bench, Justice Leventhal was in private practice from 1982 until 1994 specializing in criminal and civil litigation and appeals. Justice Leventhal is a frequent lecturer on evidence, domestic violence, elder abuse, guardianship, and other topics before bar associations, law schools, civic groups, court administrators, and governmental agencies. In 2015, he received the Brooklyn Bar Association's annual award For Outstanding Achievement in the Science of Jurisprudence and Public Service. He has been given the Brooklyn Law School Alumni of the Year Award (2009); the Distinguished Achievement Medal from the New York State Free and Accepted Masons (2008); the Brooklyn Women's Bar Association Beatrice M. Judge Recognition Award (2008) for outstanding service to the women of the bar, to the community, and to the law; the New York Board of Rabbis and Dayenu Voices of Valor Elijah Award (2008) for male leadership in ending domestic violence; and the National College of District Attorneys Stephen L. Von Riesen Lecturer of Merit Award (2008) in recognition of exceptional service in the continuing professional education of all individuals who work on behalf of domestic violence survivors, their families, and our communities. In 2005, Justice Leventhal received a special commendation from the Department of Justice in recognition of his extraordinary contribution to the prevention of violence against women.

Justice Leventhal has authored or coauthored twenty-three articles relating to criminal and civil law. His work as a judge dealing with domestic violence cases has been featured in a number of newspaper and magazine articles, including a profile in Public Lives of the *New York Times* on April 25, 2001, as well as on MSNBC.